Footprints in the Dust

The Life of the Buddha from the Most Ancient Sources

S. Dhammika

Pariyatti Press

Pariyatti Press
an imprint of
Pariyatti Publishing
www.pariyatti.org

Second revised edition and first Pariyatti edition, 2023

ISBN: 978-1-68172-596-3 (paperback)
ISBN: 978-1-68172-597-0 (ePub)
ISBN: 978-1-68172-598-7 (Mobi)
ISBN: 978-1-68172-599-4 (PDF)
Library of Congress Control Number: 2023944518

Cover photo, stupa from Kanhiri, 3rd cent. CE, courtesy of Kevin Standage

I see him in mind as if by eye
And spend the night in praising him;
Thus it is I am never away from him.

Sutta Nipāta 1142

Contents

Foreword

What was the Buddha like as a human being? How did he relate to others? With great care and an eye for detail, Venerable Dhammika pieces together the life events we can 'read' from very early texts. The result is a truly authoritative biography. It shows that as a man, as well as a teacher, the historical Buddha was remarkable indeed. The chapter headings are refreshingly original: a day in the life of, his humour, his debating style, his background. I really enjoyed thinking about Gotama Buddha simply as a person – and clearly an extraordinary one, as Ven. Dhammika shows us. I recommend this book to anyone who would like a down-to-earth, accurate and readable appraisal of the founder of this great world religion, seen through modern eyes.

Sarah Shaw
Oxford, March, 2021

Preface to the Second Edition

For this second edition of *Footprints in the Dust* I have included details about the Buddha and the world he knew which I had previously overlooked. Also, Stuart Corner and Barry Ng both patiently went through the original text making many corrections to the spelling and references, and Bryan Levman drew my attention to aspects of Pali and the Dhamma that needed clarification and in some cases correction. I am most grateful to them all for their input. I must also thank Brihas Sarathy and Steve Hanlon of Pariyatti for arranging this second edition and seeing it through the press.

Preface

In a sense, I have been writing this book for thirty-five years. Who the Buddha was and what he was like has intrigued and fascinated me since I became a Buddhist in my late teens. In my 1989 book *The Buddha and His Disciples* I looked at some aspects of his persona, his style of teaching and his relationships, and in the subsequent decades I wrote several articles dealing with other aspects of the Buddha's life: his physical appearance, his habits, his travels and even his diet. Some of that earlier work has been incorporated into the present book. To get at least some feel for the world in which the Buddha lived, I also undertook three walking tours through India that followed in his footsteps: going from Bodh Gaya to Varanasi; from Bodh Gaya to Rajgir and back again; and, longest of all, retracing the Buddha's final journey from Rajgir to Kusinara. In the last few years I have also immersed myself in Vedic literature from both the early and late periods, the better to understand the religious and social background to the Buddha's life.

In writing this book I have received generous help and encouragement from many people. Discussions with Anandajoti Bhikkhu, Peter Prins, Sarah Shaw and Peter Harvey have been enormously helpful mainly on matters related to the Dhamma. Input from Bhikkhu Khemarato, Bhikkhunī Acala, Chris Burke and Ranjith Dissanayake helped fine-tune the final draft. Bradley Smith and my brother Charles each went through the manuscript, making numerous corrections and suggestions for its improvement. Discussions with Deepak Ananda, who shares my deep interest in the ancient topography of Buddhism, kindly shared his knowledge of this subject with me. In the end though, I am responsible for everything in the book. As he has done many times before, Suhendra Sulistyo arranged for me to get access to books and monographs I needed. In writing about the Buddha in the time of the coronavirus and serious personal illness, the good cheer and encouragement of Calvin and Yandi, Padma, Ananda and Tony have also been much appreciated. I express my gratitude and thanks to them all.

Note on Usage

The Buddhist scriptures include numerous repetitions that make tedious reading for those unfamiliar with this genre of literature. I have condensed these repetitions where necessary, and where this has been done, it is indicated in the quotes themselves or in the notes. Unless otherwise mentioned, Pali rather than Sanskrit has been used throughout. A few exceptions are made to this in deference to widespread usage, the main ones being Nirvana instead of Nibbāna and *stupa* rather than *thūpa*. In Buddhist literature the conventional way of indicating a large number of things is to say that there were five hundred. This has been replaced by 'many', 'a large number' or 'several hundred.' Throughout, 'the text' or 'the earliest texts' are used interchangeably with 'the Tipitaka.' Likewise, *samaṇa*, monk and ascetic are used interchangeably. In Pali as in Sanskrit, the term 'samaṇas and brahmins' is a compound and does not usually mean both types of individuals but is a conventional way of referring to religious in general. When referring to the Buddha before his awakening, he is called by his clan name Gotama, and after his awakening he is called the Buddha.

1
Introduction

Buddhism teaches that each person comes into their present life from an earlier one and that most people will have another life when their present one ends. This process of being born, dying and being reborn is called *saṃsāra* and only ceases when one attains a state called awakening, *bodhi*, more commonly known as Nirvana. Like everyone else, the Buddha had many lives before his final one as Gotama, and the Buddhist tradition created fictional biographies of over five hundred of these former lives, recounted in a book called the Jātaka. What is unique about the Buddha is not that he had former incarnations, fictional or otherwise, but that in the centuries after he attained Nirvana devotees and admirers have continued to 'reincarnate' him in a sense, by creating new 'lives' for him, some of these more incredible than his former ones as recounted in the Jātaka.

Although physically and in a number of other ways the Buddha was an ordinary human being, some participants at the Third Buddhist Council, which took place around the middle of the third century BCE, asserted that such was his purity that his faeces had a fragrant smell. There were, however, those who maintained a more realistic view of the Buddha and who gave a common-sense rebuttal to this claim. If this were true, they argued, it would have required the Buddha to eat perfume, and it was well-known that he ate rice and other ordinary food. Furthermore, if his faeces really smelled fragrant, people would have collected it, stored it up and used it as a cosmetic, but there is no record of this ever being done.[1]

Several centuries after this, a biography of the Buddha called the *Lalitavistara* depicted him as an individual in whose presence marvels

---

1. Kv.XVIII, 4.

and wonders manifested, the way mushrooms appear after rain. To give but one example from many, when as a child he was taken to a temple for a blessing, the statues of the gods stood up out of reverence for him.

A century or two after this, the *Saddharmapuṇdarīka Sūtra* went much further and maintained that the Buddha was actually an eternal cosmic being and that the so-called human Buddha was just an apparition this cosmic Buddha used to teach humanity.[2] But even as this divine, or quasi-divine, wonder-working Buddha was well on the way to becoming standard in some quarters, more grounded voices could still be heard.

One of these was Aśvaghoṣa, who in the early second century CE wrote his *Buddhacarita*, a narrative poem of the Buddha's life from his first to his last days. In this epic, the Buddha was depicted as exceptional but still human. In about the sixth century the Hindu *Matsya Purāṇa* proclaimed that the Buddha was actually an incarnation (*avatāra*) of the god Visṇu, a claim repeated later by other *Purāṇas*. This half-hearted effort to neutralize Buddhism by absorbing it into Hinduism was never really taken seriously by Hindus and certainly not by Buddhists.

By about the tenth century a confused and fragmentary account of the Buddha's life had filtered through the Middle East into Europe, and because it depicted him as conspicuously holy it was assumed that he must therefore have been a Christian. Consequently, he was inducted into the Catholic Church as a saint under the name St. Josaphat, with his feast day being the 27th of November.

With the penetration of European powers into Asia, the Buddha underwent a new wave of 'incarnations', finally emerging as an historically real individual, although it took time to establish that he was not a god, a prophet of God, and not Chinese but Indian.

By the middle of the Victorian era, he came to be seen by the more liberal minded as a reformer of Hinduism, a rationalist or a great moral teacher just one step below Christ; a few bold souls even dared to suggest that he was equal to Christ.[3] Some proclaimed that the Buddha was an atheist or an agnostic, while others were equally sure he believed in God but said little on the subject because the Divine is beyond words.

---

2. Jain 2001, pp.87-89.
3. Philip C. Almond, *The British Discovery of Buddhism*, 1988.

In the early 1880s the eminent Dutch scholar of Indian religion Hendrik Kern published a two-volume tome in which he proved that Buddhism grew out of sun worship and that the Buddha was originally a solar deity. The twelve *nidāna* of Buddhist doctrine were the months of the year, the six wrong views were the six planets, the Buddha's Middle Way was the summer solstice in disguise, and so on. Although Kern's fellow academics had great respect for his learning, the sun soon set on his astronomical theory of the Buddha.

In 1916, just as the distinction between Buddhism and Hinduism was becoming more apparent, the art historian Ananda Coomaraswamy wrote a book claiming that the Buddha taught the Ātman and Brahman of Vedānta, although using different terminology. His book was widely read and helped perpetuate misunderstandings about Buddhism that continue even today.

Inspired by the new thinking of the Second Vatican Council, eminent theologian Karl Rahner informed Buddhists in the late 1950s that they were actually what he called "anonymous Christians" and presumably, that the Buddha was also a Christian without knowing it. As of today, no Buddhist thinker has returned the compliment by announcing that Christians are anonymous Buddhists and that Jesus was really a late-comer to the Dhamma, despite not wearing a yellow robe.

After the counter-culture movement of the 1960s and the subsequent emergence of New Age spirituality, the Buddha became an apostle of vegetarianism who had opened his third eye and taught how to become one with the universe.

At around the same time, in liberal Christian circles there were those who were claiming that if Jesus and the Buddha had ever met, they would have been the best of friends and smilingly nodded in agreement when each explained their teachings to the other.[4]

Out of step with all these curious, though generally positive, incarnations, is a recent publication revealing for the first time that

4. A good example of this claim is *Jesus and Buddha, Friends in Conversation* by Paul Knitter and Roger Haight. The former, representing Buddhism, is professor emeritus of Union Theological Seminary in New York and the latter, representing Christianity, is a Jesuit priest and theologian at the same institution. Apparently it was not thought necessary to invite a practising Buddhist scholar for their opinion.

the Buddha was actually an accomplished field general with extensive experience in commanding men in battle. Apparently he probably "witnessed so much battlefield carnage that he suffered a psychological collapse." The book also informs the reader that there is "a reasonable suspicion" that the Buddha was murdered.[5]

With so many 'Buddhas' it is hardly surprising that in the minds of many people this Indian sage is a figure hovering between myth and reality, benign and compelling but not quite real. There are, of course, and have been for at least a century and a half, studies that present more realistic or perhaps better, more conventional accounts of the Buddha, whoever he was and whatever he taught. However, nearly all these efforts, including contemporary ones, recount the Buddha's biography by padding the meagre and scattered facts from the earliest sources with legends that evolved centuries after his passing. And because even the information from these more reliable early sources is not enough for a decent-sized volume, at least half or more of such biographies typically recount the Buddha's philosophy rather than being primarily about the man himself.

Logically, the best way to know who the Buddha was and what he was like would be to examine the earliest records of him, simply because they would be closer to his time than any later ones. Such an endeavour, however, is not as easy as it sounds. Dating ancient Indian literature is a notoriously difficult and frustrating task, and there is usually diverse opinion amongst scholars about when any particular text was written. Complicating the task even further is that few ancient texts are homogeneous, with most being written at one time but undergoing expansion or revision in later centuries. There is, however, a general consensus amongst scholars that the core material in the Pali Tipitaka, sometimes also called the Pali Canon, contains the earliest accounts of the Buddha and what he taught.

The name Tipitaka is a combination of the words *ti*, meaning 'three', which refers to the three divisions of the scriptures, and *piṭaka*, meaning 'a basket.' Calling the scriptures 'baskets' relates to the fact that they were transmitted orally for several centuries, there being no

---

5. Richard A. Gabriel's *God's Generals, the Military Lives of Moses, the Buddha and Muhammad*, 2016.

writing during the Buddha's time. In ancient India labourers would move earth, grain or building materials using a relay of large, round, shallow baskets. A worker would put the filled basket on his head, walk to the next worker, and pass it to him, and then he would repeat the process. So in the minds of the early Buddhists, the passing of material in baskets from the head of one person to another was analogous to passing the scriptures from the memory of one person to another.

The three divisions of the Tipitaka are the Sutta Piṭaka, the Vinaya Piṭaka and the Abhidhamma Piṭaka. The first and most important of these contains the sermons and dialogues of the Buddha, plus a few by his monastic and lay disciples. Each of these individual sermons and dialogues is called a *sutta*, meaning a thread or string, and may have been used because the sounds strung together give the words, and the words strung together give the meaning. However, *sutta* is more likely derived from the Sanskrit *sūkta* meaning well-spoken.[6] These suttas are arranged into five collections, or *nikāyas*, the fifth of which is made up of thirteen independent books. From the language, content and style of several books in this fifth collection it can be deduced that they were composed later than the core material in the first four collections, and indeed most of them do not even claim to have been spoken by the Buddha.[7] It is also true that scattered throughout the first four collections are some suttas that date from perhaps a century or two after the Buddha, but for the most part these can be easily identified.

The second part of the Tipitaka, the Vinaya Piṭaka, contains a bare list of the rules for monks and nuns known as the Pātimokkha and is the oldest part of the Vinaya. This list of rules is embedded in a commentary explaining each rule, laying down the procedures for governing the monastic order and giving the early history of the order. Parts of this commentary are early and include information about the Buddha that is likely to be authentic, while other parts were composed a century or two after the Buddha and are less reliable.

The third part, the Abhidhamma Piṭaka, is a précis of the essential features of the Buddha's Dhamma, mostly in the form of lists enabling

---

6. Norman 1997 p.104.

7. The only ones used in the present book will be the Dhammapada, Itivuttaka, Jātaka, Sutta Nipāta, Theragāthā, Therīgāthā and Udāna.

the Dhamma to be more easily remembered and perhaps more easily taught as well. The Abhidhamma Piṭaka dates from perhaps two hundred years after the Buddha, and while it contains little that contradicts his teaching as presented in the Sutta Piṭaka, it does develop some of these teachings. However, it contains nothing that could help in constructing a biography of the Buddha either and has not been used in this book.

The Tipitaka is in an ancient language called Pali which originated in northern India roughly around the time of the Buddha. The general opinion amongst scholars about the origin and nature of Pali is that, "[w]hile it is not identical to what Buddha himself would have spoken, it belongs to the same broad language family as those he might have used and originates from the same conceptual matrix. This language thus reflects the thought-world that the Buddha inherited from the wider Indian culture into which he was born, so that its words capture the subtle nuances of that thought-world."[8] However, Prof. Richard Gombrich, the renowned scholar of early Buddhism, has recently argued against this position, saying that there are cogent reasons for thinking that the Buddha did speak Pali.[9] Perhaps the most that can be said is that the Buddha spoke either Pali or a language quite similar to it.

It is acknowledged that the Tipitaka was assembled in its present form over a period of probably several centuries and that it is an amalgam of mostly early material with lesser parts added later. But with a careful examination of this material, together with intelligent guesswork, it is possible to identify the earliest stratum within the Tipitaka. Such an approach reveals that the core material in the Sutta Piṭaka and parts of the Vinaya Piṭaka dates from the time of the Buddha to perhaps a generation or two after him.

The *Mañjuśrīmūlakalpa* claims that a decade or so after the Buddha's passing, King Ajātasattu's son and heir Udāyin, had the Buddha's words committed to writing (*tadetat pravachanaṃ śāstu lekhā-payishyati vistarm*).[10] If this were so, it would seem that the more conservative and traditional monastic communities who were the majority,

8. Bodhi, 2005, p.10. See also Gombrich 2018, pp.15-22.
9. Gombrich, 2018 and Karpik, 2019.
10. See Jayaswal p.10.

continued to rely on oral transmission. It is commonly thought that written information is transmitted with greater accuracy than memory, but the evidence shows otherwise. Before printing, books had to be copied by hand, and scribes often made mistakes as they wrote. Over time, as one book was copied from another, mistakes accumulated to the degree that sometimes it became difficult to work out what some parts of the original meant. More seriously, a lone scribe could delete or add passages to the book he was copying, which would be included in the next copy, creating confusion when compared with manuscripts without the changes.

Human memory, on the other hand, particularly if trained from childhood and in a world devoid of all the distractions we are bombarded with, can be highly accurate, and this is exactly what brahmins, the priests of India's ancient Vedic religion, did. A brahmin boy was trained from an early age to repeat the Vedic hymns over and over again until they were imprinted in his memory.[11] During various ceremonies, congregations of brahmins chanted the hymns so that, even if one of them missed a verse or mispronounced a word, his memory would be jogged or his mistake corrected by the chanting of the others. This also made it almost impossible for an individual to add or delete anything once the text was settled and 'closed.' To do so would require a widespread conspiracy, and as the texts came to be considered sacrosanct, no one would dare to do such a thing.

A significant number of the Buddha's disciples were from the brahmin caste, and they brought these skills to their new religion.[12] When someone became a monk, he would listen to the discourses being chanted and gradually learn them by heart. It is also known that some monastic congregations specialized in learning different parts of what became the Tipitaka. To help preserve the Buddha's sermons, they were edited in ways that made them more amenable to memorisation. They are replete with mnemonic devices such as numbered lists, stereotyped passages, standardised terminology, rhyming verses, and, most of

11. On the accuracy attainable through this training see Bronkhorst 2002 pp. 797-801, and Anālayo 2011, pp.867 ff.

12. An examination of the commentary to the Theragāthā reveals that, of 259 monks, 113 were brahmins; Rhys Davids 1913, p. xxviii, and also Sarao 1989 pp. 93 ff.

all, repetitions, one of the reasons why it takes time and patience to get used to their style.[13] This editing gave the Buddha's sermons a somewhat artificial and stilted form while still preserving the meaning of what he taught and sometimes quite likely the very words he spoke. Time and again while reading the Tipitaka, phrases and short passages stand out as being natural, unaffected and personal, just the kind of thing a real person would say. Thus there is no reason to doubt that the core material in the Tipitaka represents an accurate record of what the Buddha taught as remembered by his direct disciples and inherited by the immediate succeeding generation. For a detailed survey of the issues involved and evidence for the fidelity of the Pali Tipitaka, the reader can consult *The Authenticity of the Early Buddhist Texts* by Bhikkhu Sujato and Bhikkhu Brahmali.

Material evidence of the Buddha is meagre. In the year 249 BCE the Indian emperor Asoka made a pilgrimage to Gotama's birthplace at Lumbinī and had a huge stone pillar erected there with an inscription on it. The inscription reads:

> "Twenty years after his coronation, Beloved-of-the-Gods, King Piyadasi (i.e., Asoka), visited this place and worshipped because here the Buddha, the sage of the Sakyans, was born. He had a stone figure and a pillar erected and because the Lord was born here, the village of Lumbinī was exempted from tax and required to pay only one eighth of the produce."

This is the earliest undisputed mention of the Buddha outside the Tipitaka. Another piece of evidence is an inscribed relic casket found in a stupa at Piprahwa, the site of Kapilavatthu, Gotama's hometown. The inscription reads: "This casket of relics of the blessed Buddha of the Sakyas [is gifted by] the brothers Sukirti, jointly with their sisters, sons and wives." Unfortunately, as is so frustratingly common with ancient Indian records, there is disagreement among scholars about the age of this inscription. Based on its orthography, some believe it is earlier than Asoka's inscriptions, but others consider it to be contemporary with them or even later. The jury is still out.[14]

---

13. On editing the suttas in order to aid memory see Anālayo 2011, pp.14 ff.
14. A great deal has been written in the last hundred years about the

Another piece of evidence may be a passage from the *Maitrāyaṇīya Upaniṣad* condemning "... the tawny robed ones who convert others with rational arguments, examples and the jugglery of a false doctrine that denies the soul, and who teach a Dhamma that is destructive to the Vedas..."[15] This *Upaniṣad* dates from after the Buddha, although not very long after, and seems to be referring to Buddhist monks and the distinctive Buddhist doctrine of *anatta*, both of which presuppose the Buddha himself. [16]

There is no chronologically arranged narrative of the Buddha's life in the Tipitaka as there is, for example, for Jesus in the Gospels or for Emperor Augustus in *De Vita Caesarum*. However, the Vinaya includes an account of approximately the first two years of the Buddha's career, starting with his awakening at Uruvelā up to the conversion and ordination of the two men who were to become his chief disciples, Sāriputta and Moggallāna.[17] This looks like it was the beginning of an attempt to write an account of the Buddha's life but for some reason it was never completed. The longest discourse in the Sutta Piṭaka also records the events in the Buddha's life from the time he left Rājagaha to his death in Kusināra about twelve months later. These two narratives indicate that, despite scholarly opinion on the matter, the ancient Buddhists did have a sense of history and wished to portray the Buddha at a particular time and place within it. In fact, these two Tipitaka narratives are the earliest examples from India of an attempt to describe historical events and to compose a continuous, coherent story.[18]

Nonetheless, it is almost impossible to work out when most of the other events in the Buddha's career took place during the more than four decades between these two narratives. Added to this is the fact that the Tipitaka records almost nothing about the Buddha's life before he became a wandering ascetic at the age of twenty-nine. Consequently, while we know a great deal of what the Buddha

---

Lumbinī and Piprahwa inscriptions and the identification of Kapilavatthu. Good representatives of the research are Fleet1906; Allen 2008; Falk 2017; and The Piprawa Project at http://www.piprahwa.com/home

15. 7.8-9 condensed. See also Jayatilleke p.66-68.
16. Wynne 2019 and Levman 2019 argue for the historicity of the Buddha.
17. Vin.I,1-44.
18. Hinüber, 2006, p.197.

taught, where he taught it, to whom he taught it, and sometimes the circumstances that prompted him to teach it, we know very little at all about exactly when in his life it took place. Thus a biography of him from birth to death is not possible.[19]

But biographies are more than just an account of chronologically arranged events. They also include details about their subject's character, habits, attitudes, achievements and relationships with others, and the Tipitaka includes a great deal of information about such things concerning the Buddha, perhaps more than about any other person from ancient times. Most of this information is in the form of vignettes, brief asides and tangential comments made in passing, which makes them all the more compelling because most of them have no doctrinal value and are therefore likely to be genuine memories of the people who knew and interacted with the Buddha. When all this material is put together with what can be inferred about the Buddha from what he taught, it provides a surprisingly realistic and complete portrait of the man.

One thing that raises doubts about the value of the Tipitaka for providing information about the Buddha as a real person is the supernormal abilities some passages ascribe to him. Examples of this include him levitating, hearing conversations over a long distance, reading people's minds, and being visited by and conversing with heavenly beings. Although the Buddha did have remarkable psychic abilities, some of those ascribed to him are probably later embellishments, and it is also likely that many of the people who interacted with the Buddha genuinely believed that they witnessed him manifesting such powers. It is well-known that charismatic individuals are often credited with having superhuman or at least exceptional abilities, and there is little doubt that the Buddha had a great deal of personal charisma.[20] As for the later embellishments, they express a world-view of which supernormal phenomena were a part. Indeed, it is likely that this very world-view was

19. Bv-a.4 includes a list of all the places the Buddha stayed during the yearly rainy season retreat during the first twenty years of his career. Although this text dates from the fifth century CE some of the material in it may be much earlier, and I suspect this list is mostly authentic.

20. Weber, Max. *The Theory of Social and Economic Organization*, 1947. pp.328, 358ff.

partly responsible for the inclusion of such material into the Tipitaka. That and the prestige this may have given the sermons in the eyes of the intended audience, are sufficient to explain why they are there. There is no good reason for thinking that the existence of these elements shows that the transmission of the core material in the Tipitaka is unreliable.[21]

21. A paraphrase of Sujato and Brahmali, p.112.

2
An Era of Change

> To the frontier town of Kajaṅgala and nearby Mahāsālā in the east, and to the Sallavatī River in the south-east, does the Middle Land extend. To the town of Setakaṇṇika in the south, the brahmin village of Thūna in the west, and the Usīraddhaja Mountains in the north does the Middle Land extend.
>
> Vinaya I, 197

The Buddha was born in and spent his whole life in what was then called by the people who lived there the Middle Land (*majjhima desa*), an area roughly equivalent to the modern north Indian states of Bihar and Uttar Pradesh.

In about the seventh century BCE a discovery was made that was to have a profound effect on every aspect of life in this region. Iron was discovered in what is now northern Jharkhand and the hills between Agra and Gwalior. This metal had been known in India for at least a few hundred years before this, but the metal now discovered was closer to the surface and of a higher quality, meaning that it was easier to mine and smelt. Now every farmer could have an iron tip on his ploughshare and an iron hoe or spade to turn the earth where his plough could not be used. Iron sickles made harvesting less laborious, and iron nails held wooden structures together better. More significantly, it meant that the forests which covered much of the Middle Land could be cleared more efficiently, thus opening up more land for agriculture.

Up until this time, most settlements in the Middle Land were small and on or near rivers; now they gradually became larger and started appearing in the hinterland. Where once only tribal people and hunters roamed, now agriculturalists settled and laid out fields. Most of these settlements grew organically, but there is evidence that kings founded villages to hasten the development of their kingdoms. One text describes how a king had a reservoir excavated and cottages built, which encouraged farmers to move to the site from elsewhere. The ground around a nearby sacred tree was levelled for as far as its branches extended, then surrounded by a fence with arched gates so that the new settlers would have somewhere to worship.[1] The net result of these changes was a larger food surplus and a consequent growth in the population, so that small settlements grew into villages, villages into towns and towns into cities.[2] For the first time since Mohenjo-Daro, Harappa and Rakhigarhi, the great cities of the Indus Valley a thousand years earlier, large population centres became a feature of the landscape of northern India.

The Buddha described a mythical ideal city he called Kusavatī as being "twelve *yojanas* long from east to west and seven wide from north to south. It was rich and prosperous, crowded, full of people and with abundant food ... Day and night it resounded with the ten sounds; that of elephants and horses, chariots and drums, tablas and veenas, singing, cymbals and gongs, and with cries of 'Eat, drink, and eat more.'"[3] Although fanciful, parts of this description are clearly based on what one of the main metropolises the Buddha was familiar with could have been like.

In the texts, cities are described as having ramparts or walls with towers at intervals along them, gates, and sometimes as having moats around them.[4] Gatekeepers would scrutinize everyone who entered the city and would patrol the walls to make sure there was no way for anyone to creep in or out at night.[5] The east gate was usually considered the most auspicious and therefore was the main entrance into the city, while the

1. Ja.V,511. *Arthaśāstra* II,1,1-4 details how the setting up of new villages was to be done.

2. Dyson, p.37 gives an approximation of the population of some of these cities in about 100 CE.

3. D.II,170. Vin.I,254 says that Sāketa was six yojanas from Sāvatthī and as the two are about ninety kilometers apart by a relatively straight road, this would make a yojana about fifteen kilometers. However, how far a yojana was considered varied from one region to another and during different periods. See Srinivasan, pp.25-29.

4. S.IV,194.

5. S.IV,194; V,160; D.II,83.

south gate was the most inauspicious, beyond which was the rubbish dump, the charnel ground or cremation ground and execution ground. The gates were usually named after the destination they opened to.[6]

Some of the notable buildings in a city included the king's palace, the court, the treasury, the tax office and the market. The most important public buildings in any city or town were the municipal halls, which usually consisted of an open-pillared structure on a platform. Typically, there were also alms halls at each city gate, in the centre of the city, and at the entrance to the king's palace. The most basic of these halls were provided with benches and water jars,[7] and during festive occasions or religious events alms would be distributed from these halls to the poor, the indigent and wandering ascetics. They also provided shelter for travellers who had nowhere else to stay and for ascetics who might be passing through. There were also halls for entertainment (*kutūhala sālā*), which served as venues for popular events, including religious debates. Queen Mallikā of Kosala built such a hall next to a line of Tinduka trees in her park in Sāvatthī, and the Tipitaka records an occasion when some three hundred ascetics of different sects assembled there.[8]

Most ordinary houses were made of wood, wattle and daub or unfired brick and roofed with thatch or with tiles for those who could afford them. The Buddha described a prosperous citizen's residence as "a peak-roofed house plastered inside and out and with well-fitted doors and shutters keeping the draft out. Inside there might be a couch spread with woollen blankets and covers, a fine antelope skin, with a canopy above and crimson pillows at either end, an oil lamp burning and four wives attentive to their master's pleasure."[9] Archaeological investigation of early cities such as Rājagaha, Vesālī, Kosambī and Bhita show that houses typically had two floors and did not abut each other but always had a small gap between them, probably so that during fires one house could be cleared without destroying the adjacent one.[10]

---

6. Agrawala, p.140.
7. Ja.I,199.
8. D.I,178; M.II,22. The Tinduka tree is the Indian Persimmon, *Diospyros malabarica*.
9. A.I,137.
10. *Arthaśāstra* III 8,13 recommends a gap between houses, probably for this reason.

Although there is no mention in the Tipitaka of fires sweeping through cities or towns, such disasters must have periodically happened, given that most buildings were of wood, all cooking was done on open fires and all lighting at night was by lamp. There was a custom, or in some cities or towns a law, that each household had to have five pots of water available to fight fires that might break out.[11] Once, it was reported to the Buddha that the women's quarters in Kosambī's royal palace had caught fire, resulting in numerous deaths.[12]

As nearly all the cities of the time were on the banks of large rivers, another danger they were subject to was flooding. Archaeology has uncovered evidence of massive flooding in Patna, and Hastinapura was flooded so many times that it was eventually abandoned for several centuries. It is not surprising that the Buddha frequently mentions fire and floods as two of the dangers to a family's hard-earned wealth.[13]

With large numbers of people living close to each other and sanitary arrangements rudimentary at best, another problem cities faced was the outbreak and spread of disease. What might be one of the few mentions of such occurrences was when Ānanda informed the Buddha that a monk, a nun and ten lay disciples had recently died in Nādikā, perhaps because there had been an epidemic of some kind in the town.[14]

Another feature of the cities was parks and gardens, some of them private and others open to the public, a few within the cities but most in their environs. There is evidence that some of these parks included flowers, bushes and trees planted for ornamental purposes, ponds beautified with water lilies and lotuses, bowers of flowering creepers, and benches. The royal pleasure garden in Sāvatthī included an art gallery (*cittāgāra*) which was open to the public, at least sometimes.[15] The Veḷuvana, the Bamboo Grove, just beyond the north gate of Rājagaha, had places where people could come to feed the squirrels and peacocks.[16] Most of these parks and gardens, however, or at least

---

11. Mil. 43. This is also mentioned at *Arthaśāstra* II 36,18.
12. Ud.79.
13. A.II, 68; IV,281-82.
14. D.II,91.
15. Vin.IV,298.
16. M.I,145; II,1.

the ones open to the public, were just small pockets of forest which had been preserved as the suburbs expanded. They were popular places for the many ascetics of the time to lodge or meet with other ascetics or lay folk who were interested in what they had to say. There are numerous references to the Buddha or his monastics staying in or spending the day in such parks and being visited by people wanting to converse with them. Encountering the Buddha at the Añjana Park at Sāketa, the ascetic Kuṇḍaliya described for him how he spent his time:

> "After I have finished my breakfast, it is my habit to amble from one park or garden to another, and while there I observe various ascetics and brahmins discussing how they can defend their position during a debate and criticise the positions of others."[17]

The Buddha praised one such place, Rājagaha's Bamboo Grove, as being "not too near the city, not too far, convenient for coming and going, quiet, secluded from people, good for sitting without being disturbed and conducive to spiritual practice."[18] So associated were gardens with wandering ascetics of all sects, including Buddhist monks, that the word *ārāma*, garden or park, actually took on the double meaning of monastery or hermitage.

There were no temples at this time, but there were religious shrines (*cetiya*): trees or rock formations in which gods or spirits were believed to dwell and earthen mounds (*thūpa*, Sanskrit *stūpa*) raised over the ashes of long dead saints or heroes. The ashes of Mahāvīra, the leader of the Jains, were interred in a stupa, and King Muṇda raised a stupa over the ashes of his queen, perhaps because he had great love and esteem for her.[19] Vesālī had such shrines at each of the four directions around the city and at a number of other locations within it. The Buddha once visited the Maṇimālaka Cetiya in Rājagaha, where the spirit (*yakkha*) Maṇibhadda was believed to reside.[20] This shrine, much rebuilt and renovated over the centuries, still exists and is now known as Maniyar Math.

---

17. S.V,73.
18. Vin.I,39.
19. M.II,244; A.III,62.
20. S.I,208.

The evidence from Buddhist texts and other contemporary sources indicates that the cities and towns of the Middle Land supported a lively civic and cultural life. Philanthropic individuals had large reservoirs excavated in which people could bathe, wash and do laundry and from which they could fetch drinking water. These reservoirs were sometimes lined with stone, had steps leading down into them, and could be planted with lotuses to beautify them. Vesālī had several such reservoirs, and the Sumāgandha Pond in Rājagaha was one of the sights of the city, as was Queen Gaggarā's Lotus Lake in Campā. One Jātaka story recounts how a wealthy individual endowed his city with what would now be called a civic centre. After consulting with architects and designers, he had a complex built with accommodation for travellers, the homeless and the sick, with one section for males and another for females. There were venues for sports, for religious activities and for hearing court cases, and outside the complex was a reservoir with bathing steps, surrounded by a garden. When the whole complex was completed, the donor engaged artists to cover all the walls with paintings.[21] Although this story is perhaps exaggerated, there is little doubt that the wealthy sometimes did establish such places.

Poetry was already a highly developed art, and recitals took place in small groups and at various public gatherings. The Buddha had some interest in and knowledge of poetry. He was familiar with poets composing in four different genres, conversant with prosody, and mentioned that the most popular hymn was the *sāvittī*.[22] His appreciation of poetry was probably the reason why some of his disciples were either accomplished poets or became so, e.g., Vaṅgīsa, who composed a series of beautiful verses in praise of the Buddha, and also Ambapālī, India's first poetess.

It was common to see itinerant entertainers in city streets – pole acrobats, snake charmers, magicians and minstrels. Brief references to actors, dancers, mimes and bards, and of performers' managers, suggests that such entertainment had reached a sophisticated level.[23]

---

21. Ja.VI,333.

22. S.I,38; A.II,230; Sn.568. The *sāvittī*, now known as the Gāyatrī mantra, has three lines and twenty-four syllables, Sn.457.

23. Ja.II,430 S. IV, 306; Vin.IV,285.

Every year in Rājagaha there was an event called the Hilltop Festival (*giraggasamajja*), at which there was much eating, drinking and theatrical performances.[24] Occasionally there also seems to have even been something like informal beauty pageants, where the winner would be designated the fairest in the land. The Buddha described crowds of people jostling each other to see such a winner and urging her to sing and dance for them.[25]

The cows that wandered through city streets could sometimes injure or even kill people, as happened to Bāhiya just after his discussion with the Buddha. To minimize this hazard, cattle would sometimes have their horns removed.[26] It was normal to throw human waste, rubbish and food scraps into the streets which were as a result, odorous, dirty and usually only cleaned just before festivals.[27] We read of "the drains and rubbish heaps in the alleys" at Kusinārā.[28] With no street lighting, being out at night, especially late, could be problematic and was something the Buddha advised his disciples to avoid.[29] Walking through a city or town in the dark, one might fall into a cesspit or sewer, stumble over a sleeping cow, or encounter delinquents intent on crime or a prostitute offering to expose herself for a small coin.[30]

Occasional civil disturbances were not unknown either. There is a mention of a minor riot over a prostitute by a group of youths and widespread public drunkenness during some festivals.[31] Occasionally some of the wandering ascetics of the time would come into the cities and towns to try to get some basic necessities, like cast-off clothes, salt, medicine or just food. They could be seen standing at doors with their alms bowls or sitting at strategic locations with their hands out asking for alms.

While the new and growing cities and towns in the Middle Land could have large populations, the majority of people still lived in

24. Vin.II,107. For more on drama in ancient India see Wijesekera pp.13 ff.
25. S.V,170.
26. Ud.8; A.IV,376.
27. Vin.IV,265. A toilet similar to that described at Vin.II,222 is displayed in Vesālī's site museum, Acc. No.244. See also Roy 1987 pp.341-350.
28. D.II,160.
29. Vin. IV, 265; D.III,183.
30. M.I,448; Vin.II,112.
31. Ud.71.

villages. The inhabitants of most villages were farmers, although the texts have frequent references to villages of potters, fisherman, reed-cutters, smiths, salt makers and carpenters, reflecting the division of labour that was taking place at the time. Typically, a village would be surrounded by a fence, sometimes of mud bricks, wood or thorny tree branches as a protection against wild animals and thieves, and be entered through a gate.[32] The village's boundary, which included its fields and common land, were also clearly defined, to avoid conflicts with neighbouring villages and for taxation purposes.[33] The repetition and drudgery of the farmer's life was described by the Buddha's cousin Anuruddha like this: "Having brought in the crop, exactly the same thing has to be done the next year and exactly the same the year after that. The work never ends; there is no end in sight to it."[34]

Burdensome taxation, banditry and, worst of all, the vagaries of the weather meant that life was hard for rural folk. While the ancient law books stipulated that a fair tax on the harvest should range from a sixth to a twelfth, in reality rulers, whether kings or council elders, could raise as much revenue as they wanted, on top of imposing levies and charges for numerous other things.[35] But it was the unpredictability of the weather that posed the greatest threat. A drought might cause food shortages for city-dwellers, but it could mean death for rural folk. The texts mention a famine in Kāsi because of the monsoon's failure three years in a row, so that the land looked "as if scorched by fire."[36] The Buddha spoke of how a drought in one region would cause hungry people to flee to another region, where they would have to live in crowded conditions in what we would call refugee camps.[37] Even when the monsoons were late by only a week or two, people would be haunted by what were called the three fears (*tīṇi bhayāni*): fear of drought, of famine and of disease.[38] And in a cruel irony, sometimes it was not

32. Vin.III,52.
33. Vin.I,110. See Agrawala pp.143-144.
34. Vin.II,181.
35. E.g., *Manusmṛti* 7,130; *Gautama Dharmasūtra* 10,24.
36. Ja.V,193.
37. A.III,104.
38. Ja.II,367. The Buddha referred to the four fears as fires, floods, kings and bandits, A.II,121.

lack of rain causing the problem but too much, so that the subsequent floods destroyed crops, resulting in famine.[39] Someone once asked the Buddha why in the past the population was large enough that "villages, towns and royal capitals were so close together that a rooster could fly from one to another," whereas now there were far fewer people. He replied that peoples' excessive greed had caused civil strife, droughts and malevolent spirits, all of which had made the population decline.[40] As the Buddha saw it, "life is short, limited and fleeting, and only rarely does anyone live to a hundred."[41]

The Buddha observed that if a man had been away from his village for an extended period and he were by chance to meet another man from his village, he would anxiously ask whether things back home were safe, whether there had been any epidemics, food shortages or attacks by gangs of bandits; such was the precariousness of rural life.[42] So that his disciples would not become complacent, the Buddha asked them to occasionally reflect that, while now the harvests were good and food plentiful, this situation could easily change, and thus they should make full use of the good times to practise the Dhamma.[43]

Of course, life could not have been all work and want, at least not for everyone, everywhere and all the time. There were occasional opportunities for relaxation and revelry, even at religious events. The Buddha spoke of one such religious gathering that took place in the southern districts, which included food and drink, singing, dancing and music.[44] Also, he said that with good government the land could be at peace, and banditry could be suppressed so that happy people, with joyful hearts, would be able to dance with their children in their arms and keep their homes unlocked.[45]

---

39. Ja.II,135.
40. A.I,159-160. Concerning droughts, the Buddha accepted the common belief that widespread immorality or an unjust ruler could adversely affect the weather.
41. D.II,52.
42. M.II,253.
43. A.III,104.
44. A.V,216.
45. D.I,136.

City folk tended to consider villagers to be unsophisticated boors and looked upon them with a degree of contempt. In ordinary parlance the term *gamma*, 'of the village', meant something low and crude. In keeping with this common usage the Buddha described sexual intercourse, going to see various spectacles and idle chatter to be "*gamma*." Although the deeper and more philosophical aspects of the Buddha's teachings would have held little interest for the average villager, his moral and social teachings certainly did, and it was probably these aspects of the Dhamma that he taught during his tours, when he would often stay in villages.

The increasing food surplus, the growth in population and the rise of cities stimulated another major change in the Middle Land, and that was the expansion of commerce and the beginning of long-distance and transcontinental trade. Previously, village communities were almost entirely self-sufficient, growing their own food and having most of their other necessities made by local craftsmen. Their few other essentials they obtained from neighbouring villages, from the nearby forest or from the occasional peddler or small-time trader who passed through with his donkey or bullock cart. Exchange was mainly by barter.

There are numerous references in the Tipitaka to caravans of wagons carrying goods from one city or region to another. While the Buddha was still at Uruvelā just after his awakening, he met the two merchants Tapussa and Bhallika who were from Ukkalā, probably somewhere in Orissa.[46] The texts do not mention these two men being attached to a caravan, but, coming from such a long distance, they would have been. The wealthy businessman and patron of the Buddha, Anāthapiṇḍaka, travelled from his home base in Sāvatthī to Rājagaha and back on business and had a business estate in Kāsi.[47] There is mention of several hundred wagons carrying jars of sugar along the main road between Rājagaha and Andhakavinda, and when the Buddha rested at the foot of a tree while on his way to Kusinārā, a caravan of carts forded a nearby stream.[48] Caravans would sometimes halt in one location for months,

46. Vin.IV,4. Buddhist artefacts and early Brahmi inscriptions mentioning the names Tapussa and Bhallika have been found in Tarapur, Jaipur District in Orissa, see Mohanty pp.1-11.

47. Vin.II,154 ff; IV,162.

48. Vin.I,224; D.II,128. When Tavernier was in India in the 17th century he

acting as a trading post for districts in the vicinity. The Jātaka includes a story about a young merchant whose caravans travelled "now from east to west, and now from north to south."[49] One wagon in his caravan carried large clay jars of water for when passing through areas where no water was available, and at night the wagons would be arranged in a circle for protection. A similar story tells of a caravan that passed through a desert, probably Rajasthan's Thar Desert, so hot that the caravan could only travel at night, and the pilot navigated by the stars.[50]

Kings and chiefdom administrations set up custom posts at river crossings, mountain passes and city gates to collect fees from caravans. Special government officials manned customs posts and were sometimes ensconced in large caravans to make sure they paid duty at the designated places.[51] Once, the Buddha scolded a monk for being the beneficiary of a fraud because he had travelled with a merchant's caravan knowing that it intended to bypass a customs post and thereby avoid paying duty.[52] We read of merchants from a handful of countries meeting together to elect a president, probably to establish an international trading house, and of a city providing a place where foreign merchants could temporarily store their goods.[53] The Buddha characterized such merchants and traders as always thinking: "I will get this from here and that from there."[54]

Merchants and craftsmen formed guilds (*seṇi* or *pūga*) to oversee and protect their interests. Traditionally, there were said to be eighteen guilds, and their presidents or aldermen had direct access to the king or the ruling council and sometimes even held the position of finance minister. The Buddha mentions guilds conducting courts to arbitrate disputes between their members.[55]

---

witnessed caravans of up to 12,000 bullock carts. Sometimes oncoming traffic was obliged to wait two or three days for them to pass; *Travels in India* by Jean Baptiste Tavernier,1886, Vol.1 pp.39-40.

49. Ja.I,98.
50. Ja.I,107.
51. Vin.IV,131.
52. Vin.IV,131.
53. Ja.VI,333.
54. M.II,232.
55. M.I,288.

Concurrent with the growth in trade, the first currency in India appeared in perhaps 600 BCE: countable units of copper, silver and gold coins, with punch marks rather than legends. The standard denomination was the *kahāpaṇa*, and these were issued by trading houses, guilds and governments.[56] The use of money created professions such as accounting, auditing and calculating (*mudda, gaṇanā, saṅkhā*) which, along with trade and farming, the Buddha considered legitimate livelihoods.[57]

Beyond village-based producers such as carpenters, smiths, potters and basket weavers, the Tipitaka mentions other workers and craftsmen which suggest the existence of disposable income and the demand for luxurious non-essentials. These include goldsmiths, jewellers, ivory-workers, garland-makers and florists, silk weavers, coach-builders, confectioners and perfumers. One much sought-after luxury was the embroidered fabric known as Kāsi cloth manufactured in Bārāṇasī which the Buddha described as being smooth on both sides, having a beautiful colour, being pleasant to the touch, and so valuable that even when it was worn out it was used to wrap gems in or kept in a scented chest. He also mentioned that as a layman his turban, tunic, waist cloth and wrap-around scarf were all made of Kāsi cloth.[58] There were assessors (*agghakāraka*) who valued elephants, horses, precious stones, gold and other high-priced articles for royal courts and the affluent, artists who did paintings on the walls of buildings, on cloth and on polished wooden panels, and weavers who made silk cloth with gems sewn into it.[59]

Products were imported into the Middle Land from far beyond it: horses from Sindh; sandalwood from south India; a type of crimson coloured blanket and wine from Gandhāra; fine Siveyyaka cloth from Sivi; conch shells from the far south, to name but a few. The Tipitaka also mentions high-value, low-volume items such as pearls, beryl, lapis lazuli, quartz, red coral, ruby and cat's-eye, most of which also made their way into the Middle Land by way

---

56. On the various coins and their values see Agrawala, pp.259-274.
57. M.I,85; D. I,51; S.IV,376; Ja.IV,422; Ud.31-32.
58. D.II,110; A.I,248-249;145.
59. Ja.I,124; S.II,101-02, A.I,181.

of trade.[60] The Buddha opined that trading was a livelihood which had certain advantages over more traditional ones such as farming:

> "Agriculture is an occupation with much to do, many duties, much forethought, great problems and which, if it succeeds, yields great profit… Trading is an occupation which requires little work, fewer duties, planning and problems, and if successful yields greater profit."[61]

Like much else in the Middle Land during the sixth to fourth centuries BCE, momentous changes were also taking place in politics. The few details recorded in the Tipitaka enable us to say that the old republics or chiefdoms (*saṅgha* or *gaṇa*) were gradually giving way to monarchies (*rājaka*). The main kingdoms were Magadha, Kosala, Vaṃsā and Pañcāla, and the chiefdoms were the Vajjian confederacy and those of the Mallas, Cedis, Videhas, Koliyas, and the Buddha's clan the Sakyas, all of them small.

While kings could rule as they liked, restrained perhaps to some extent by precedent and tradition, the chiefdoms had participatory governments, although this was only open to the men of high-status families. The Mallas of Kusinārā for example, had a governing body of eight counsellors (*pāmokkha*).[62] The chiefdoms' cities, towns and even villages had council halls where the business of the state or the community was conducted. The Buddha was invited by the Mallas of Pāvā to inaugurate their new council hall by spending the night in it.[63] Apparently it was considered auspicious to have a revered person 'open' such buildings by doing this.

One text describes how the gods conducted business in their celestial council hall, which gives a clue to the way such assemblies were conducted in their earthly equivalent. The participants were seated in a specific order; after the chairman had presented business to the assembly, others spoke on the issues involved, and then there was more voting and discussion until a majority or a unanimous decision was reached.[64]

---

60. Ud.54; Vin.I,278. Sivi is now Sibi in Pakistan's Balochistan.
61. M.II,197-99.
62. D.II,160.
63. D.III,207.
64. D.II,208-209.

Terms such as party or faction (*vagga*), party whip (*gaṇapūraka*), motion (*ñatti*), arbitration (*ubbāhikā*), constituency (*sīmā*), referendum (*yebhuyyasikā*), and rules of the council (*sabhādhamma*) indicate that there were accepted procedures for conducting such assemblies. In some councils at least, ballot tickets, literally 'sticks' (*salākā*), were used to cast votes (*chandaka*), and there could be open voting (*vivaṭaka*) or secret voting (*gūḷhaka*). The Buddha adopted many of the procedures and rules of the chiefdoms in the running of the monastic Saṅgha. Less formal were the town and village meeting days (*negamassa samayo*) presided over by the headman (*gāmaṇī*), at which the population would gather and discuss matters concerning their general welfare.[65]

There are references to some of the kingdoms going to war with each other but none of the chiefdoms doing so. Before Gotama's birth, or perhaps during his childhood, King Vaṅka of Kosala had invaded and annexed Kāsi. Later records say that the Sakyan country was incorporated into Kosala after a swift and bloody campaign, probably within a few years of the Buddha's demise. The most aggressive kingdom of the time was Magadha, which had already annexed Aṅga, again probably during Gotama's youth. Later, when Ajātasattu was on the throne of Magadha, he invaded Kāsi, initially defeating Kosala's army but then being driven out by a Kosalan counter-attack.[66] The Tipitaka has a brief reference to Ajātasattu strengthening Rājagaha's fortifications, fearing that King Pajjota of Avanti might invade and, in the last months of the Buddha's life, of him building fortifications at Pāṭaligāma in preparation for a planned conflict with the Vajjians.[67] Within a century of the Buddha's passing, Magadha emerged as the paramount power, firstly in northern India and eventually in most of the subcontinent.

It is hard to know how large or destructive these and the few other inter-state conflicts were, but even brief skirmishes could have been bloody, as the Buddha's comments on war testify. He spoke of how "men take up swords and shields, buckle on bows and quivers, and both sides fling themselves into battle and, with arrows flying, knives waving

65. Vin.III,220.
66. S.I,82-85.
67. M.III,7; D.II,86.

and swords flashing, they pierce with arrows, wound with knives and decapitate with swords and so suffer death or death-like pain."[68] He also described how a soldier might "lose heart, falter or be unable to brace himself" on seeing even the dust thrown up by the opposing army's approach and how those besieging a fortress or city could be "splashed with boiling oil or crushed by heavy objects" thrown down on them.[69]

The process whereby a chief might transform himself firstly into a despot and eventually into a monarch is unclear but it probably happened through irregular or contested means. The political systems in most of the chiefdoms were not like Athenian democracy but were rather oligarchic, where certain elites or families dominated political power. Nevertheless, an unpopular chief, even though duly elected, might have to bend to popular opinion or risk being overthrown.

This was the world Gotama was born into, although it is unlikely that he was aware of much of it until he became a wandering ascetic, his homeland being on the outer edge of and relatively uninfluenced by much of what was going in the rest of northern India.

---

68. M.I,86-7.
69. A.III,89.

3
Gods, Brahmins and Ascetics

The majority of people in the Middle Land during the Buddha's time were not Hindus, as is commonly supposed, but rather animists. Because this animism was an informal, unstructured religion, it has left few traces of its presence, but something of it can be culled from Brahminical, Jain and Buddhist sources and to some degree from contemporary Indian folk religion.

There were no temples at this time, but there were shrines to various gods and spirits or sometimes revered kings, heroes or people deemed saintly. The Buddha observed that "many people go for help to sacred hills, groves, trees and shrines."[1] People believed that the spirits who inhabited such places or the energy emanating from them had a protective power or would respond to the prayers or offerings made at them. Milk and water were poured on the roots of sacred trees, garlands were hung on the branches, lamps of scented oil were burned around them, and cloth was tied around their trunks.[2] A type of red or ochre-coloured paste (*vaṇṇaka*) would be smeared on shrines and flowers placed before them.[3] There is mention of animal and occasionally even human sacrifices being made to sacred trees. The victim's blood was poured around the foot of the tree, and the entrails were draped over the branches.[4] As today, the trees that were most likely to be inhabited by gods were pipal trees or banyan trees, particularly old and majestic ones.

The belief in and worship of various spirits, such as *yakkha*s (and their female equivalents *yakkhinī*s), *bhūta*s, *nāga*s, *rakkhasa*s, *kumbhaṇḍa*s, *pisāca*s and *picācillikā*s was also common. These beings

1. Dhp.188.
2. Ja.II,104.
3. D.II,142.
4. Ja.I,260; III,160.

lurked in cemeteries, remote stretches of forests and along lonely roads and encountering one at night would be enough to make one's hair stand on end.[5] Some were benevolent, but more usually they were menacing and had to be propitiated with offerings of flowers and incense or, for the more malevolent ones, with meat and alcohol.[6] A yakkha, a type of ogre, could possess people, which was a "fierce, terrible and horrifying" experience, causing the victim to cry out in alarm: "This yakkha has possessed me, harmed and hurt me, and will not let me go!"[7] One later text says that yakkhas named Kāla and Upakālaka were worshipped in Kapilavatthu, the Buddha's hometown.[8] *Nāgas* were semi-aquatic beings inhabiting deep lakes or lonely jungle pools. They could adopt a human form one minute and a serpent-like one the next. Generally kindly when treated with respect, *nāgas* could quickly change if crossed and kill with their poisonous breath or incinerate with their laser-like gaze.

Gods (*devas*) were seen as being in some sense separate from and higher than the various spirits. Pāṇini made a distinction between the 'official' gods of the Vedas and worldly (*laukika*) gods of folk beliefs, such as earth spirits (*bhumā devā*).[9] But by the fifth century BCE it was becoming more difficult to separate the two, as Brahminism gradually assimilated many local deities into its pantheon, usually by claiming that they were a different 'aspect' of a Vedic god or simply a god's alternative name. Many of the local or regional gods and goddesses were associated with fertility, rain and the protection of crops. Some of the more popular of these, such as Śri, the goddess of good fortune, and Vessavaṇa, the king of the directional gods, were later merged into the Hindu pantheon as Lakshmi and Kubera.

The formal religion during the Buddha's time was Brahminism, which, in the centuries after the Buddha, gradually morphed into Hinduism. Those who practiced this religion were known as Vedists (*vaidika*). Brahminism had a priesthood, a canon of scriptures, a liturgical language, and various clearly defined doctrines and rituals.

---

5. D.II,346; Ja.I,99; Vin.II,156-157.
6. Ja.I,425; 489.
7. D.III,203-4. There are no examples of the Buddha performing exorcisms.
8. See Sircar, p.268.
9. *Aṣṭādhyāyī* VI.3,26; M.I,210.

Its sacred texts were the three Vedas – the *Ṛgveda*, *Yajurveda* and the *Sāmaveda* – with the first of these being the oldest and most important. A collection of spells, incantations and magical charms called the *āthabbaṇa* was known to the Buddha in the fifth century BCE and came to be accepted as a fourth Veda, the *Artharvaveda*, some centuries later.[10]

The Vedas consist of hymns addressed to various gods, praising them and calling upon them for help. The most popular of these gods were Pajāpati, Soma, Indra, Yama and Agni, although there were many others. The sacrifices (*yāga*) during which the hymns were chanted were the central sacrament of Brahminism. They were elaborate rituals conducted by a number of brahmin priests and arranged by a sponsor hoping to gain wealth, progeny, the love of a woman, victory over rivals or other worldly gains from one or another of the gods. The sacred fires that were the focus of the sacrifice were ignited, and offerings of ghee, milk, grain, cakes and flowers were thrown into the flames and carried aloft to the gods in the smoke. There were sacrifices marking the passing of the seasons, to consecrate rulers, to ward off calamity, to bring rain, to guarantee victory in war and for a hundred other matters. In more important sacrifices, animals were slaughtered and offered to the fire. The Buddhist texts describe one such sacrifice in which hundreds of bulls, bullocks, heifers, goats and rams were slaughtered.[11] During other sacrifices a hallucinogenic drink called soma was consumed by the brahmins and shared with the gods, although by the fifth century BCE the plant from which this drink was made seems to have disappeared. There were also much smaller and less elaborate domestic sacrifices which were done daily in the home and conducted by the family.

Vedic Brahminism had its origins perhaps a thousand years before the Buddha, beyond the western edge of the Middle Land in what is now northwestern Pakistan and adjoining areas of Afghanistan. This region was called Āryāvarta, and its inhabitants were a semi-nomadic people who called themselves Aryans (*āryas*), noble ones. One of the most notable features of the Aryan's religion was the belief that humans

10. Sn.927.

11. A.IV,41. This number of victims is "hyperbole far beyond actual *vaidika* practice" and no doubt ment for affect, Pollock, 2005, p.403.

were of four different kinds: brahmins or priests; warriors (*khattiya*); traders/farmers (*vessa*); and menials (*sudda*, Sanskrit *śūdra*). Below these groups were forest-dwelling peoples who were beyond the pale of Aryan society and were considered untouchables. The first three castes were called twice-born (Sanskrit *dvija* or *dvijāti*) because at a certain age a male underwent an initiation rite which cemented him into his caste and its practices and obligations; but the fourth caste, the menials, could not participate in any Vedic rituals, and untouchables and foreigners had no place in Brahminical religion at all. According to the *Ṛgveda*, each caste had been created from different parts of Pajāpati's body: the brahmins from his mouth; warriors from his arms; traders/farmers from his thighs; and the menials from his feet.[12] No explanation was offered for the origins of the untouchables.

To the Aryans, the people of the Middle Land to their east were demonic and "as stupid as cows" because they did not follow Aryan customs, worship the Vedic gods or honour brahmins.[13] According to some Brahminical texts it was improper to perform the sacrifice in the east, i.e., the Middle Land. Worse still, Easterners were lax in their practice of caste, the cornerstone of the Vedic social order, and thus were ritually impure. Nevertheless, for several centuries the Aryans had been gradually moving east, bringing their culture and religion with them, so that by the Buddha's time Brahminism was on the way to being integrated into the culture of the Middle Land, transforming it and to some extent, being transformed by it. Brahmins recommend themselves to kings and local rulers, giving them legitimacy, offering to perform rituals that could guarantee victory in war, regular rainfall and male progeny; and acting as administrators and advisors. In return, they were granted estates and certain privileges, and their social theories, particularly the fourfold division of society, were given theoretical justifications that led them to becoming accepted as the norm. The Buddhist scriptures mention both brahmins living in their own villages and of brahmins coming "from the north," implying

---

12. This belief became central to Hindu social life and is mentioned at *Ṛgveda* X, 90; *Atharvaveda* XX.6, 6; *Taittīyrīya Saṃhitā* 7,1, 1, 4-6; *Manusmṛti* I, 31; *Bhagavad Gīta* IV,13; *Mahābhārata* 12. 73, 4-5 and in several *Purāṇas*.
13. *Śatapatha Brāhamaṇa* 13.8.1.5; *Mahābhārata* III p.368.I,20.

that they were purer and more ritually potent having come from the Āryavata rather than in the inferior Middle Land.

Over the centuries, and certainly by the Buddha's time, the meaning of the Vedic sacrifice had changed and, with it, how the ritual was performed. The hymns came to be seen more as magical spells that, if pronounced absolutely correctly, would compel the gods to grant requests. What had been relatively simple rituals became increasingly complex and expensive and entailed significant amounts of offerings being thrown into the sacred fire. The fees brahmins required for performing these and other rituals had also become exorbitant. The growing dissatisfaction with these changes resulted in some people, at least, beginning to reinterpret certain Brahminical doctrines, a trend reflected in the early *Upaniṣads*, and encouraged an openness to the broader religious culture of the Middle Land.

Brahminism was very much a community-centred, family-orientated religion. The ideal setting for the twice-born's life was living amongst his kin in a village, and his goal was to have a faithful wife who could give him sons and to be rich in land and cattle. The new cities that were sprouting up were repugnant to brahmins. One text states: "They say that a man who disciplines himself well will attain final bliss even though he lives in a city, with his body, hands and face covered with its dust. But this is impossible!"[14] A similar attitude is echoed in another text: "He should avoid a main city as he would…the boiling caldron of hell."[15] Some brahmins even maintained that the sacrifice would not work if it was performed in a city. Brahminism was a religion of the countryside; as we shall see, Buddhism was more a religion of towns and cities.

Not a religion as such, but a religious movement which had a presence throughout the Middle Land, probably for centuries already before the Buddha's time, was that of a class of ascetics most commonly called *samaṇas*.[16] These ascetics were also known variously as wanderers (*paribbājaka*), because of their homelessness; ford-makers (*titthakara*), because they were endeavouring to find or claimed to have found a way

---

14. *Baudhāyana Dharmasūtra* 2.6,33.

15. *Nāradaparivrājaka Upaniṣad* 7, 95. *Manusmṛti* 4, 107; *Āpastamba* 1. 32, 21; and *Gautama Dharmasūtra* 16. 45 make this same point.

16. On the origin and meaning of the word see Olivelle 1993, pp.11-16.

to cross the raging river of conditioned existence; mendicants (*bhikkhu* or *piṇḍola*), because they begged for alms; or silent ones (*muni*), for their penchant for being quiet and retiring. As well as being itinerant and mendicant, most *samaṇas* were also celibate. The Buddha said of the typical samaṇa that, "having accepted sufficient alms, he goes his way, as a bird, when it flies here or there, takes nothing with it but its wings."[17] He described his senior disciple Sāriputta as an ideal samaṇa because he was one "with few wishes, contented, secluded, solitary, energetic and devoted to developing the higher mind."[18] Although most *samaṇas* were males, there were smaller numbers of females who had chosen the life of renunciation. According to which sect they belonged to, some of these women wore their hair in a topknot. Having men and women in the same group together could lead to problems, and the Buddha reported some male wandering ascetics saying: "Real happiness is the downy soft arms of a female wanderer."[19]

It has been argued that the samaṇa tradition was a response to disaffection and alienation caused by the new urbanization taking place at this time and thus that it was a recent phenomenon, but it is more likely that it was an ancient tradition indigenous to the Middle Land. Others have argued that Buddhism started as a reaction against Brahmanism but this theory is increasingly being called into question too.[20]

In contrast to the brahmins, the *samaṇas* generally rejected the Vedas and most Brahminical beliefs and practices and gave precedence to personal experience over dogma and scriptural authority. They experimented with meditation, self-mortification, yogic breathing, fasting and extended periods of isolation. The two movements also aspired to different goals. Brahminism was concerned with success in this world and heaven in the next, while the *samaṇas* renounced all worldly concerns, believing that some forms of ecstatic mystical experience were achievable either here and now or after death. A few *samaṇas*, however, taught a materialist philosophy or were sceptical

17. D.I,71.
18. Ud.43.
19. M.I,305, also Ud.43. On the frequent sexual harassment Jain nuns had to endure see Jain 1984, pp. 220-222.
20. See Schlieter pp.137ff.

of all philosophical viewpoints, and, of the seven most prominent teachers of the time, none of them taught a form of monotheism.

A samaṇa who believed he had attained some kind of spiritual realization might attract disciples, and thus a sect or school would come into being; others lived in small, informal bands, and a few lived alone in forests. According to which discipline or ideology they subscribed to, there were *samaṇas* who went naked, symbolic of their rejection of all social norms and values, while others wore animal skins or robes made out of rags, usually dyed tawny brown or yellow. Some shaved their heads, others tore their hair out, and still others let their unkempt hair grow so that it formed matted dreadlocks.

By the fifth century BCE, there were at least a dozen major samaṇa fraternities or sects in the Middle Land, such as the Muṇḍaka Sāvakas, the Jatilas, the Māgaṇḍka, the Tedaṇḍikas, the Aviruddhakas and the Devadhammikas. *Samaṇa* teachers who were attracting attention included Pūraṇa Kassapa, Ajita Kesakambalī, Pakudha Kaccāyana, Sañjaya Belaṭṭhaputta, Mahāvīra, and, of course, the two teachers who guided Gotama's early explorations, Āḷāra Kālāma and Uddaka Rāmaputta.[21] Most of these sects, their founders and the doctrines they espoused soon faded into obscurity and were forgotten. Other than the Buddhists, the only ones to last more than a few centuries were the Ājīvakas and the Jains, then known as the Nigaṇṭhas, the Bondless Ones.[22]

The Ājīvakas had been founded by Makkhali Gosāla, who had originally been a companion of Mahāvīra, the Jain leader, before falling out with him and starting his own movement. Only a few scattered and partly contradictory references to Gosāla's doctrine survive, but it seems to have been a kind of rigid determinism and included many magical practices. The Buddha's repudiation of such practices, particularly astrology, was probably an indirect criticism of the Ājīvaka teachings. The Ājīvakas garnered considerable support for a few centuries and then went into a long period of decline, finally disappearing in about the thirteenth century.[23]

---

21. A.III,276; D.I,157.
22. The term *jina*, 'victor', the origin of the English Jain[ism], only came into widespread use after the 9th century. See Jaini 1998, p.2 note 3.
23. See Balcerowicz and Basham,1951.

Jainism had been founded by the sage Pārśva in about the seventh century BCE, and was then reformed, reformulated and revitalized by Mahāvīra, the Buddha's older contemporary, called Nātaputta in the Buddhist texts. Those who adhered to Pārśva's original doctrine and discipline still existed during the Buddha's time and, outwardly at least, differed from Mahāvīra's disciples, who went naked, by wearing a small cloth over their genitals – hence their name, 'They of the One Cloth' (*ekasātaka*).[24] Their leader, Keśin, accepted an invitation to meet with a senior disciple of Mahāvīra to discuss their differences, which were eventually resolved, resulting in the two branches of the religion agreeing to unite. Apparently, a large crowd of ascetics of different sects had gathered to listen to the discussion.[25]

Despite being the two most prominent teachers of the time and their disciples often engaging in polemics with each other, it is strange that Mahāvīra and the Buddha never met. It is stranger still to learn that on occasions they stayed in the same location at the same time – for example once in Vesālī and on another occasion in Nāḷandā – and that they both spent the same three months of a rainy season in Rājagaha, and yet never took the opportunity to meet and debate their respective views.[26] It would appear that neither man wanted a face to face encounter with the other.

In many respects Jainism was similar to Buddhism, but a major difference, and one from which several other differences arise, was the idea in Jainism that every act, intentional or not, created kamma.[27] It also accepted the reality of a soul, something which Buddhism rejected. Jainism has survived in India until today, and although its adherents have always been small in number, they have had a profound and positive influence on Indian thought and culture.

By the Buddha's time a small but significant number of brahmins had adopted some samaṇa practices, particularly renunciation, forest living and meditation. Known as *vānaprastha* or *vaikhānasa*, they were usually identified by their matted hair (*jaṭila*) and the deer skins

24. Ud.65. Thi.107.

25. *Uttarādhayayana* XXIII,1-19. Some centuries later Jainism split again into the Digambaras and the Śvetāmbaras.

26. M.I,371-373; II,2; A.IV,79-80.

27. M.II,214; see also Jain 2014, pp.111 ff.

(*ajina*) they wore.[28] However, seemingly unable to completely let go of worldly life as traditional *samaṇas* did, some spent the day at the edge of their village or in the nearby forest tending the sacred fire and returned to their homes in the evening, while others lived permanently in the forest but kept their wives and children with them. The layman Potaliya thought of himself as a true renouncer because, although living at home, he had handed over all his property and obligations to his sons and was content with being fed and clothed by them. Nonetheless, he became irritated when the Buddha kept addressing him as "householder" during a conversation the two had, and protested that he was no longer a layman but a renunciant. The Buddha told him that being a genuine renunciant required much more than that.[29]

The life of renunciation was such a threat to Brahmanism's theology and values that the *Baudhāyana Dharmasūtra* claimed that it was actually a demonic plot to deprive the gods of the sustenance they received from sacrificial offerings and thus destroy them. It would be centuries before renouncing family and society became fully accepted as a part of Hinduism.[30]

Most samaṇa fraternities or sects looked back to founders who they believed had lived in the distant past, some of whom were mythical and others possibly real. As mentioned before, the Jains looked back to Pārśva. The Buddha once mentioned six "ford makers" from the past whose names were still recalled with reverence.[31] He saw himself as the most recent of these previously awakened Buddhas, who had rediscovered and reformulated the essence of their teachings. He explained it like this:

> "Suppose a man wandering through the forest were to see an ancient road or path traversed by people in days gone by and he were to follow it until he came to an ancient city once inhabited by people, with parks and groves; reservoirs and walls—a really

28. The hide of the blackbuck, *Antilope cervicapra*. This beautiful animal had a particular significance in Vedic thought. The open grasslands of Punjab, Haryana and semi-deserts of Rajasthan where it roamed were part of the sacred land of Brahminism, *Manusmṛti* 2, 22-3. On the mythology surrounding the blackbuck see Stella Kramrisch's *The Presence of Siva*,1981, p.40-50.

29. M.I,360.

30. 2.11,28.

31. S.II,5ff. In later centuries the Buddhist tradition created many more.

beautiful place. Then that man would inform the king or one of his ministers about it and say, 'Sir, restore that city!', and they would, and in time it would become rich and prosperous, crowded and full of people, so that it would grow and flourish again. In the same way I saw an ancient road or path traversed by fully awakened Buddhas in the past. And what is that ancient path, that ancient road? It is the Noble Eightfold Path."[32]

The Buddha's immediate predecessor was Kassapa Buddha, again possibly a real person although with legends built around his life and doctrines attributed to him which he may or may not have promulgated. The Tipitaka even contains a few verses supposedly spoken by this Kassapa Buddha.[33]

Although most people treated *samaṇas* with respect and sometimes even with awe, not everyone did. The attitude of a few was: "I cook, but they don't. It is not right that I who cook should give to those who do not."[34] When a samaṇa stood at someone's door waiting for alms, the lady of the house might politely refuse him, pretend not to see him so she did not have to give him anything, coolly dismiss him with leftovers, or send him away with a hail of abuse.[35] According to the Buddha: "Being an alms-gatherer is the lowest of callings. To say, 'You are an alms-gatherer, wandering about bowl in hand' is an insult in today's world."[36]

Not all *samaṇas* were worthy of respect either. There are places in the Tipitaka where the Buddha berated those *samaṇas* who preyed on people's devotion or gullibility by claiming to be able to predict the future and interpret dreams and omens, or who practiced astrology, or dispensed nostrums "while living off food provided by the faithful."[37] One of the people the Buddha was having a discussion with described the discourses of many ordinary ascetics and brahmins as nothing more than chitter chatter (*vilāpaṃ vilapitaṃ*).[38] A few *samaṇas* were

32. S.II,105-6.
33. Sn. 239-252.
34. A.IV,62.
35. M.II,61-62; S.I,114.
36. It.89.
37. D.I,8-11.
38. M.I,234.

prepared to pander to the powerful in the hope of obtaining their patronage, and for their part the powerful were not averse to using *samaṇas* for their own ends. Because *samaṇas* travelled widely and were generally trusted, or at least thought of as innocuous, they made useful informants and spies. King Pasenadi actually admitted to the Buddha that he employed certain *samaṇas*, or people disguised as them, to gather intelligence for him.[39] On the whole, though, most *samaṇas* lived simple, harmless lives dedicated to the quest for ultimate freedom, even if they never achieved it.

Given the *samaṇas*' rejection of the Vedas and the respect they received, it is not surprising that the more orthodox followers of Brahminism, particularly brahmin priests, regarded them as rivals, heretics and as little more than outcastes. The Tipitaka records numerous incidents of brahmins belittling *samaṇas*, the Buddha and his monks included. The antagonism between the two was highlighted by Patañjali (circa. 150 BCE), who wrote that *samaṇas* and brahmins were "like cat and mouse, dog and fox, snake and mongoose," meaning that they were polar opposites in both their lifestyles and their approaches to spirituality. He added that "the opposition between the two is eternal."[40] While this was not always the case, these observations do point to the tension and competitiveness between the two, which is reflected in the literature of the time, including the Tipitaka.

From the beginning, the Buddha saw himself firmly within the samaṇa tradition and his Dhamma as antithetical to Brahmanism, not a reform of or a restatement of it, but an alternative to it. When he embarked on his quest for truth he did not seek out a brahmin teacher to study the Vedas with, rather he seems to have taken it for granted that the way of the *samaṇas* would lead him to the goal he aspired to. Throughout the Tipitaka the Buddha is addressed as or referred to as "the samaṇa Gotama," and he asked his monks to identify as *samaṇas* too. "Samaṇa, samaṇa, that is how people perceive you. So when you are asked, 'What are you?' you should reply that you are samaṇas."[41] He either rejected, reinterpreted,

39. Ud.65-66. *Arthasāstra* I,11ff recommends using ascetics as spies.
40. *Mahābhāṣya* II,4,9.
41. M.I,281.

criticized or ignored almost every Brahmanical doctrine and practice. He even forbade his Dhamma being rendered into Sanskrit, mainly so it would be understandable to everyone but probably also so it could maintain its non-Vedic distinctiveness.[42]

42. Vin.II,139. For a detailed and in-depth study of some of the distinctions between Buddhism and Vedic teachings see Pollock 2005 pp.400 ff.

4
The Sakyans

My lineage is Ādicca, I am Sakyan by birth,
and it is from this family I have gone forth.

Sutta Nipāta 423

Paralleling the Himalayan foothills that define the modern India-Nepal border is a strip of terrain called the Terai. The whole region is flat, and the soil is a rich fertile alluvium. The numerous rivers and streams that flow down from the hills to the north sink into the gravel and then percolate to the surface in the Terai, creating pools, marshes and swamps. For centuries most of the Terai was made up of thick malarial forest, but beginning in the late nineteenth century it has been deforested and given over to rice cultivation. To get some idea of what it was like before the deforestation, one has to visit the Katarniaghat and the Suhelva sanctuaries, Dudhwa National Park or Valmiki National Park. Elephants, one-horned rhinoceros, the beautiful chital deer, tigers, leopards, monkeys, wild buffalo and hyenas roam through stands of sal, rosewood, khair, champak and bahera trees and areas of tall grasses. During the monsoon, when the rain has washed the dust from the atmosphere, the snowy peaks of the Himalayas can be clearly seen on the horizon to the north.

In the fifth century BCE one of the ethnic groups who inhabited parts of the Terai were the Sakyans, and it was into this group that the person who was to become the historical Buddha was born. Nothing in the early texts suggests that the Sakyan homeland was anything other than a small and unimportant chiefdom, and it would never have become famous or even been remembered had the Buddha not been born there.[1] In a number of places in the Tipitaka sixteen of the main states in the Middle Land are listed, but Sakya is not amongst them. The Tipitaka also records the names of a mere ten villages in the Sakyan country, again suggesting that it covered a modest area and probably that it was sparsely populated.[2]

The Sakyans claimed to be descendants of the sons of the semi-mythical King Okkāka, who had been driven into exile by the machinations of his second queen.[3] Wandering through the forest, they came to the hermitage of the sage Kapila who invited them to settle down nearby. Out of gratitude to him, they named the settlement they established Kapilavatthu, although the name is more likely derived from 'place of' (*vatthu*) and 'monkeys' (*kapi*), and it became the Sakyan's principal town. Because this settlement happened to be in a grove of *sāka* trees, the exiles became known as Sakyans – at least that's what Sakyan clan history said.[4] The name Sakya, sometimes Sākya, is more likely to be derived from *śak*, meaning "to be able" or "capable." The Sakyans also claimed to be of the Ādicca lineage, which supposedly went back to the Vedic sun god, and to be of the warrior caste.

Although nominally independent, the Sakyans were under the influence of the kingdom of Kosala, their larger and more powerful neighbour to the south and west. The Tipitaka says: "The Sakyans are vassals of the king of Kosala; they offer him humble service and salutation, do his bidding and pay him homage."[5] This explains why the Sakyan land, "the land of [the Buddha's] birth" (*jātibhūmaka*), was described as belonging to the king of Kosala and why the king once said to the

---

1. *Mahāvaṃsa* II,1 ff and *Mahāvastu* I, 338 ff give genealogical data about the Sakyans, and the *Viṣṇu Purāṇa* IV,22,3 mentions Suddhodana, the Buddha's father, but not the Buddha himself. However, these texts were composed centuries after the Buddha, and there is no way of knowing if their information is reliable.

2. In 1962 an archaeological survey in what had been Sakyan territory located over two dozen ancient sites dating from the 6th to the 2nd centuries BCE, some of them possibly the remains of these villages. See Mitra pp.205-249.

3. D.I,92.

4. The sal is *Shorea robusta*.

5. D.III, 83; Sn.422.

Buddha that the two of them were Kosalans.[6] One text mentions the king being driven into Sakyan territory in his state carriage to the town of Medaḷumpa, which would have only happened if he had suzerainty over the Sakyans.[7] Tradition says that, towards the end of the Buddha's life, or more likely after his death, the Sakyans' *de jure* independence came to an end when their lands were formally absorbed into Kosala.

The Sakyans' neighbors to their east were the Koliyans. The border between their territories was the Rohiṇī River which has its source in the Himalayan foothills and flows into the Rapti River a little west of the modern town of Gorakhpur. A later, although plausible, legend claims that, during a summer drought, the Sakyans and Koliyans nearly came to blows over the use of the water in this river, an argument which was later arbitrated by the Buddha.[8] The Tipitaka preserves only a few scraps of information about the Koliyans: the Buddha visited the chiefdom on a few occasions; they had a form of government similar to that of the Sakyans; they had a kind of police force which had a distinctive uniform and a reputation for extortion and high-handedness; and they were one of the claimants for the Buddha's ashes after he died.[9] Later texts also claim that the Sakyans were related to and sometimes intermarried with the Koliyans, which again seems quite plausible.

The Sakyans had a reputation for pride and impulsiveness and were considered rustics by their neighbours. A group of Sakyan youths are reported as saying of themselves, "We Sakyans are proud," and Upāli, himself a Sakyan, described them as "a fierce people." Taking a more positive stance, the Buddha said his kinsmen were "endowed with wealth and energy."[10] When an arrogant young brahmin complained to the Buddha that during a visit to Kapilavatthu the Sakyan youths did not give him due respect, the Buddha defended his kinsmen, saying: "But even the quail, such a little bird, can talk as she likes in her own nest."[11] The Buddha's comparison of Sakyans with a little bird is further evidence of their country's diminutive size and unimportance.

---

6. M.I,145; II,124; also Sn.422.
7. M.II,118.
8. Dhp-a.III,254; Ja.V,412ff.
9. S.IV,341; D.II,167.
10. Sn.422.
11. D.I,91.

There are only a few scattered references to what the main Sakyan town Kapilavatthu was like. There was some kind of school and a council hall (*santhāgāra*) where the elders of the clan would meet to discuss matters pertaining to the running of the chiefdom. The texts mention that after the construction of a new council hall and the Buddha was invited to inaugurate it by spending the night in it: "the floor was spread; [12] seats were arranged; a large pot of water was put out; and an oil lamp was hung up."[13] Within walking distance of Kapilavatthu was the Nigrodhārāma, a park where the Buddha would stay during his occasional visits. From there he could walk to the Mahāvana, the Great Forest, indicating that the town was surrounded on some sides by this extensive forest which reached into the Himalayan foothills and stretched all the way to Vesālī and probably beyond.[14] Another place where he would sometimes stay was the mango orchard owned by the Vedhañña family, of whom nothing else is recorded.[15] Although Kapilavatthu was almost certainly a small town, one of the few detailed references to it describes it as being "rich and prosperous, crowded and full of people, its streets busy," which seems to suggest that it was something more than a small place.[16] Archaeology can help resolve the apparent disparity between these two descriptions.

In the 1980s archaeologists conducted surveys of ancient settlement sites in the Kanpur district of Uttar Pradesh dating from between the seventh to the third century BCE. They found eighty-one settlements of less than two hectares and calculated that these could have had a population of not more than 500 people. There were fourteen settlements covering an area of between two and four hectares, and these could have had a population of between 500 and 1000. Four settlements were more than four hectares and could have accommodated between 1,200 and 1,300 inhabitants.[17] All these population centres were much

12. This probably refers to spreading a thin layer of cow dung over the floor, still commonly done in village homes. When dry, it prevents the feet getting dirty from the earthen floor. See also Vin.III,16.

13. S.IV,182-183.

14. S.III,91.

15. D.III,117.

16. S.V,369.

17. See Lal, 1984 a and b.

smaller than the main cities of the time, and they would qualify as villages today. If Kapilavatthu had a population of 1,300, it would have been big enough to be described as bustling and crowded, especially if it was also a centre of commerce and the seat of government. Excavations conducted at the site of Kapilavatthu in the early 1970s confirm the impression that it was a modest place. They revealed that the area it took up was small, although the whole site could not be explored because some of it was under cultivation. All structures dating from the Buddha's time had mud walls, while those made of baked brick were from a much later period. Kapilavatthu was nothing like the grand royal capital as described in later Buddhist legend.[18] Numerous contemporary biographies of the Buddha repeat the inaccuracy that Kapilavatthu was in the Himalayan foothills. In fact, the terrain around it is as flat as it is possible to be; the first line of hills only starts about thirty kilometers further north.[19]

It has been said that "the Buddha was born, grew up and died a Hindu," a claim apparently based on the assumption that because most Indians today are Hindus, they must have been in ancient times too.[20] In reality, we have no idea what religion prevailed amongst the Sakyans and thus might have influenced the young Gotama. Certainly, there is little evidence of a brahmin presence in the Sakyan country. Only one village in the chiefdom, Khomadussa, had some brahmins living in it, and when the Buddha visited the place they gave him a cool reception.[21]

As mentioned previously, Brahminism, the precursor of Hinduism, had been moving from its traditional sacred land into the Ganges Valley for at least three hundred years and was in the process of establishing itself in the region. Kings such as Bimbisāra of Magadha had taken some brahmins as court advisors and functionaries, but on the other hand one of his cousins had become an Ājīvaka ascetic, suggesting

---

18. Srivastava, 1986.The description of Kapilavatthu having high circling walls with strong battlements and gates at Tha.863 must be fanciful, as no such walls, not even modest ones or even a defensive ditch, has been revealed by archaeological investigation.

19. Sn. 422 says the Sakyan country was flanked by, or beside (*passa*) the Himalayas.

20. *2500 Years of Buddhism*, edited by P. V. Bapat, 1956, p. ix.

21. S.I,184. See Pandey, pp.119-120.

that some of the elite were maintaining their allegiance to the non-Vedic samaṇa tradition.[22] Peoples such as the Sakyans, who were on the fringes of the major states, were probably still relatively uninfluenced by Brahminism. This is probably why, when the four castes are mentioned in the Tipitaka, the warrior caste is always placed before the brahmin caste. This suggests that the clan-based chiefdoms were still either resisting or ignoring the brahmin concept of caste hierarchy. The only hint we have of the religious life of the Sakyans is the brief comment that the Buddha's uncle Vappa was a follower of the non-Vedic Jains.[23] The majority of Sakyans, like most people in the Middle Land, were probably what would now be called animists worshipping their own local spirits and gods.

We have some information about the political life of the Sakyans. Legend claims that the Buddha's father Suddhodana was a king, although there is scant evidence in the Tipitaka to back up this claim. Nowhere is the Buddha called a prince (*rājakumāra*), nowhere is he or his family said to live in a palace,[24] and only once is his father called *rāja*, a word usually translated as king.[25] Although by the fifth century this word had come to be used for kings, in the Buddha's time it still retained its earlier meaning of an elected chief or consul, without any regal connotations.[26] Even in the very places where one would expect the Buddha to call his father a king or himself a prince, he did not do so. For example, when asked by King Bimbisāra about his birth and kin, he simply replied that he was from a Sakyan family.[27] The Tipitaka says that the Sakyans had a body of men called 'chief-makers' (*rājakattāra*). Such groups are mentioned in other early Indian texts, and it is clear they elected a chief to rule over them, either for a set

---

22. Vin.IV,74.
23. A.II,196.
24. *Pāsāda* could also be translated as mansion, villa or manor house. Archaeology has shown that two-storied houses were quite common in the towns and cities. At Sn.685 Suddhodana's abode is referred to simply as a *bhavana*, a residence.
25. D.II,7. At Vin.I, 82 he is referred to as just Suddhodana the Sakyan.
26. See Jayaswal p.11.
27. Sn.422-4.

period or for as long as he had their confidence.[28] The council hall the Buddha had inaugurated in Kapilavatthu was the very kind of place where the chief-makers and clan elders would gather to conduct business, with the chief presiding over their meetings as *primus inter pares*.[29] So while the Buddha was almost certainly from a ruling class family, he was not royalty in the sense that came to be understood in later centuries, or as it is today.

Suddhodana had two wives, Mahāmāyā, Gotama's mother, and her sister Mahāpajāpatī Gotamī, although whether they were co-wives or he married the latter after the death of the former cannot be determined. Sororate marriages were recognized in ancient India and are mentioned in later law books. The second part of Mahāmāyā's name has given rise to a particularly uninformed theory. While *mahā* means 'great', *māyā* is widely known to mean illusion, and the theory is that her name is evidence of a connection between Buddhism and Advaita Vedānta with its concept that what is taken to be real is actually just an illusion. However, several early meanings of *māyā* include 'wisdom', 'extraordinary' and 'supernatural power', any one of which would have been unremarkable as part of a girl's name, especially one coming from an elite family. Only later did 'illusion' become the primary meaning of *māyā*.[30]

It is also worth noting that Suddhodana gets only five brief mentions in the Tipitaka.[31] Other than him, the only person mentioned as being a Sakyan chief is Bhaddiya. After becoming a monk, he said that when he was chief he lived in constant anxiety and had to have guards both inside and outside his residence.[32] Sakyan politics, it seems, could sometimes be dangerous.

Other than giving birth to Gotama and dying seven days later, the Tipitaka records no other information about Mahāmāyā. It does, however, tell us a little more about his stepmother, Mahāpajāpatī

---

28. D.II,233. See Majumdar, pp.97 ff; 223 ff and Roy, pp.23 ff.
29. S.IV,182.
30. See Monier-Williams' *Sanskrit-English Dictionary*,1899.
31. D.II, 52; Sn.685; Th. 534, Vin.I,82-83, and at M.I,246, where he is not named. Not included are references to him in the Buddhavaṃsa or Apadāna, both late additions to the Tipitaka.
32. Vin.II,180-182; Ud.18-19.

Gotamī. "As his mother's sister, she was his nurse, his stepmother, the one who gave him milk. She suckled the Lord when his own mother died."[33] Later, she became a nun which will be further discussed in Chapter 10.

Neither the Tipitaka nor early tradition mentions Gotama having any brothers or sisters, but the Tipitaka does refer to six of his half-brothers and cousins. Ānanda, Anuruddha and Mahānāma were sons of his father's brother; Devadatta was the son of his mother's brother; Tissa was the son of his father's sister (*pitucchāputta*); and Nanda was the son of his father's second wife Mahāpajāpatī Gotamī (*mātucchāputta*). The *Manorathapūraṇi* also mentions a half-sister named Nandā, possibly a sibling of Nanda. Several women so named are mentioned in the Tipitaka but it is not clear which of them, if any, were related to Gotama. All these individuals eventually became monks except Mahānāma, and Nandā, who became a nun.

It is interesting to note that when the Buddha was talking to lay people, whether or not they were his disciples, he always addressed them as 'householder' (*gahapati*). When he was speaking with other ascetics he would usually use their clan names, and when speaking with royalty he normally used a title, i.e., king or prince.[34] When speaking with his fellow Sakyans, however, he always used their personal names. He required ascetics who left their sect to become monks under him to undergo a four-month probation. However, if they were Sakyans, he granted them a "special privilege" (*āveṇiyaṃ parihāraṃ*) of needing no probation and being ordained immediately.[35] All this suggests that the Buddha had a closeness, a familiarity, perhaps even a favouritism, towards his own kin.

The Pali Tipitaka records almost nothing about Gotama's life until he left his home to become a wandering ascetic. This did not stop later generations of Buddhists from filling in the gaps, and they did so with enthusiasm and considerable aesthetic skill. The stories they created about Gotama's birth are as charming as those that make up the Christian nativity story.

---

33. M.III,253.
34. When talking with King Pasenadi he always addressed him as *mahārāja* but when talking with Queen Mallikā he addressed her by her name.
35. Vin.I,71.

Almost every account of the Buddha's life recounts the incidents that supposedly occurred at his birth: his mother dreaming of a white elephant before or as she conceived; giving birth to him while grasping the branch of a tree; and he emerging from her right side. Some later accounts even add that Mahāmāyā was a virgin when she gave birth. None of these stories are mentioned in the Tipitaka.

The only discourse dealing with Gotama's birth, the Acchariyābbhūta Sutta, is admittedly late, including as it does several wondrous events that supposedly occurred before, during and immediately after the event.[36] However, not all the details it recounts should be dismissed as fantastic exaggerations; some may have been based on fact, while others may have had a didactic purpose. For example, the discourse claims that Mahāmāyā gave birth while standing, which is by no means improbable. Little is known of ancient Indian birthing practices, but delivering while sitting or lying down (*nisinnā vā nipamā*) was common and standing was not unknown. Interestingly, Britain's Royal College of Midwives recommends upright birthing and says that it is quite safe if the midwife and other attendants are properly trained and prepared for it.[37]

The discourse also says that a brilliant light appeared when Gotama was born – not a star, as with the Christian nativity story, and not a light identifying a particular location, but one which allowed beings to think differently about each other. The discourse says:

> "When the Buddha came forth from his mother's womb, a great immeasurable light more radiant even than the light of the gods shone forth into the world... And even in the dark, gloomy spaces between the worlds where the light of our moon and sun, powerful and majestic though they are, cannot reach, even there did that light shine. And the beings that are reborn in that darkness became aware of each other because of that light and thought: 'Indeed there are other beings here.'"

It would seem that this story was not meant to suggest that an actual light appeared when Gotama was born. Rather, it is a literary device, an

---

36. M.III,119 ff.
37. In the West, giving birth while prone is a relatively recent practice. See Lauren Dundes' 'The Evolution of Maternal Birthing Position', in *American Journal of Public Health*, Vol.77, No. 5,1987.

allegory, a way of saying that the advent of the Buddha would enable beings to become aware of each other, thus making empathy and understanding between them more likely.

Almost the only thing that can be said with certainty about Gotama's birth is that it took place in Lumbinī, which was in a district of the Sakyan lands somewhere between Kapilavatthu and Devadaha, the main Koliyan town.[38] The birth is always depicted as happening in the open, with Mahāmāyā standing and grasping the branch of a tree, but as Lumbinī was a village (*gāma*) it is much more likely to have taken place in one of the village houses or at least under some type of shelter.[39] The location of Lumbinī was identified with certainty in 1896 with the discovery of a monolithic pillar erected there by the emperor Asoka in 249 BCE after he made a pilgrimage to the place.

The only other details about Gotama's birth concern the ascetic Asita. This ascetic was living in the forest and had matted hair, things often associated with, but not exclusive to, Brahminical ascetics. He was also known as Kaṇhasiri, Dark Splendor, suggesting that he was from a low caste, or at least not a brahmin.[40] One day Asita noticed that the gods were particularly jubilant. When he asked them why this was, they replied it was because a very special child had been born amongst the Sakyans. Consequently, Asita went to Suddhodana's residence, where he was shown the child and given him to hold. Being accomplished in prognostication and spells (*lakkhaṇa manta*), Asita could see that the child would grow up to be a great spiritually accomplished individual, but then tears welled up in his eyes. Fearing that Asita had seen some misfortune in the child's future,

---

38. M.II,214 says that Devadaha was in the Sakyan country, which must be a mistake. Some fifty kilometers north-east of Lumbinī is the village formerly called Saina-Maina which Nepalese authorities renamed Devadaha in the 1960s and since then have claimed is the hometown of the Buddha's mother. As yet there is no archaeological evidence that the place was Devadaha. On Saina-Maina see Mitra, pp.221-222.

39. Sn.683. Asoka's Lumbinī inscription also refers to it as a village. The site of the village is about two hundred meters south-west from the pillar and archaeological investigation has shown that it was occupied from about the twelfth century BCE to the seventh century CE. See Strickland, pp.1-17.

40. Sn.689.

Suddhodana asked him why he appeared upset. He replied: "This boy will attain complete awakening, the highest purified vision, and with compassion for the many he will set moving the wheel of truth, and his teaching will become widespread."[41] Later legend says Asita predicted two futures for the boy: that he would become either a great spiritual teacher or a great political leader. However, Asita does not make this either/or prediction.

41. Sn.679-694.

5
Towards the Light

The doors of the Deathless are open.
Let those who can hear respond with faith.

Majjhima Nikāya I, 169

Modern biographies usually give great attention to their subject's upbringing, the idea being that a person's formative years will hold clues to and explain their traits, behaviour, achievements or beliefs in later life. The ancient Indians did not think like this, and consequently they had little or no interest in Gotama's life until after he became a wandering ascetic. Thus we discover that, of the well-known stories about Gotama's youth, colourful and engaging though they be, few are found in the most ancient texts. The story about Gotama undergoing a name-giving ceremony; the wonderful one about him saving a wild goose from his cousin Devadatta; about him winning athletic and martial competitions; about him courting and then marrying Yasodharā; about his luxurious lifestyle, and so on, are all later creations. In fact, apart from the Asita story, there are only three brief scraps of information about Gotama's childhood, youth and early adulthood.

Once, in later life, when reminiscing about this period, the Buddha said that he was "delicately brought up, most delicately brought up, exceptionally delicately brought up" in that he wore fine silks and perfumes, had a troupe of female musicians to entertain him, an umbrella-bearer to accompany him when he went out and sumptuous food to eat. He went on to say that he had three mansions to live in, one each for the summer, winter and the rainy season, again confirming that he was from a wealthy and privileged background.[1]

1. A.I,145.

Another piece of information, again provided by the Buddha himself, is more significant. One day, while he sat in the shade of a jambu tree watching his father work, he had what might now be called a mystical experience. Apparently quite spontaneously, he fell into a meditative state which he would later call *jhāna*.[2] This experience was to have a profound influence on his awakening years later and will be discussed in detail below.

Gotama must have been married, probably in his early teens, as was the custom of the time, although there is no mention of either this marriage or his wife's name in the Tipitaka.[3] According to tradition her name was Yasodharā, although she is only ever referred to by the epithets Bhaddakaccā or Rāhulamātā, i.e., Rāhula's mother.

Whatever her name, the texts mention that Gotama had a son named Rāhula, although they include almost no information about him until he became a monk. After Rāhula ordained, the Buddha sometimes gave instructions to him, went alms gathering with him and praised him for his readiness to learn, and for his part, Rāhula described his father as "the torchbearer of humanity" (*ukkādhāro manussānaṁ*).[4] Curiously, in only one place is Rāhula's relationship with his father unambiguously stated.[5] Curious also is Rāhula's absence from significant events in the Buddha's career, most noticeably during his final journey and at his deathbed.

That Gotama had only one offspring raises an interesting question: if he was married in his teens and renounced the world as a mature adult – he said he was twenty-nine – how is it that he and his wife had only one child? There are a number of possible answers to this question. It occasionally happens that a couple have sexual relations for years

---

2. M.I,246. Most modern accounts of this incident follow the commentary in saying that Gotama was watching his father ploughing at the time, while the text simply says his father was 'working', *kammante*. In later centuries, and certainly by the time of the commentary, it was believed that Suddhodana was a mighty king and amongst the few manual tasks kings did was the annual ceremonial first ploughing. Thus working, which could have included a range of activities, became ceremonial ploughing.
3. On the marriage customs of the time see Wagle 1995, pp.127 ff.
4. M.I, 414; 421; Sn.336.
5. Vin.I,82-83.

without pregnancy occurring, and then eventually it unexpectedly happens. There can be multiple causes for this phenomenon. However, this scenario seems unlikely in Gotama's case because it was a common practice to divorce a wife who failed to conceive after several years.[6] And the family would have decided, not the young husband. Another scenario might be that there were other children, but only Rāhula is mentioned because only he became a monk. However, this explanation has problems too. The Tipitaka records the Buddha dialoguing with members of his family (for example, his father, uncle, stepmother, stepbrother and nephew), so if he had children other than Rāhula, it is likely there would be some mention of him meeting with and talking to them. A more likely scenario is that Gotama and his wife did produce several children, but they all died either at birth, in infancy or later. No information is available about infant mortality rates at any period in Indian history until the nineteenth century, but it was probably very high.[7]

According to the tradition, the turning point in Gotama's life was his encounter with what is known as the four signs (*catu nimitta*). The story goes that, to prevent the young Gotama from knowing anything of the ugly realities of life and thereby becoming a renunciant sage, as Asita had predicted, his father had him confined in a beautiful palace, provided with every means of sensual gratification. One day, however, with the help of his page Channa, he managed to slip out of the palace and drive through the streets of Kapilavatthu, where he saw a man bent with age, another suffering some hideous disease, and a corpse being taken for cremation. Having never seen such things before, he was deeply shocked, and even more so when Channa told him that such things were an inevitable part of life. As the two drove back to the palace, they passed an ascetic clad in a yellow robe. Gotama asked what he was, and Channa explained that he was one of those individuals

---

6. According to Vin.III,144, husbands could divorce their wives simply by saying "Enough!" although the grounds for doing this is not stated. Some law books stipulate that a wife can be divorced if she is barren, continually miscarries, produces only girls, or if she does not produce a son after a certain period. See e.g., *Manusmṛti* 9,81; *Baudhāyana Dharmasūtra* 2.4.6, etc. Whether such laws and customs prevailed amongst the Sakyans is not known.

7. Dyson, pp.16 ff.

who had given up everything in order to search for a state beyond old age, sickness and death. It was these four encounters, legend says, that triggered Gotama's decision to take the momentous step that he did. Joseph Campbell rightly called this episode "the most celebrated example of the call to adventure in the literature of the world," and as a metaphor it certainly is.[8] Unfortunately, it does not appear in the Tipitaka as having happened to Gotama, but rather to one of the former Buddhas, Vipassī.[9] It would seem that the story was later grafted onto the Buddha's post-Tipitaka legendary biography.

The Buddha described his ruminations about and decision to renounce the world in far briefer and less dramatic terms.

> "Before my awakening I thought like this: 'Being myself subject to birth, ageing, sickness, death, sorrow and defilement, and having understood the dangers in them, I should seek after the unageing, unailing, deathless, sorrowless, and undefiled security from bondage, Nirvana.' So later, while still young, with black hair, endowed with the blessings of youth and in the prime of life, despite my mother and father objecting with tear-stained faces, I shaved off my hair and beard, put on the yellow robe and went forth from the home into homelessness."[10]

In the traditional version of this episode, Gotama left his home stealthily, disappearing into the night while the palace slept. But as the passage just quoted shows, his parents were aware of his decision, and they reacted badly: as well as the tears, it is possible that there was also raised voices, pleading and recriminations.

Something else about the Buddha's account of his renunciation does more than contradict the legendary version; it also raises questions concerning his parents. He said that his mother and father objected (*akāmakānaṁ mātāpitūnaṁ*) to his decision to abandon his home life, and his father may well have done so, but his mother certainly could not have because, according to the Tipitaka, she had died after giving birth to him. Did the Buddha refer to his stepmother Mahāpajāpatī

8. Joseph Campbell, *The Hero with a Thousand Faces*, 2008 p.46.

9. D.II,24.

10. M.I,163. On the Buddha's return home some years later, his father told him his leaving had caused "not a little grief" (*anappakaṃ dukkhaṃ*), Vin.I,82.

Gotamī as his mother, as a child in the same circumstances might do so today? This seems unlikely. Pali texts use terms for kin relationships very carefully and precisely, as does all Indian literature. Thus one would expect him to refer to Mahāpajāpatī as his mother's sister or aunt (*mātucchā*). Then, is the story about Mahāmāya dying seven days after giving birth to Gotama just a legend? This seems unlikely too because it would serve no good purpose to make this claim if it were not true.[11]

The next we hear of the young Gotama was as a tawny-robed samaṇa staying on the east side of Mount Paṇḍava on the edge of Rājagaha and of him walking from there into the city for alms. King Bimbisāra happened to see him in the street and was impressed by the young ascetic's demeanour, particularly how he walked keeping his eyes cast down, his gaze a plough pole's length in front of him. The king ordered a servant to follow Gotama, find out where he was staying and report back. When this was done, the king drove out in his chariot, and the two men met and had a brief conversation.[12]

At some point after this, no doubt after a period of adjusting to being homeless and learning the etiquette and mores of the *samaṇas*, Gotama began looking for a teacher. He met with and asked to become a student under Āḷāra Kālāma, who must have had some renown, although he is not mentioned in the lists of well-known teachers of the time. Furthermore, other than what can be deduced from the goal of the meditation he taught, we do not know what other things he taught or what philosophy he espoused.[13] Kālāma maintained that the goal of the ascetic life was to attain a state of consciousness he called the sphere of nothingness (*ākiñcaññāyatana*), that he had realized this state, and he taught his students that, under his guidance, they could

11. I thank Anandajoti Bhikkhu for drawing my attention to this point.

12. Sn.408-421.

13. Karen Armstrong claims that Āḷāra Kālāma probably taught Sāṃkhya philosophy, that the Buddha incorporated elements of it into his Dhamma, and that he could have even been influenced by it before becoming a monk because Kapila, the founder of Sāṃkhya, "had links with Kapilavatthu," pp.44-46. There is no evidence for any of this, and it is unlikely that Sāṃkhya existed during the Buddha's time or even that this Kapila was a real person; Bronkhorst, 2007, pp.63-64.

attain it too.[14] When Gotama requested to become a disciple, Kālāma said to him: "This teaching is such that an intelligent man can very soon experience what the teacher has, attain it and abide in it through his own direct knowledge." First Gotama had to learn the theory, the foundation of the practice.

> "Very soon I mastered this teaching so, as far as lip-service, repeating and the opinion of the elders were concerned, I could say with confidence and certainty that I know and see, and I was not the only one."

Having done this, Kālāma now initiated him into the actual practices that would lead up to the sphere of nothingness. Again, within a short time Gotama had attained this state. When he went to report this, Kālāma examined him and was satisfied that he had in fact attained it:

> "You know the teaching that I know, and I know the teaching that you know. As am I, so are you, and as are you, so am I."

Pleased with such an accomplished student, Kālāma invited Gotama to become his co-teacher, but the young ascetic declined the offer: he was not convinced that being reborn into this sphere of nothingness was the highest state, and he would not be satisfied with anything short of complete awakening.

So he left and proceeded to seek out another teacher, this time one named Uddaka Rāmaputta.[15] Uddaka was the son of the samaṇa teacher Rāma and had apparently taken over his father's community after the latter's death. Rāma had taught meditational practices which led to a state he called the sphere of neither perception nor non-perception (*nevasaññānāsaññā*). While Uddaka taught and practiced what his father had bequeathed to him, he had not actually attained this state himself. As before, Gotama mastered the theory and the practice within a short time and went on to attain the actual goal of it, which must have astonished Uddaka as well as been an embarrassment to him. In fact, Uddaka actually offered to step aside and allow Gotama

14. Wynne 2007 pp.108 ff, has attempted to reconstruct Kālāma's philosophy.
15. M.I,163-66. That Rāmaputta was known to the Jains gives credence to the claim that he was a real person. See *Isibhāsiyāiṃ* 23; Schubring p.44.

to become the teacher of both himself and the other disciples but, as before, Gotama declined the offer and for the same reason.

The Tipitaka includes two curious snippets of information about the Buddha and other disciples of his two teachers. At some point later in the Buddha's life (exactly when cannot be determined), he happened to be in Kapilavatthu and, not being able to find other suitable accommodation, he stayed at the hermitage of the ascetic Bharaṇḍu Kālāma, who happened to be his fellow student when he was studying with Āḷāra Kālāma.[16] And while on his way to Kusinārā just days before his death, the Buddha had a chance meeting with the Mallan Pukkusa, who had also been a disciple of Āḷāra Kālāma, although whether as an ascetic or a layman is not clear.[17] The mention of these two individuals adds nothing to the context in which they appear. The Buddha's brief reconnection with them seems to have been recorded simply because they were considered interesting, although minor, episodes in his life.

Now fully integrated into the samaṇa tradition and with a good grounding in meditational disciplines, Gotama wandered off and, perhaps out of frustration or uncertainty about what to do next, he decided to try an approach popular at the time: self-mortification (*attakilamatha*). There were a number of theories behind such a discipline. Amongst Brahminical ascetics, the belief was that self-mortification was a penance (*prāyaścitta*), a way to purify oneself from or make amends for neglecting some taboo or ritual requirement.[18] A widely accepted belief amongst non-Vedic samaṇa sects was that subjecting the body to severe stress and pain would create a kind of spiritual heat (*tapa*) which would unleash an energy, giving one power over oneself and even over the external world. The Jains' justification for self-mortification was related to their particular understanding of kamma. They believed that every experience one had was the result of actions done in the past. Thus any pain one experienced now, even if self-inflicted, must be the result of some evil kamma done in a former life, and so the more one tortured oneself, the more negative kamma

---

16. A. I,276; D.II,130.
17. A. I,276; D.II,130. The texts say Bharaṇḍu had been a *brahmacāriya* and Pukkusa had been a *sāvaka*.
18. See e.g., *Gautama Dharmasūtra* 24,1-11; *Vāsiṣṭha Dharmasūtra* 22,1-16, etc.

would be expunged.[19] The Buddha never gave his reasons for deciding to subject himself to self-mortification, but it was probably because he accepted one of these theories or at least was willing to give some of them a try. Whatever his reasons, for the next few years he embarked on a program of gruelling self-torture that became ever more extreme.

In later life the Buddha described some of the painful mortifications he undertook during this time.

> "Such was my asceticism that I went naked, rejecting conventions, licking my hands,[20] ignoring requests to come for alms, refusing food specifically prepared for me or an invitation to a meal...I took food only once a day, or only once every two days, or only every three, four, five, six or seven days. I was an eater of sal leaves, millet, wild rice, hide parings, rice bran and the scum from boiled rice, of sesame pomace, grass and even cow dung. I foraged for forest roots, fruit or the fruit that had fallen from the tree...I was one who pulled out my hair and beard [rather than shaving], I remained standing or squatting for extended periods, I slept on a bed of thorns, I immersed myself in the river three times a day, sometimes at night. Just as grime and dust on a tree stump peels off and flakes off, like that the grime and dust that had adhered to my body over the years peeled off and flaked off, and yet it never occurred to me to wipe it off...I went on all fours to the cow kraals after the cows and cowherds had gone and ate the dung of the suckling calves. As long as my own faeces and urine lasted, I consumed my own faeces and urine. I would plunge into the fearful forest, fearful enough to make one's hair stand on end if one was not free from lust. During the cold winters I would spend the night out in the open, and during the summer I would spend the day similarly..."[21]

After years of such mortification and self-denial, his physical condition deteriorated dramatically.

---

19. M.I,92-93; II,214 ff.

20. This refers to the practice of refusing to use a bowl to receive alms food, requiring it to be put in one's cupped hands from which it would be licked up.

21. M.I,77 ff, condensed. On these and other extreme ascetic practices see Olivelle,1992.

"Because I ate so little, my backbone looked like a string of beads, my ribs like the rafters of an old shed, my eyes sunk into their sockets, and the gleam in my eyes looked like the gleam in the water at the bottom of a deep well. Because I ate so little, my scalp shrivelled and dried up like a gourd withered in the sun. If I tried to touch the skin of my belly, it was my backbone I touched, and if I tried to touch my backbone, it was the skin of my belly I touched. I would get up to urinate or defecate and fall down on my face, and if I stroked my limbs, the hair, rotted at its roots, fell out."

The Buddha claimed that, at one point during all this, even the gods thought he would die and offered to feed him nourishment through his pores so that, technically, he would not break his fast. He refused.

While subjecting himself to such a punishing regimen, Gotama was also attempting to control his thinking processes.

"[W]ith my teeth clenched and my tongue pressed against my palate, I crushed, subdued, and suppressed my mind using my mind."

Sweat ran from his armpits, and he became overwrought and exhausted. Another method he tried was breath retention meditation (*appāṇakaṃ jhānaṃ*), holding his breath for as long as possible and persisting with it for hours on end. He said that when he did this he could hear a rushing sound of air in his ears, and he suffered from splitting headaches.[22]

As much as possible he tried to avoid any human contact, choosing instead to forage for roots, berries and leaves in the forest so he would not have to go to a village for alms.

"Such was my isolation that I would enter some forest and remain there. If I saw a cowherd or a shepherd, a grass-cutter, twig gatherers or a woodsman, I would flee from one grove

22. M.I,242-247, condensed. This was something like what came to be called *prāṇāyāma* which involved controlling (*āyāma*) the breath as described in works such as the *Baudhāyana Dharmasūtra* 4.1.22-4, 28-30 and the *Āśvalāyanaśrauta Sūtra* 2.7. The pain and exhaustion it caused was believed to purify the evil deeds one had done.

> or thicket to another, from one gully or upland to another, so that they would not see me or I them."[23]

The strain of no human company for months on end must have been considerable, but it was not the only difficulty he had to confront and overcome. He also had to deal with the very real possibility of being attacked by a wild animal.

> "While I dwelt [in the forest], a wild animal would prowl somewhere near me, a peacock would snap a twig or the wind would rustle the leaves, and I would think, 'Here comes that fear and dread. Why am I staying here getting nothing but fear and dread? I will master it and remain without moving.'"[24]

Gotama's fears were quite justified, as north India's forests harboured lions, tigers and leopards, wolves, hyenas and sloth bears, any one of which could have done him great harm.[25] At other times cowherd boys would notice him and, knowing that he would not retaliate, would try to provoke him by urinating on him, throwing things at him or poking twigs in his ears.[26]

Most later sources say that Gotama underwent these austerities for six years, but this would mean that he stayed with Āḷāra Kālāma and Udaka Rāmaputta for only a few months at most.[27] That he could have attained the exalted states he did under their guidance so quickly seems unlikely. He must have been with these two teachers for at least a year or two, meaning that he practiced austerities for less than six years, although exactly how long cannot be determined. The only thing the Buddha said on the matter was that he practiced self-mortification for a number of years (*nekavassagaṇika*), without stipulating how many.[28] The most that can be deduced from the texts is that, from the time Gotama abandoned his home to his awakening, six years elapsed.

---

23. M.I,79.
24. M.I,20.
25. Vin.I,220 mentions monks sometimes being attacked by such animals.
26. M.I,79. Mahāvīra suffered similar abuse, see Wujastyk 1984, pp. 189-194.
27. E.g., *Buddhacarita* 12.95; *Jātaka* I.67; *Lalitavistara* 17,22; *Mahāvastu* II,241.
28. M.I,78.

At some point during this terrible time a group of five other *samaṇas* attached themselves to Gotama, their names being Assaji, Bhaddiya, Koṇḍañña, Mahānāma and Vappa. Impressed by the unremitting rigor of his austerities, they were sure that sooner or later he would realize some exalted state and, when he did, they would be the first to receive his teaching. Again, the impression usually given is that his five companions waited on him throughout this period, but that may not be correct either. According to his own words, Gotama spent extended periods in isolation in the forest. A possible scenario is that his companions would seek him out every few days to give him food and water and then return to the forest edge where they resided, leaving him to his grim solitude.

After several years of ever more gruelling self-punishment, it finally occurred to Gotama that he was getting nowhere. It seemed to him that he had undertaken all the accepted austerities and many of the mind-control techniques current at the time but that, despite his fierce determination, none of them had worked. It was time for a reassessment, to reconsider the notion that pain was the way to liberation.

> "I thought, 'Why am I afraid of that happiness that has nothing to do with sensual pleasures and unskilful states of mind?' And I thought, 'I am not afraid of that happiness.' Then I considered further, 'It is not easy to attain that happiness with such a severely emaciated body. I should eat some solid food, some boiled rice and barley porridge.' And so I did..."

His five companions were shocked by Gotama's change of direction and, seeing it as a betrayal, lost their faith in him. "When I ate some solid food, those five monks were disgusted and left me, saying, 'The samaṇa Gotama now lives in abundance. He has given up striving and has returned to the life of abundance.'"[29]

Apparently no nearer the goal than when he had left his home, this must have been a period of disappointment and even despair for him. He spent time recovering, eating properly, resting, and regaining his strength and then set off walking through the Magadhan countryside until he came to the small riverside village of Uruvelā. His now refreshed mind enabled him to appreciate the lovely rural scene that unfolded

29. M.I,247.

before him. This was not the grim and fearful forest that had been his home until just recently but a cultivated countryside in which familiar and homely sounds, like the lowing of cattle and human voices, could be heard. It lifted his spirits.

> "Then, being a seeker for the good, searching for the incomparable, matchless path of peace, while walking on tour through Magadha, I arrived at Uruvelā, the army village. There I beheld a beautiful stretch of ground, a lovely woodland grove, a clear flowing river with a delightful ford and a village nearby for support. And I thought, 'This is a good place for a young man set on striving.' So I sat down there."[30]

It is worth noting that while both ancient tradition and modern biographies never fail to mention that Gotama settled down to do his meditation under the spreading boughs of a pipal tree, known nowadays as the Bodhi Tree, this detail is given almost no attention in the Tipitaka. In the six accounts of Gotama's awakening, this tree is only mentioned in a brief text repeated twice.[31] Although there are reasons for believing that this passage is a later addition, it is quite likely that Gotama did sit under or near such a tree. To this day, almost every Indian village will have its tree shrine – typically a pipal tree, *Ficus religiosa*, or a banyan tree, *Ficus benghalensis* – in the vicinity. Positioning himself at the foot of or nearby such a tree would be the very thing an ascetic such as Gotama would have done. He would have known that sooner or later someone would come to pray to the deity of the tree, see him, and either give him their offerings, if it was food, or go home and return with some food for him. It is even possible that a simple credulous villager might think that such an ascetic was actually a spirit or tree god. Indeed, an early non-canonical legend says that when a servant woman went to Uruvelā's local sacred tree to prepare for making offerings to it at the request of her mistress Sujāta, she saw Gotama and thought he was the god of the tree.[32]

---

30. M.I,166–67.
31. Ud.1-2 and Vin.I,1. In another context it is mentioned at D.II,52-53 where it is just referred to as *assattha*.
32. Ja.I, 69.

Gotama sat down determined that it was now or never, that he was going to marshal all the patience, endurance and meditational experience he had developed during the last six years and try to make a final breakthrough. He made this resolution: "Gladly would I have my skin, sinews and bones wither and the flesh and blood of my body dry up if I can persist until I attain that which may be attained by human strength, human exertion, human striving."[33] Reviewing his life until then, he recalled the experience he had as a youth when he spontaneously slipped into a profoundly peaceful state of mind. He explained it like this.

> "I recalled that when my Sakyan father was working and I was sitting in the shade of a jambu tree with my mind completely secluded from sensual pleasures and unskilled states of mind, I entered and remained in the first jhāna which has a joy and happiness born of seclusion together with applied and sustained thought. And I thought, 'Could this be the way to awakening?'... And I decided that indeed, this is the way."

He now tried to reduplicate this state within himself, succeeded in doing so and then took it further.

> "Tireless energy was aroused in me and continuous mindfulness, my body was calm and untroubled, my mind concentrated and unified. Then, quite secluded from sensual pleasures and unskilled states of mind, I entered and remained in the first jhāna, which has a joy and happiness born of seclusion, together with applied and sustained thought. Then, with the ceasing of the applied and sustained thought, I entered and remained in the second jhāna, with inner tranquility, oneness of mind, an absence of applied and sustained thought and has joy and happiness born of concentration. With the fading of that joy, equanimous, mindful and with the body at ease, I entered the third jhāna, experiencing the happiness of which the worthy ones say, 'Happily lives he who is equanimous and mindful.' Then, with the giving up of both happiness and sorrow, pleasure and pain, I entered and

33. A.I,50.

remained in the fourth jhāna, beyond pleasure and pain and with a mindfulness purified by equanimity."[34]

It is difficult for one who has not experienced it to imagine what these states were like, but their culminating qualities were a penetrating, observing but utterly detached mindfulness purified by equanimity.

Gotama had not yet attained awakening (*bodhi*), which would only come when several profound insights became apparent to him. That this jhānic state he had attained was not a passive one is clear from what he said next. With his mind now "focused and purified, cleansed and bright, pliant and free of defilements, malleable, stable, firm and imperturbable,"[35] he turned it or directed it (*cittaṃ abhininnāmeti*) to certain subjects. The first of these concerned whether or not rebirth was a reality, as some claimed, and he experienced what he called the knowledge of past lives (*pubbenivāsa ñāṇa*), wherein he saw with great clarity and in dramatic detail the long parade of some of his former lives.[36] This experience allowed him to verify the reality of rebirth directly and personally. This led to a second insight, which he called the knowledge of the arising and passing away of beings (*cutūpapāta ñāṇa*), allowing him to understand how rebirth takes place according to the complex and subtle workings of kamma. Later, he said that, while an ordinary person may believe in and accept the reality of rebirth and kamma, only an awakened person actually has a personal and direct knowledge of its working.[37] The third and most crucial of these insights he called the knowledge of the destruction of the mental defilements (*āsavakkhaya*

34. M.I,21-23; I,246-48.
35. M.I,248.
36. This seems to have been an extension of, and in some way related to, what psychologists call a life review experience (LRE), where a person who has a close brush with death sees their whole life instantly flashing before them. For a scientific evaluation of this phenomena see Judith Katz and Noam Saadon-Grosman's 'The Life Review Experience: Qualitative and Quantitative Characteristics', *Consciousness and Cognition* Vol. 48, February 2017. So far, the most credible studies of rebirth are those of Ian Stevenson, late Professor of Psychiatry and Director of the Division of Personality Studies, University of Virginia. His decades of research are summarised in his two-volume *Reincarnation and Biology*, 1997.
37. A.III, 348ff.

ñāṇa).[38] In the deepest regions of consciousness, he saw the ultimate cause of desire and hatred, clinging and aversion and all their diverse and subtle manifestations, and in seeing them they dissolved. Now, what had been half-remembered experiences, glimpses of knowledge and scattered inklings became a sharply defined understanding which, when it merged with these three insights, gave him a complete picture of reality and the individual's position in it. "Light arose, vision arose, seeing arose," and the young ascetic Gotama became the fully awakened Buddha.[39] There is no indication of how long this overwhelming and liberating process took, but he may have been sitting, completely still, eyes closed, totally absorbed in the process for perhaps many hours. Nor did he say exactly when it occurred, other than "during the third watch of the night" (*rattiyā pacchi yāme*),[40] i.e., towards dawn, although since ancient times the event has been celebrated during the full moon day of Vesākhā, the second month of the Indian calendar.

At some point during this whole process, probably towards the beginning of it, the Buddha claimed that a kind of apparition he called Māra appeared before him. Initially this Māra tried to get him to give up his quest, return to normal life and just be a good person by making merit. When this did not work, Māra assembled an 'army' around him and attacked him. The Buddha said that he overcame these attacks with insight, i.e., seeing them as they really were, and by unshakable resolve.[41] Did he see this form or vision, whatever it was, with his actual eyes, or with his inner eye, his imagination, or was he simply dramatizing his final struggle with worldly desires in language that would be understandable to others? In the Tipitaka's account of this struggle, Māra seems to be a metaphor for, or perhaps a personification of, the physical and psychological barriers to awakening, the conditioned mind's final

38. D.I,81-3.

39. On the other accounts of the Buddha's awakening experience see Norman 1990, 25 ff.

40. M.I,249. In later centuries at least, the first watch (*purima yāma*) was divided into six *ghāṭikas*: the middle (*madhyayāma*) into two; and the third (*paścima yāma*) into four *ghāṭikas*. The duration of each would have differed according to the season, and its difficult to know how they were calculated.

41. Sn.442-3.

attempt to resist the light.[42] The name itself comes from the Sanskrit root *mṛt* meaning 'death' and is linked to the causative form *māreti* meaning 'causer of death.' It is clear from this and the constituents of Māra's 'army' that this explanation is the most plausible. The 'army' consisted of sensual pleasures, discontent, hunger and thirst, craving, sloth and torpor, fear, doubt, hypocrisy and obstinacy, gain, honour and fame, desire for reputation, and exalting oneself while disparaging others.[43] In three or four other discourses there are references to Māra's daughters, and again their names point to them being personifications of negative mental states rather than actual beings. The daughters were named Craving (*taṇhā*), Discontent (*aratī*) and Lust (*ragā*).[44] It is perhaps also worth pointing out that Māra's appearance is not mentioned in the four most detailed accounts of the Buddha's awakening.

The Buddha's awakening has sometimes been described as a mystical experience, although exactly what constitutes mysticism is difficult to define. Looked at from the perspective of modern psychology, most, if not all, experiences usually labelled mystical have four characteristics: they have an intense emotional component; they are triggered by physical or psychological stress (despair, longing, fasting, suppressed sexuality, long vigils, etc.); they never contradict the mystic's theological beliefs (Christians do not have visions of Krishna, Muslims never have a glimpse of the Trinity, etc.); and they are interpreted as having been caused by or being in some way related to an external agent (God, angels, the Absolute, Henosis, the Holy Spirit, etc.) The Buddha's description of his awakening does not fit well into this definition or with those given in seminal works on the mysticism experience.[45]

Gotama had fully recovered from his austerities, mentioning that he had been eating decent food, was rested, and had regained his strength (*balaṃ gahetvā*).[46] Prior to beginning his meditation in the

---

42. Sn.425ff. On metaphors, (*pariyāya*), in the Tipitaka see Gombrich, 2009, p.6.

43. Sn.436-8.

44. S.I,124.

45. E.g., William James' *Varieties of Religious Experience* 1902; Rudolf Otto's *Mysticism East and West* 1932; and Evelyn Underhill's *Mysticism* 1911.

46. M.I,247.

hours before his awakening, he appears to have been calm and poised.[47] Neither is there evidence that he had any idea about the doctrines he would later formulate as central to his philosophy (the Four Noble Truths, the Noble Eightfold Path, Dependent Origination, etc.) before his awakening. In fact, he claimed that the truths he had realized and later taught had "not been heard about before" (*pubbe ananussutesu dhammesu*).[48] He never described his awakening as a result of divine grace, as being 'at one with the universe', merging with the Absolute, as ineffable or any of the other terms typically associated with what is called the mystical experience. He always insisted that a person can attain awakening "through their own knowledge and vision" (*sayaṃ abhiññā*), by "human strength, human exertion, human striving" (*purisa thāmena, purisa viriyena, purisa parakkamena*).[49]

There are three accounts of what the Buddha did in the immediate aftermath of his awakening. One says he lingered at Uruvelā for four weeks, during which time he encountered a brahmin, a nāga, two merchants and a deity from the Brahmā world, one of the highest heavens.[50] The second says he stayed for three weeks and encountered the brahmin mentioned in the first version.[51] Both these accounts look like elaborations of another one in the Ariyapariyesanā Sutta which gives no time frame for his stay, recounts only his encounter with the deity from the Brahmā world, and is probably the oldest version of the Buddha's post-awakening Uruvelā sojourn.

Recalling this experience years later, the Buddha said he thought like this:

> "The truth I have realized is profound, difficult to see and understand, peaceful and sublime, impenetrable by mere reasoning, subtle, and accessible only to those who are wise. But people nowadays delight and rejoice in the things of the world, and it would be hard for them to see this truth, that is, how things come into being according to conditions. It would be

47. M.I,247.
48. S.V,422.
49. D.III,55; A.IV,190.
50. Vin.I,1-8.
51. Ud.1-3.

hard for them to see this truth, that is, the stilling of all mental constructs, the letting go of all attachments, the destruction of craving leading to dispassion, cessation, Nirvana. If I were to teach this truth to them, they would not understand me, and that would be wearisome and troublesome for me."

Therefore, he decided that he was not going to teach others but spend the rest of his life in peaceful obscurity enjoying what he called the joy of awakening. As the Buddha recounted it, the beings in the highest heaven, the Brahmā world, became aware of these thoughts, and one of them, Brahmā Sahampati, dismayed by them, appeared before him, bowed and said:

"Lord, teach the Dhamma, let the Happy One teach the Dhamma. There are beings with little dust in their eyes who are wasting away through not hearing it. There will be those who will understand it."

The Buddha said that, in response to this appeal, he surveyed the world with his 'Buddha eye' and this prompted him to reconsider.

"In a pond of blue, pink or white lotuses some sprout and grow in the water but never reach the surface, others grow up but remain on the surface, and a few grow above the surface and stand there untouched by the water. In the same way, I saw beings with little dust in their eyes and much dust, quick witted and slow witted, with good dispositions and bad ones, amenable to instruction and resistant to it, only a few of them seeing the danger in doing wrong and its results in the future."

For the sake of this last group, though few in number, he resolved to proclaim his Dhamma to anyone who would listen.[52]

The Buddha's next thought was whom he should teach first and the obvious candidates were his former teachers Āḷāra Kālāma and Uddaka Rāmaputta. In his estimation, both men were "intelligent, discerning and with only little dust in their eyes" although he later came to believe that some of Rāmaputta's pronouncements were "meaningless" (*anattha saṃhitaṃ*) and his claim to have attained high spiritual states

52. M.I,168-69.

was delusional.[53] Having come to know that both of them had died since he had last seen them, the next people he thought of were his five former companions, and, knowing that they were at Bārāṇasī, he set out to find them. As he was going along the road between Uruvelā and Gayā on his way to Bārāṇasī, an Ājīvaka ascetic named Upaka happened to be coming in the other direction. Even from a distance Upaka noticed the Buddha's mindful deportment, serene sense faculties and radiant complexion and was deeply impressed by it. When the two met, Upaka asked: "Who is your teacher? Whose doctrine do you follow?", a conventional greeting when wandering ascetics met, although in this case there was some admiration and curiosity in Upaka's words as well. The Buddha replied: "I have no teacher. In all the world, its gods included, I am unique and without counterpart." Upaka must have been taken aback by this claim. Certainly he was sceptical of it and replied: "According to what you say you must be the universal victor!" The Buddha responded that he was indeed a victor in that he had conquered all evil states of mind. Upaka then walked off shaking his head, saying as he did: "It may be so friend."[54]

The Buddha arrived in Bārāṇasī and then headed for Isipatana, a reserve for deer where he had heard his companions were staying.[55] The five ascetics saw the Buddha approaching in the distance and agreed amongst themselves that they would cold-shoulder him, neither standing up for him nor offering him a seat, although they would not object if he joined them. He had dashed their expectations, and they would not give him their respect. As he got closer, however, the haggard, emaciated ascetic they had known now looked completely different; his complexion was radiant, and he held himself with poise and confidence. So impressive was the man who approached them that they forget their decision to withhold their respect and, one by one, rose

53. D.III,126; S.IV,83.

54. M.I,170-172.

55. *Mahāvastu* III,324 and *Lalitavistara* XXVI,6-7 give the Buddha's itinerary from Uruvelā to Isipatana, but the only place they mention which can still be identified is Lohitavastuka, or, as it is called in the *Lalitavistara*, Rohitavastu, which corresponds to Rohita Vihar in modern Sasaram. This indicates that the Buddha made his way to Bārāṇasī via the Uttarāpatha which today's Highway19 roughly follows.

to their feet. When he got to them they took his bowl and offered him a seat, although they were still reticent to show him marks of respect beyond that.[56] He told the five that he was now a fully awakened being and that, if they were to follow his instructions, they could become awakened too. Both these claims were met with scepticism. "Friend Gotama, even though practicing austerities, you failed to attain any elevated states, any higher knowledge or vision worthy of saints. As you have now given up striving and reverted to the life of abundance, how could you have achieved such a state now?" The Buddha replied: "Have you ever known me to say something like this to you before?"

This unexpectedly personal appeal, drawing on their years together, made the five monks pause and think, and they admitted that, indeed, Gotama had never made such a claim in all the time they had known him. Disapproval was now put aside, and they agreed to listen to what he had to say. Over the next few days the Buddha and his five companions held what would now be dubbed a workshop, with some receiving instruction while others went alms gathering, and all six eating what was collected.[57]

What the Buddha imparted to them was later summarised into two suttas called the Discourse Setting into Motion the Wheel of the Dhamma and the Discourse on the Sign of Not-self, which together present a point by point, easily digestible account of the central features of what was to become Buddhism: the Four Noble Truths, the Noble Eightfold Path and the concept of no phenomena being a permanent self or its possession.[58]

What happened to the five monks – Assaji, Koṇḍañña, Bhaddiya, Mahānāma and Vappa – after their sojourn with the Buddha at Isipatana is something of a mystery. The Buddha had asked them to wander through the land proclaiming to others what he had taught them, but other than Assaji and Koṇḍañña, they get almost no further mention in the Tipitaka. A few months after leaving Isipatana, Assaji was in Rājagaha, where he met Sāriputta, not yet a disciple of the Buddha, who asked him who his teacher was and what he taught.

56. M.I,171-173.

57. M.I,173.

58. Vin.I, 13-14; S.V,420-424.

Assaji gave him the briefest account of the Dhamma, saying that he was not yet conversant with the teaching.[59] We hear of him only one more time, in Vesālī, where an ascetic asked him what the Buddha taught, and once again he replied with only a short outline of the Dhamma.[60] Koṇḍañña met the Buddha after a long absence on one other occasion and gets two more brief mentions.[61] Being the first monks ordained by the Buddha and thus senior to all the many others who were to come, one would have expected the five to be held in particularly high regard and their careers to be fully documented, but this is not the case. Were they retiring types who spent the rest of their lives in solitude and meditation, or did they die shortly after their ordinations? We do not know.

59. Vin.I,39 ff.
60. M.I,228.
61. S.I,193-194; A.I,23; Tha. 674-688.

6
A Teacher of Gods and Humans

> The Lord is awakened; he teaches the Dhamma for awakening. The Lord is tamed; he teaches the Dhamma for taming. The Lord is calmed; he teaches the Dhamma for calming.
>
> Majjhima Nikāya I, 235

The Buddha's awakening experience (*bodhi*) and the subsequent transformation it brought about within him led him to believe that he was a completely different type of human being, psychologically and ethically far above others, although still human.[1] He believed himself to be a Buddha and often referred to himself as being an Arahant or a Tathāgata. The epithet 'Buddha' comes from the past participle of the noun *bujjhati*, which means 'to awaken' or 'to be awake' and, when used in reference to a person, means one who has awakened to or realized something. *Arahant* was a pre-Buddhist term for those in positions of power or authority and means something like 'worthy one.' It came to

1. Numerous commentators have maintained that when the Buddha was once asked if he was a human being, he denied it. This claim is based on an early translation of the discourse in which the incident occurs where *bhavissati* was wrongly taken to be "Are you...," whereas it is actually the future tense "Will you become..." A.II,38. The Buddha was being asked if he would become, i.e., be reborn as, a human being, to which he answered 'no', affirming that he had freed himself from the process of birth, death and rebirth. The passage was rendered correctly in F. L. Woodward's 1933 translation of the Aṅguttara Nikāya and appears correct in all subsequent translations. Despite this, both academic and popular writers continue to use the mistranslation to prove or disprove various claims about the Buddha, usually that he saw himself as divine rather than human.

be used for any respected ascetic, and the Buddha used it to refer to himself and also to monks and nuns who had attained awakening.[2] 'Tathāgata' is an unusual word in which *tatha* could be used as an adjective meaning true or real or as the adverb *tathā* meaning thus or so. The former is probably meant. Further, if the word is arranged *tathā* + *āgata* it can mean 'he who has come to the truth' or *tathā* + *gata*, 'he who had thus gone.' Whatever its exact meaning or significance, Tathāgata was a word that seems to have been a Buddhist creation, quite possibly coined by the Buddha himself. The Buddha was usually addressed by the honorific 'Bhante' meaning 'Sir' or 'Reverend' or as 'Bhagavā' meaning 'Blessed One' or 'Auspicious One' and in this book is translated as 'Lord.'

For at least two thousand years it has been assumed that the Buddha's given name was Siddhattha, meaning 'he who achieves his goal', although this name appears nowhere in the Tipitaka in connection to him. Perhaps it was an epithet for him later mistaken for his name. That his given name is never mentioned may be because the editors of the Tipitaka were conforming to the widespread belief that it was presumptuous and disrespectful to refer to one's teacher by his name or to address him by it.[3] His clan name (*gotta nāma*) was Gotama, meaning 'best cow', a brahmin name, which has caused some confusion because the Sakyans, the Buddha's family, were of the warrior caste, not brahmins. Brahmins of the Gotama linage traced their origins back to a sage of that name, one of the authors of the Vedas. Today's sociologists use the term Sanskritization for the process by which low caste Indian communities sometimes adopt higher caste rituals, customs and names in the hope of raising their status. It is possible that as Brahmanism became increasingly dominant in the Middle Land, the Sakyans did something like this, laying claim to a brahmin linage while not realizing or not caring that it clashed with their claim to also be of the warrior caste.[4]

According to the Buddha's understanding, anyone could realize what he had through their own effort and determination. His role

2. See Rhys Davids 1921, Vol. III pp.3-4.
3. Vin.I,92-93; Ja.III,305.
4. For more on the Sakyan's caste affiliation see Levman 2013, pp.159-160.

was to draw their attention to truths which were, in a sense, already available to anyone who was able to clarify their perception enough to see them. He put it like this:

> "Whether Tathāgatas appear in the world or not, this order exists: the fixed nature of phenomena, their regular pattern and their general conditionality. The Tathāgata discovers this and comprehends it and, having done so, he points it out and teaches it, explains and establishes it, reveals, analyses and clarifies it and says 'Look.'"[5]

Thus the Buddha saw himself primarily as a teacher – not the aloof and distant type, but one motivated only by a deep compassion for humanity. He said of himself:

> "There is one person who is born into the world for the welfare of the many, for the happiness of the many, out of compassion for the world, for the welfare and happiness of both gods and humans. Who is that person? It is the Tathāgata, the Worthy One, the fully awakened Buddha."[6]

He reminded his disciples that when he reproached or even scolded them, his motive was always a compassionate concern for their well-being: "Whatever has to be done by a teacher out of compassion for his disciples and for their welfare, I have done for you."[7] Even those who had only a passing contact with the Buddha noticed that compassion and kindliness were the most noticeable features of his character. The physician Jīvaka said this to him: "Sir, I have heard it said that Brahmā abides in love, but with my own eyes I have seen that the Lord abides in love."[8] Thus, first and foremost the Buddha considered himself to be a fully awakened human being who taught the truths he had awakened to out of an abiding love and compassion for others.

The Buddha's compassion was seen as similar to that of a caring and concerned physician who restores an ailing patient to health. There were three main types of medical practitioners in fifth century BCE

5. S.II, 25.
6. A.I,22.
7. M.I,46.
8. M.I,369.

India: professional physicians (*bhisakka* or *vejja*); surgeons (*sallakatta*, literally 'arrow extractors'); and informal or folk healers (*tikicchaka*). Some physicians specialized in treating poisonings (*visavajja*) caused by poison arrows, snake bites and scorpion stings.[9] The Buddha observed that despite these medics' best efforts, their interventions only worked sometimes, but the 'medicine' he prescribed, the Dhamma, never failed if taken as instructed.[10] It is not surprising therefore that the Buddha often compared himself with and was seen by others as being comparable to a medic. He was praised as "the healer of the world" and "the compassionate teacher, the supreme physician and surgeon" who extracts the poison arrow of craving.[11]

The popular perception of the Buddha, even by Buddhists themselves, is that he was a semi-recluse who spent most of his time alone in forest glades and mountain caves. This perception is not supported by the Tipitaka, which depicts him as most commonly residing within walking distance of the large cities and towns of the time and frequently communicating with people. Even when he was travelling through rural areas or had gone to forest retreats, he was always near a village or hamlet, which he relied on for his food.

His audience came from all backgrounds, although typically they were city-dwellers or towns-folk, often from the economic, religious and political class. They included merchants, ascetics of various sects, military men, and occasionally even royalty. Sunidha, Vassakāra and Ugga were each senior government ministers, Jīvaka was a physician, Sīha a general, Abhaya a prince, Cundi and Sumanā were both princesses, Gaṇaka Moggallāna was an accountant, and Ambapālī a courtesan. Many of the brahmins he dialogued with were the leaders of their clans and communities or eminent scholars, and a small but significant number of them became his disciples and even monks. Others, such as Anāthapiṇḍaka, Ghosita, Kukkuṭa, Kālaka and Pāvārika, were wealthy businessmen. Such people were typically familiar with and interested in the various religious and philosophical

9. Ja. IV,496. M.II,216 and 259 describe in detail the extraction of poison arrows and the after-treatment of the wounds.

10. A.V,218.

11. E.g., It.101; M.II,258; Mil.112; 233, 247; Sn.560; Tha.722.

theories being aired at the time and in some cases were quite capable of discussing the finer points of these different teachings.

This should not be taken to mean that the Buddha had nothing to say to ordinary folk, that his Dhamma was not relevant to or was of little interest to them. The carpenter Pañcakanga had a long talk with the Buddha and another with the monk Anuruddha, and he was confident enough of his grasp of the Dhamma to correct another monk's misunderstanding of it.[12] Both Sunīta and Ariṭṭha were from the very bottom of the social ladder before becoming monks, the first a scavenger and the second was a vulture killer.[13] The Buddha had talks with Pessa and Kesi, both of them animal trainers, and with the village headman Asibandhakaputta, the son of a snake charmer. The nun Puṇṇika had been a water-carrier and another nun, Subhā, was a blacksmith's daughter. A female servant in the harem of King Udena named Khujjutarā never actually spoke with the Buddha but attended many of the talks he gave in Kosambī and absorbed much of what she heard. The Buddha lauded her for her deep learning and esteemed her as a disciple that others should look up to and emulate.[14] He once said that, for whomever he taught, even if it was a humble beggar or a hunter, he would do it carefully and respectfully.[15]

The Buddha often engaged in dialogues with one or more of the people who came to hear him or ask him questions, sometimes while those who accompanied the interlocutor listened in. These encounters typically began with courteous small talk, during which people found the Buddha "polite, genial and pleasantly spoken, not at all stern,

---

12. M.I,396 ff; III,145.

13. M.I,130 ff; Tha.620-631. Exactly why Ariṭṭtha killed these birds is not clear but their large flight feathers were used to make fans and flights for arrows, and their quills were used as needle cases and containers for such things as such as gold dust.

14. A.I,26; II,164; S.II,236. The tradition credits Khujjutarā with being responsible for preserving the discourses later compiled in the Itivuttaka. Unfortunately, the monks who recited, edited and transmitted the Tipitaka did not consider it worthwhile to record any other details about this interesting woman.

15. A.III,122, *sakkacca* and *gārava*.

clear-mouthed and first to open the conversation."[16] Like all such communication, the Buddha used these initial brief exchanges to let people know that they were meeting him on a basis of friendliness and mutual respect. Such openings were accompanied by polite physical gestures: joining palms in the *añjali* gesture and sitting down at what was considered an appropriate distance from him. As for brahmins, some admired the Buddha, others were cautious of him, having heard of his attitude towards aspects of their religion, and some were reluctant to be seen conversing on equal terms with someone they considered their inferior. Meetings with them might go like this:

> "Some greeted the Lord and sat down at one side, some greeted him and chatted briefly in a courteous and friendly manner and then sat down, some put their hands together in the añjali gesture and sat down, some announced their names and clan and sat down, and some sat down at one side without saying anything."[17]

On rare occasions, those who did not like or who disapproved of the Buddha, and there were some, might forgo the accepted pleasantries, and on at least one occasion the Buddha took issue with this. A group of young brahmins, including one named Ambaṭṭha who had excelled in his Vedic studies, went to see the Buddha. On meeting him they all exchanged greetings except Ambaṭṭha, who muttered something in an off-hand manner and walked up and down while the Buddha was sitting, a deliberate breach of etiquette. Deciding not to let this rudeness pass, the Buddha asked him:

> "Well, Ambaṭṭha, would you behave like this if you were talking with learned brahmin elders, teachers of teachers, as you do with me?"
>
> "No, good Gotama. A brahmin should walk with a walking brahmin, stand when he is standing, sit when he is sitting and recline when he is reclining. But with those shaven petty menials, the black scrapings of Brahmā's foot, it is fitting to act and speak as I do with you."

---

16. D.I,116.
17. M.I,401.

This added insult to ill-manners, and the Buddha replied:

> "Well, Ambaṭṭha, you came here for some reason, and whatever it was you should turn your attention to that. This Ambaṭṭha thinks he is well-trained, when in fact he shows a lack of training which can only be due to youthful inexperience."[18]

At this the young man became angry and then disparaged the Buddha's clan, the Sakyans. This tense exchange continued until the Buddha pointed out that Ambaṭṭha's family was of mixed caste, something the young man either knew and was sensitive about or perhaps was unaware of until then. Having humbled him, the two proceeded to have a long and fruitful discussion.[19]

After the introductions and small talk were over, and depending on whom he was talking to, the Buddha would ask questions of the visitor, or they would question him and he would answer, usually taking the opportunity to explain some aspect of his Dhamma in detail. Before giving a more detailed explanation of his position on some subject, he would often begin by asking for the interlocutor's full attention, saying: "Listen, pay attention and I will speak."[20] At other times, if he decided that they were amiable to his Dhamma, he would give what was called a talk on basics (*anupubbikathā*), i.e., on generosity, morality, heaven, and the disadvantages of sense pleasures and how to overcome them, before presenting the deeper aspects of his teaching.

To overcome any shyness or hesitation on the interlocutor's part about expressing their opinion, the Buddha would occasionally encourage them to speak up by praising any questions they might ask. "Good, good! Your intelligence is excellent and so is your inquiry. Your question is a good one."[21] Such encouragement meant that questions and comments kept coming, giving interlocutors the opportunity to express their views and the Buddha the opportunity to formulate his answers in a way that took into account their views. Inevitably, towards the end of such a back and forth, the Buddha would fully explain his perspective on whatever

---

18. D.I,90.
19. On the mixed caste Ambasṭhas in Brahminical/Hindu law see *Manusmṛti* 10, 8-13; 13-15.
20. A.IV,429.
21. A.II,177.

subject was being discussed. Some of his monologues were quite long. They were usually conducted in a polite manner and only rarely became heated, as for example those with Ambaṭṭha, Assalāyana and Caṅkī.[22]

The Buddha often used parables (*upamākathā*) or similes (*upamā*) in his talks. While presenting some aspect of his Dhamma, he would sometimes add: "I will give you a simile, because intelligent people understand better because of a simile" and then do so.[23] No one has ever counted all the Buddha's similes and parables, but there are at least several hundred. They draw on a wide variety of elements, ranging from natural phenomena to travelling, country life, the landscape, business, animal taming, royalty, metallurgy, household articles and duties, to name but a few. Their richness, diversity and realism suggest a creative communicator and a careful observer with wide experience. Three examples using the imagery of a river will suffice to demonstrate this.

One of the more famous of these is the Parable of the Raft. The Buddha saw his Dhamma mainly in utilitarian terms, as something used to accomplish a specific goal, i.e., awakening, after which it would be redundant. To explain what he meant, he told a story of a man who, in the course of a journey, came to a wide river and, knowing the country on his side to be dangerous and the other side to be safe, was determined to cross over. With no ferry or bridge available, he improvised a raft of grass, foliage and branches and, using his hands and feet, paddled to the further bank of the river. Having done this and thinking how useful the raft had been, he decided to hoist it onto his head and carry it with him for the remainder of his journey. Then the Buddha asked his monks if they thought this was an intelligent thing for the man to do. They answered that it was not, and then he concluded by saying: "Monks, when you understand that the Dhamma is similar to a raft, you will let go of what I have taught, even more so things I did not teach."[24]

Another of the Buddha's parables also used the image of crossing a river, although to make a different point. A man once asked the Buddha what he thought of those who claimed that liberation could be achieved through self-mortification. In answer to this the Buddha said:

22. D.I,87ff; M. II,147 ff; M.II,163 ff.
23. S.II,114.
24. M.I,134-5. See Gombrich 1996, pp.23-26.

> "Suppose a man wanting to cross a river were to take an axe, go into a forest and chop down a young, straight tree, one without any knots. He would lop off the crown, strip the foliage and branches off, shape the log with the axe, trim it with an adze, smooth it with a scraper, then polish it with a stone ball and, having done so, set out across the river. What do you think? Would he be able to cross that river?"

The man answered:

> "No sir, he would not. Because although the log had been well shaped on the outside, it had not been cleaned out on the inside."

The Buddha agreed and then said that, unless someone had "cleaned the inside" by cultivating psychological purity, he or she would not be able to attain awakening.[25]

A third riverine parable was used by the Buddha to explain his role in helping humankind to see the problems involved in ordinary conditioned existence:

> "Imagine a lovely, delightful river and a man being carried along it by the current. Then imagine that a perceptive man standing on the bank were to see this and call out, 'Hey sir! Further downstream there are rapids and whirlpools, crocodiles and demons, and if you end up there you will suffer death or death-like pain.' Hearing this, the man in the river would struggle against the current with his hands and feet."

The Buddha then explained that each element of the parable represented an aspect of the spiritual life – e.g., the river for craving, struggling against the current for renunciation, and the perceptive man on the river bank for himself.[26]

An aspect of the Buddha's approach to teaching which rarely gets mentioned is its gentle humour. His discourses and dialogues are replete with puns, humorous exaggerations, wordplay, irony and occasional satire. None of this would have caused guffaws or giggles, but some of

25. A.II,201.
26. It.114.

it may well have raised a smile. Unfortunately, for the most part this humour is not apparent to the modern reader. The American monk Thanissaro writes:

> "One of the reasons why the Canon's humour goes unrecognized relates to its style, which is often subtle, deadpan and dry. This style of humour can go right past readers in modern cultures where jokes are telegraphed well in advance, and humour tends to be broad. Another reason is that translators often miss the fact that a passage is meant to be humorous, and so render it in a flat, pedantic way."[27]

Further, it is never easy to retain humour in a text when translating it from one language to another, but even taking this and the linguistic and cultural differences between the Buddha's world and our own into account, his humour can sometimes shine through.

At one time, King Ajātasattu went to visit the Buddha and asked him if he could tell him an advantage of the monastic life that was observable here and now. The king had only recently murdered his father and was starting to feel increasingly regretful and uneasy about it. He may also have started to consider that he had set a dangerous example for his own son, which later happened to be the case. The Buddha asked the king what he would do if one of his slaves ran away and became a monk, and he later came to know where the fugitive was. Would he, the Buddha inquired, have the monk arrested and returned to bondage? "No," answered the king. "On the contrary, I would stand up for him, bow to him and offer him alms." The Buddha replied: "Well, there you are! There is one of the advantages of the monk's life that is observable here and now."[28] This unexpectedly whimsical answer to a serious question must have at first surprised the king, but then made him smile. Having lightened his mood and put him at his ease, the Buddha proceeded to answer his question more seriously.

On those occasions where a particular way of thinking has made a problem look unsolvable or a burden appear unbearable, making a joke of the situation can sometimes open up a different way of looking at it and suggest a solution. Humour can also trigger a catharsis,

---

27. Thanissaro, p.5.
28. D.I,51-61. For more examples see Gombrich, 2009, pp.183ff.

a therapeutic release from anxiety, tension or fear, or lift one out of depression. This incident may be an example of the Buddha doing this.

A number of the Buddha's similes and parables include humour, sometimes by juxtaposing two incongruous but related elements. For example, he said that having strong determination but faulty understanding would be like tugging a cow's horn in an effort to get milk. Likewise, a dull student will learn nothing, despite having a good teacher, any more than a ladle will taste the soup it holds.[29] To illustrate how futile it would be to investigate the constituents of individuality in the hope of finding an eternal underlying self, the Buddha related a parable about a certain king who, on hearing the music of a veena for the first time, asked his courtiers to bring him the instrument so that he could examine the music that had so enchanted him. As tactfully as they could, the courtiers explained that the music was the result of the various parts of the veena and the effort of the player. Failing to understand this, the king got a veena, chopped it up, splintered the pieces, burned them and then winnowed the ashes in an effort to find the music. Bewildered and irritated at not finding it, he expressed his disgust for veenas.[30] Those listening to this tale must have found it comical that a king, usually seen as a formidable and grave person, could act so foolishly.

Despite such occasional light-heartedness, the Buddha is never described as laughing or causing others to laugh, although he often smiled.[31] Likewise, his monastics were certainly not jocular, but those who were "sensitive, polite, who speak nicely, have lovely smiles, and on first being met bid you welcome" (*saṇhā sakhilā mihita pubbañgamā ehisvāgatavādino*) were generally appreciated.[32]

One of the most important ways the Buddha communicated his Dhamma was by participating in the public debates (*vivāda*) that were a feature of the time. So popular were these events that they attracted large crowds, and some towns even used their public halls to hold them. The Tipitaka and other sources from around the same period and later give some idea of how these debates were conducted.[33]

29. M.III,141; Dhp.64.
30. S.IV,196-197. *Vīṇā*, sometimes translated as harp, arched harp or lute.
31. E.g., A. III, 214; M. II, 45; 74; S. I, 24; Tha. 630.
32. Vin.II,11.
33. See Prets, 2000.

If, on being asked a legitimate question three times, an opponent would be warned that his head would shatter into seven pieces if he did not answer, which is to say, be defeated.[34] Participants were expected to use recognised arguments and adhere to accepted procedures, and a moderator (*pañhavīmaṁsakā*) tried to make sure they did. To dodge a question by asking another question, change the subject, make an unproven assertion, drop it when challenged and then take up another one, or ridicule the questioner, were considered improper. Likewise, to shout down an opponent, catch him up when he hesitated or, for the audience, to interrupt from the side lines, were also unacceptable.[35]

The popularity of these events gave rise to individuals who were adept at promoting and defending their thesis in the public arena. One particular Jain monk named Saccaka was described as "a debater, a clever speaker much esteemed by the general public." Like some others who participated in these encounters, he revelled in displaying his rhetorical and dialectical skills and once proclaimed: "I see no samaṇa or brahmin, no leader or teacher of any sect or denomination, including the ones claiming to be spiritually accomplished or fully awakened, who would not shiver and shake, tremble and sweat from the armpits if he were to take me on in a debate." After a discussion with a Buddhist monk and an arrangement to meet the Buddha later, he made this boast before a large assembly of Licchavis:

> "Today there will be some discussion between myself and the samaṇa Gotama. If he maintains before me what one of his well-known disciples, the monk Assaji, maintained before me just a while ago, then as a strong man might grab a shaggy ram by the fleece and drag it to and fro, this way and that, so too in debate I will drag the samaṇa Gotama to and fro, this way and that."[36]

Saccaka did go to confront the Buddha, followed by a group of Licchavis interested to see what would happen. The discussion started

34. M.I,231. See Witzel pp.363-415. Having the head crushed for offenses such as misrepresentation, perjury or fraud may have been the origin of this threat.

35. M.II,168; A.I,197-199.

36. M.I,227-228.

out amiably enough, but the Buddha's probing of Saccaka's assertions soon had him contradicting himself and finally reduced to silence. As the Tipitaka tells it, he ended up becoming one of the Buddha's disciples, although we hear no more of him.

With reputations on the line and the possibility of attracting patronage and disciples, there were debaters prepared to resort to trickery and deceit in order to win. Before an encounter, a participant might plot with his supporters to think up fallacious questions or double propositions (*ubhatokoṭikaṁ pañhaṃ*) in the hope of confounding the opponent.[37] One ascetic was known to have worked out numerous arguments to use against his opponents, and he must have had some success with them because he had come to be known as 'the Pundit.'[38] One Buddhist monk, the Sakyan Hatthaka, was not averse to using underhand tactics to win, or at least to give the appearance of winning. Having been bested in one encounter, he arranged to meet the same opponent for a second round at a particular time and place. After advertising this upcoming event but giving a quite different venue and time for it, when the opponent did not turn up he boasted that the man was actually too frightened to appear. Asked about this deceit by his fellow monks, Hatthaka justified himself by saying: "These followers of other sects holding other views should be defeated one way or another. Victory should be denied them." When the Buddha came to know of this, he sternly rebuked Hatthaka for his dishonesty.[39]

The Buddha noted that some teachers avoided debating out of fear of being publicly humiliated, but if compelled to explain themselves, they would resort to evasive statements, while others, who were dubbed eel-wrigglers (*amarāvikkhepika*), would not allow themselves to be pinned down to any particular position.[40] The Indian teachers of the Buddha's time were as argumentative and hair-splitting, as sophistic, subtle and penetrating, as their equivalents in ancient Athens were at around the same time.

---

37. M. I, 392-3; S.IV,323.
38. A.V,229.
39. Vin.IV,1-2.
40. D.I,24-5.

Success or failure in a debate did not always depend on the veracity of one's thesis or the logic of one's arguments. As there was not always a moderator, it could be the attitude of the audience that decided who had come out on top. The Buddha pointed out that if a protagonist supported a false doctrine but was able to silence an opponent who was using valid arguments, the audience might still support the former and noisily shout: "It is he who is the wise man!"[41] On the other hand, if the audience was appreciative of a teacher's rhetorical skill and the strength of his arguments, it would applaud him and mock the loser. There is a description of a participant on the losing end of a debate with the Buddha being "reduced to silence, his head lowered, his eyes downcast, at a loss, unable to make a reply," while the audience "assailed him on all sides with a torrent of abuse and poked fun at him…"[42] Mahāvīra said to one of his disciples, who failed to refute the Buddha on some point, that he was like a man who went off to castrate someone but came back having been castrated himself.[43] This comparison of emasculation with defeat in such public encounters gives some idea of how humiliating it was thought to be.

It was by no means the case that all these debates were just exercises in sophistry or intellectual entertainment; many who participated in them were genuinely interested in testing their ideas against others in order to plumb the truth. That at least some of those who attended these events did not just want to be entertained but took an intelligent interest in them is suggested by the questions a group of townsfolk from Kesaputta put to the Buddha during one of his visits.

> "Sir, some samaṇas and brahmins come to Kesaputta and proclaim and explain their own doctrine and then criticise, condemn, deride and clip the wings of the doctrines of others. Then other samaṇas and brahmins come and do the same to what the earlier

---

41. A.V,230-1. In later centuries, being defeated in state-sponsored debates could result in exile or even death. In the case of debates held in royal courts, it was often the whim of the king or his personal belief that decided the outcome. See Verardi, pp. 25-26, 205-207, 218-219, etc. and Bronkhorst 2011, pp.170 ff.

42. A.I,187.

43. M.I,383.

ones had said. We are in doubt, we are confused as to which of these respected teachers is speaking the truth and which falsehood."[44]

The Buddha responded that he understood the people's confusion and advised them to be cautious of arguments based on revelation, tradition, hearsay, appeals to scriptural authority, spurious logic, inference, analogies, speculation, someone's supposed expertise, or even out of respect for a particular teacher, but rather they should rely on their own experience and knowledge while taking into account the opinions of the wise.[45]

Because debates could get heated and sometimes even end in the protagonists or the audience exchanging blows, the Buddha avoided such assemblies during the early part of his career. He observed: "Some debates are conducted in a spirit of hostility and some in a spirit of truth. Either way, the sage does not get involved."[46] As a consequence, early on he was accused of being unable to defend his philosophy in the face of scrutiny. One critic said of him:

> "Who does the samaṇa Gotama speak with? From whom does he get his lucidity of wisdom? His wisdom is destroyed by living in solitude, he is unused to discussions, he is no good at speaking, he is completely out of touch. The samaṇa Gotama is like an antelope that circles around and keeps to the edges."[47]

For a long time, the Buddha was content to let his Dhamma speak for itself, but as people began to seek deeper explanations of it and it started to be criticised and even misrepresented, he was compelled to participate in public debates and discussions. He soon earned a reputation for being able to explain his Dhamma with great clarity and to effectively defend it against criticism. He also began to subject the doctrines of others to hard questioning. So successful

44. A.I,188-189.
45. A.I,188-189. The Buddha considered it acceptable for a student to correct or question a teacher if he or she genuinely thought the teacher was wrong, e.g., Vin.I,49.
46. Sn.780. The *Caraka Saṃhitā* mentions and describes both these types of debates, see Prets, p.371-373.
47. D.III,38.

was he at disarming his critics, and even influencing many of them to become his disciples, that some suspected he was using occult powers to do this.[48]

The Buddha's aim in debating or engaging in one-on-one conversation was never to defeat an opponent, silence a critic or even to win disciples but to lead people from ignorance to clarity and understanding. He emphasised this point often: "Truly, the good discuss for the purpose of knowledge and certainty"; and again: "The spiritual life is not lived for the purpose…of winning debates …Rather, it is lived for the purpose of restraint, giving up, dispassion and cessation."[49]

In one of the most heartfelt appeals the Buddha ever made, he said:

> "I tell you this. Let an intelligent person who is sincere, honest and straightforward come to me, and I will teach him Dhamma. If he practices as he is taught, within seven days, and by his own knowledge and vision, he will attain that holy life and goal. Now you may think that I say this just to get disciples or to make you abandon your rules. But this is not so. Keep your teacher and continue to follow your rules. You may think that I say this so you will give up your way of life, follow things you consider bad or reject things you consider good. But this is not so. Live as you see fit and continue to reject things you consider bad and follow things you consider good. But there are states that are unhelpful and defiled, causing rebirth, fearful, distressful and associated with birth, decay and death, and it is only for the overcoming of these things that I teach the Dhamma."[50]

For the Buddha, any discussions on philosophical or religious questions, formal or not, should be conducted in a civil, calm and respectful manner. The good protagonist, he said, will acknowledge their opposite's strong points without disparaging their weak ones (*subhāsitaṁ anumodeyya, dubbhaṭṭhe nāpasādaye*). They will avoid a hostile or arrogant tone (*aviruddho anussito*), not verbally intimidate or try to overwhelm (*nābhihare nābhimadde*) the other, or indulge in rhetorical trickery (*na vācaṁ payutaṁ bhaṇe*). In short, they will state

48. M.I.381.

49. A.I,199; II,26.

50. D.III, 55-6, condensed.

what they know (*sammad-aññāya bhāsati*) and debate or discuss for the sake of knowledge and understanding (*aññānatatthaṁ pasādatthaṁ, sataṁ ve hoti mantanā*), not just to get the better of the other.[51]

Apart from participating in debates and talking with individuals or small groups, the Buddha occasionally gave talks to large crowds of people, sometimes many hundreds who had assembled specifically to hear him. These public sermons must have been organized by his devotees and advertised beforehand. An attendee of one such sermon expressed his admiration for how quiet such a large crowd could be, as they sat utterly attentive to what the Buddha was saying:

> "Once, when the samaṇa Gotama was teaching the Dhamma to many hundreds of disciples, one of them coughed and another one nudged him with his knee, saying, 'Hush! Keep quiet! The Lord, the teacher, is expounding the Dhamma for us.' So even when he is teaching many hundreds, there is no coughing or clearing of throats for the disciples are waiting in anticipation."[52]

Sakuludāyin, a great admirer of the Buddha, once told him that during such talks, he and the others in the audience would sit with their eyes fixed on the Buddha's face.[53] This probably means that the participants were fully concentrated on what was being said, although it may also have been the case that in a large crowd it was not always easy for those further back to hear what the Buddha was saying, so it helped to be able to read his lips.

There are occasional vignettes of the Buddha teaching and engaged in discussions scattered throughout the Tipitaka that are unlikely to be literary creations but that reflect how the Buddha actually conducted himself during such encounters. For example, during one debate in front of a large audience, the Buddha's interlocutor asserted that the

---

51. A.I,199. To the claim that debates and discussions on conflicting ideas should be avoided as they lead to agitation and ill-will, one early Buddhist text, the *Upāyahṛdaya*, argued that debates were necessary. One could, it said, argue in a courteous and measured manner thus avoiding such problems, and to leave the false unchallenged would allow confusion and ignorance to prevail. See Gillon pp.22-23.

52. M.II,4-5, condensed.

53. M.II,30.

individual's body and mind are a person's true self, something quite contrary to the Buddha's understanding. When the Buddha asked him if he really believed such a thing, the protagonist replied: "Not only do I believe it, this large crowd does too," probably making a sweeping gesture towards the audience as he did. This appeal to majority opinion did not impress the Buddha, who responded: "What has this large crowd got to do with it? Confine yourself to what you believe!"[54]

The brahmin Esukārī confidently asserted to the Buddha that, according to what his religion taught, his caste was superior, and other castes were obliged to render service to brahmins. The Buddha punctured this conceit by asking: "And does the whole world agree with the brahmins?" Nonplussed by this, Esukārī had to admit that it did not.[55]

Halfway through a back-and-forth with the Buddha, his interlocutor, an ascetic, appeared to contradict himself, and the Buddha quickly pointed this out, saying: "Think carefully, Aggivessana, think carefully about how you reply! What you said before does not agree with what you said afterwards, and what you said afterwards does not agree with what you said before."[56]

There are ample examples of the Buddha being asked questions and, instead of answering them, gently brushing them aside or saying something non-committal so as to avoid an argument or having to comment on a matter of no real importance. Two *lokāyatika* brahmins once mentioned to him that the teachers Pūraṇa Kassapa and Mahāvīra both claimed to be omniscient, and yet they each taught something different about the nature of the cosmos. They asked: "Their claims being contradictory, who is speaking the truth and who falsehood?" The Buddha replied: "Enough of that; let it be! I will teach you Dhamma."[57]

Another brahmin once mentioned to the Buddha that he had heard that sacrificing animals brought great spiritual benefits, expecting

---

54. M.I,230.
55. M.II,178.
56. M.I,232.
57. A.IV,428-429. *Lokāyata* was a branch of Brahminical learning although exactly what, is disputed. It is mentioned at D. I,11; I,114; S. II,77; Vin.II,139; Ud.32, etc. See Rhys Davids, 1899, pp.166 ff and Jayatilleke, pp. 49 ff and 89 ff.

the Buddha to give his opinion on the matter. The Buddha realized that if he said what he really thought, the brahmin would be upset, so he simply commented that he had heard this claim too. The brahmin interpreted this noncommittal response as an agreement and cheerfully announced: "On this matter, good Gotama and I are in agreement." Ānanda was watching this encounter and, seeing the problem, suggested to the brahmin not to say what he had heard but to ask the Buddha what he thought would be the best way to conduct a sacrifice. The brahmin did this and, seeing no way to avoid the truth, the Buddha said that even before igniting the sacrificial fires or erecting the sacrificial post, one would create negative consequences for oneself because an essential feature of the ritual was to kill. He then told the brahmin that rather than igniting the three sacrificial fires, the most positive thing he could do would be to extinguish three fires – the fires of greed, hatred, and delusion (*lobha*, *dosa* and *moha*).[58] Here and elsewhere, the Buddha was analogising the three fires of the Vedic sacrifice – the Āhavanīya, the Gārhapatya, and the Dakṣiṇāgni – with the three major psychological negativities.

One of the most skilful ways the Buddha taught was to initially agree with assertions about an accepted concept or practice but then redefine it so that it fitted with his philosophy. He did the same with brahminical terms, using them but giving them different, usually ethical, meanings. For example, he agreed that brahmins were worthy of respect but that he and his disciples qualified to be "true brahmins" because they led exemplary lives, not because of their family background. He enumerated all the virtues that made one worthy of being considered a brahmin, but none of them included being born into the brahmin caste, reciting the Vedas, performing the sacrifice or ritual washing.[59] Likewise, the person who lacked virtue and principles was the real outcaste, not someone so designated by the caste system.[60] When the young man Sigāla told the Buddha that he worshipped the six directions at the request of his dying father, the Buddha said that he taught his disciples to worship the directions too, but in a different

58. A.IV,41-42.
59. Dhp.396-423.
60. Sn.116-134.

way. He explained that, in his Dhamma, each direction represented the people one had a relationship with – parent, spouse, friend, teacher, employee, clergyman – and that one 'worshipped' them by treating them with respect and kindness.[61] A government minister explained to the Buddha that he considered a great man (*mahā purisa*) to be one who had certain qualities, which he then listed and with most being worldly accomplishments. The Buddha replied: "I neither agree nor disagree with your assertion." Then he proposed different, more spiritual accomplishments which he considered would qualify one to be a great man.[62]

On very rare occasions the Buddha responded to a questioner with silence. Remarkably, this has been inflated by popular and even academic writers into the claim that maintaining an enigmatic silence was a significant aspect of his teaching style and a technique he used to transmit his more profound insights.[63] The Buddha did advocate silence as an alternative to the idle chatter that often takes place in a social context and in the face of anger or provocation but not as a response to sincere and meaningful questions.[64] Occasionally he refused to answer questions he considered to be trivial or irreverent, but he always explained his reasons for doing so. Only twice in his long career did he say nothing at all on being asked a question. In the first of these instances, the ascetic Uttiya once asked him how many people will free themselves from the continual rounds of birth, death and rebirth by following the Dhamma. "Will the whole world get out of saṃsāra, or half of it, or a third?" The Buddha was silent. Ānanda observed what was happening and, thinking that Uttiya might get the impression that the Buddha was stumped by the question, decided to give an answer on the Buddha's behalf. He said, in effect, that the number of people who attained awakening was irrelevant and that the important thing was how it could be done, and that was by following the Noble Eightfold Path.[65]

---

61. D.III,180 ff. On the different ways of and reasons for worshipping the directions, see e.g., *Bṛhadāraṇyaka Upaniṣad* 3.7,10 and *Chāndogya Upaniṣad* 1.3, 11; 5.6; 5.20,2. Sigāla was probably worshipping the directional gods as advocated at *Gautama Dharmasūtra* 5,11.

62. A.II,35-36.

63. On the Buddha's supposed silence, see Dhammika, 2018c, pp.85-89.

64. M.I,161; S.I,162.

65. A.V,193-195.

In the second example, an ascetic named Vacchagotta asked the Buddha: "Is there a self?" The Buddha gave no answer. Vacchagotta continued: "Then is there no self?" and again the Buddha did not respond. Perhaps annoyed or disappointed by this, Vacchagotta rose and left. When Ānanda asked the Buddha why he met these questions with silence, he replied:

> "If, when asked if there is a self, I had answered 'yes', I would have been siding with those teachers who are eternalists. And if I had answered 'no', I would have been siding with those teachers who are annihilationists. If I had answered 'yes', would this have been consistent with the knowledge that everything is without self?"
>
> "No Lord," replied Ānanda.
>
> "And if I had answered, 'No, there is no self', an already bewildered Vacchagotta would have been even more so and would have thought, 'Before, I had a self, and now I don't have one.'"[66]

In this incident the Buddha declined to give an answer, thinking that Vacchagotta did not have the background knowledge or perhaps the intelligence to understand the doctrine of Not-self (*anatta*).

The Buddha was quite conscious of the fact that the way language is used can lead to misunderstandings, and he was careful how he phrased his questions and how others phrased their questions to him. Once, he was teaching a group of monks his doctrine of the four nutriments that maintain a living being: material food; contact; mental volition; and consciousness. One of the monks asked: "Who consumes the nutriment of consciousness?" Phrased in this way, the question presupposes the existence of an entity, a self. The Buddha responded immediately: "That is not a valid question. I am not saying 'one consumes'...But if someone were to ask me, 'What arises conditioned by consciousness?', then that would be a valid question."[67] The monk rephrased his question and the discussion continued.

---

66. S.IV,400.
67. S.II,13.

While usually direct in how he spoke to others, probing in the questions he asked and precise in how he answered questions, the Buddha could also be a gracious interlocutor. A wonderful example of this is a three-way discussion that took place between him, Ānanda and Saṅgārava. As the discussion proceeded, Ānanda asked Saṅgārava a question which he could not answer without admitting that what he had said earlier was wrong, so he changed the subject. Ānanda, however, would not let Saṅgārava off the hook and kept pressing his question. Seeing Saṅgārava's discomfort and feeling sorry for him, the Buddha interrupted the discussion and asked Saṅgārava what had been happening of late in the royal court. Much to Saṅgārava's relief, he answered the Buddha's question, and Ānanda, taking the hint, stopped pressing his.[68] This incident shows the Buddha's skill in unblocking an impasse but also his attitude that it is not always necessary to win an argument, particularly with a courteous and genuine interlocutor.

While the Buddha was conversing with some learned and senior brahmins once, a young member of their group kept interrupting. When the Buddha had had enough of this, he turned to the youngster and said: "Stop interrupting this conversation with the senior brahmins. Wait until it is finished." One of the brahmins defended the youth: "Good Gotama, do not reprimand the young student Kāpaṭhika. He is an intelligent and learned clansman. He speaks well and is quite capable of taking part in our discussions with you." The Buddha realized he had misjudged the youth and shortly afterwards asked him a question, thereby including him in the conversation.[69]

Although the Buddha appreciated and praised some aspects of Brahminism, there were other aspects of it that he criticised, and two of these related to teaching. The nature of Brahminism was such that its priests, the brahmins, did not instruct the laity in Vedic religion the way Buddhist monks, Christian pastors or Jewish rabbis have always done with their religions. Rather, brahmins performed the required rituals while the laity were merely passive onlookers, and the brahmins lived off the fees charged for their services. Their teaching role was to train young brahmin boys to recite and remember the

---

68. A.I,168-170.
69. M.II,168-169.

Vedic hymns and how to conduct the various rituals. After the completion of their education, the students had to collect what was called the teacher's fee (*ācariyadhana*).[70]

There were three aspects of this system that the Buddha rejected and with which he contrasted his Dhamma: keeping the Vedas secret; charging for conducting the rituals; and requiring payment for training the students. In the distant past the Vedas were supposed to be available to the first three castes, the so-called twice-born, while menials, untouchables, and foreigners were not even allowed to hear the hymns being chanted. But long before the Buddha's time brahmins had secured a monopoly on the Vedas and kept them secret, in part because they believed the hymns would become impure if pronounced or even heard by other castes and because their income depended on their exclusive knowledge of them. The penalty for a brahmin divulging the Vedas to anyone other than a brahman was truly draconian.[71]

The Upanisadic sages of the time were radically reinterpreting Brahmanism but still expected to be paid for expounding their ideas, just as orthodox brahmins required payment for conducting the rituals. For example, when the renowned teacher Yājñavalkya was asked if he had come to an assembly to have a stimulating discussion or to acquire wealth, he answered "Both!" When Raikva was offered a large herd of cows, gold and a chariot by Jānaśruti to teach, he made it clear that this wasn't enough: "You can keep your cows and other things, you menial!" It was only when Jānaśruti added more cows and threw in his daughter as well that Raikva finally consented.[72]

The idea that one should have to pay to learn or even hear the Dhamma was repugnant to the Buddha. He remarked: "Do not go about making a business out of the Dhamma" (*dhammena na vaṇī care*).[73] He considered the truth to be a gift, not a commodity. Equally repugnant to him was the idea that the Dhamma should be restricted to an exclusive in-group. The truths he taught were understandable to all, relevant to all and should be available to all. He said: "Three things

70. On the high fees Upaniṣadic teachers charged for the knowledge they imparted, see Black, pp.112-113.

71. *Gautama Dharmasūtra* 20.1-7.

72. *Bṛhadāraṇyaka Upaniṣad* 4.1,1; *Chāndogya Upaniṣad* 4.2.

73. Ud.66.

shine openly, not in secret. What three? The orb of the moon, the orb of the sun, and the Dhamma and training taught by the Tathāgata."[74] He reiterated this same point just before his final passing when he said that he had proclaimed the Dhamma without any idea of secret and open (*anantaraṃ abāhiraṃ*) and that he did he not have a "teacher's fist" (*ācariya muṭṭhi*) which holds something back.[75] The Buddha expected nothing more from his disciples or his audience than respect for the teaching and attentiveness while he taught it.[76] To this end he laid down five principles of what might be called his ethics of teaching:

> "It is not easy to teach the Dhamma to others, so when you do so establish these five things in yourself first. Teach the Dhamma to others, thinking, 'I will teach in a gradual way. I will teach keeping the goal in mind. I will teach out of kindness. I will not teach for personal gain, and I will teach neither to my own detriment or the detriment of others.'"[77]

The Buddha made a number of extraordinary claims about himself, which is hardly surprising. Throughout history, the founders of most religions or religious movements have done this: claiming to have miraculous powers; being able to communicate with the gods or a god; or even that they were a god themselves. The Buddha's most significant claim was that he had awakened to the nature of reality. However, what set him apart from all the other claimants to spiritual authority was that he did not require his followers to have complete faith in him and unquestioning acceptance of what he taught. In fact, he actually invited people to suspend judgment about his claimed attainments until they had thoroughly examined him to see whether he had them or not.

Knowing that most people were not mind-readers, he asked those thinking of becoming his followers to first scrutinize his behaviour to see if it was consistent with what he taught. While doing this, they should also take note of what their ears might reveal about him – from

---

74. A.I,283.

75. D.II,100. Mil.94 adds *arahassakārinā bhavitabbaṁ niravasesakārinā bhavitabbaṁ*, that the genuine teacher "keeps nothing secret and holds nothing back."

76. A.V,347.

77. A.III,184, also III,196.

the comments of those who had spent time with him and perhaps from what he said and how he said it. With typical insight, he pointed out that religious leaders can start out being sincere but gradually be corrupted by success and adulation, and so he said that this scrutiny of him should continue over a period of time. He then made the equally insightful observation that a teacher could be very impressive when in front of an audience but quite different behind the scenes, and thus where possible one should examine the Buddha in all situations. In reality this would have been easy to do because there was no 'public' and 'private' Buddha, no phalanx of close disciples who kept others at bay. He was almost always available to anyone who wanted to meet him. He was confident that if someone carried out these and other examinations and inquiries, they would see for themselves that his behaviour was consistent with his claim to be fully awakened. Any faith or confidence they developed in him and what he taught as a result would be, he said, "based on reasons, supported by empirical experience, strong and unshakable..."[78]

78. M.I, 320.

7
A Day in the Buddha's Life

The Tipitaka provides enough information to get some idea of what a normal day in the Buddha's life might have been like. Of course, this would have changed at different times of the year. For example, during the rains he was sedentary, and the rest of the year he would travel. And it would have changed over time – for example, when he was young and as he grew older. But any one day would have included activities such as those enumerated in what follows.

The Buddha described his usual morning routine like this:

> "When I am dwelling dependent on a village or town, I dress in the morning, take my robe and bowl and enter that village or town for alms. After eating, I go into a nearby grove, make some grass or leaves into a pile and then sit down, crossing my legs and keeping my back straight, arouse mindfulness in front of me."[1]

The three things mentioned in this passage are the Buddha's attire, his food and how he obtained it, and his meditation. Each of them is worth detailed examination. The Buddha's dress consisted of three separate pieces of cloth: a rectangular piece wrapped around the waist and secured by a belt; a larger rectangular robe draped around his whole body, over the left shoulder and under the right arm; and a double-layered robe for use during the winter. These three garments were made up of pieces of cloth sewn together, thus lessening their value and making it less likely that they would be stolen, and each of them was dyed tawny brown or reddish-yellow. The three together were called *ticīvara* or *kāsāva*. When the Buddha needed to lie down, he would often fold his double-layered robe into four and lie in it, using it as a kind of

---

1. A.I,182.

thin mattress.[2] During the years when the Buddha experimented with various austerities, and perhaps occasionally during the years after his awakening too, he wore robes made of scraps of cast-off cloth and rags picked up in the streets or charnel grounds, which was the norm amongst many ascetics. There is at least one reference to him wearing an old robe made of scraps of hemp cloth.[3] He wore such attire later too, but if given robes made of new cloth, he had no objection to using them. The stricter ascetics thought it inappropriate to wear purpose-made robes rather than those made of rags, but the Buddha pointed out that what really mattered was the quality of one's mind and not what type of attire one wore.[4] Where the particular style of robe the Buddha used came from is unknown, but it was probably standard dress for certain samaṇa sects, and the Buddha adopted it simply because it was convenient and adequately covered and protected the body.

Many *samaṇas*, the Buddha and his monks and nuns included, obtained their food by means of a practice called alms gathering (*piṇḍacāra*), which was not begging, as is often said, but something less intrusive.[5] Beggars plead or importune for alms, while alms gathering involved standing quietly at the door of a potential donor, bowl in hand, eyes downcast, waiting for something to be offered.[6] After waiting for an appropriate time, the monk or nun moved on without a word, whether they had received something or not. As cooking at this time was usually done in the evening, when supper, the main meal of the day, was prepared together with the following day's meals, the best time to go for alms was early in the morning.[7]

---

2. E.g., D.II,134; M.I,354.
3. S.II,221. *Sāṇa* is the rough fibre of *Crotalaria juncea*. At A.I,240 the Buddha lists some of the material ascetics of other sects used as clothing.
4. M.I,282; Dhp.142.
5. Sn.710-12. *Piṇḍa*, a ball or handful of rice; *cārita*, to go.
6. Alms bowls could be made of either iron or clay, and were either large, medium or small, each with a capacity of half a *āḷhaka*, a *nālika* and a *pattha* respectively of cooked rice, and about a quarter less of raw rice, Vin.III,243. Unfortunately, what these units of capacity represent cannot be determined.
7. M.I,448, but see A.III,260. Numerous ancient texts show that cooking was done and the day's main meal was taken at different times from one region to another and during different periods, see Prakash.

Although alms gathering was the main way the Buddha obtained his food, he would occasionally be invited for a meal at the house of a disciple or an admirer, and this occurred more often as his following and his renown grew. The Tipitaka includes a detailed description of how the Buddha conducted himself during one such invitation. A donor would invite him to a meal the following day, and if he accepted, someone would come at the agreed-upon time, inform him that the meal was ready, and accompany him to the house. While waiting for the meal to be served, during it and afterwards, the Buddha did not fidget or sit in a slovenly manner but maintained a comportment of grace and dignity and did everything purposefully. Before eating he would wash his hands. He ate without rushing, chewing each mouthful fully before swallowing it, and did not take more food until he had finished the previous mouthful. It was said that he experienced the flavour but without being greedy for it. After finishing the meal, he washed his hand and bowl, sat silently for a few minutes and then gave thanks to the people who had provided it for him.[8] It can be assumed that the Buddha's behaviour here was in keeping with how a polite and cultured person would be expected to conduct themselves during a meal if they were a guest in someone's home.

Depending entirely on the generosity of others for sustenance meant that one might receive just broken rice grains, sour gruel, leftovers or, sometimes, nothing.[9] There are several references to the Buddha alms gathering and receiving nothing, and one text mentions that he went to one particular village and "came back with his bowl as clean as when he went."[10] A more serious problem with relying on alms gathering for one's food was being given what he described

---

8. M.II,138-9.

9. A.IV,392. Brahmanism recognized three types of leftover food – that from the pots in which the meal was cooked, that from the receptacles from which it was served, and that left on the plate after the diner had finished eating. The first two types might be given to the household servants, the third type (*ucchiṭṭha*) was given to beggars or slaves and was considered repulsive and polluting, on a par with vomit or excrement, and one of the reasons many brahmins despised non-Vedic ascetics who ate such food. On the rules concerning leftovers in Brahminism, see Olivelle 1999, p.354, note 3.27.

10. S.I,114.

as "the unrecognisable scraps of strangers" that were spoiled and becoming ill, or even dying, from food poisoning.[11]

Ascetics also had to be careful not to turn up for alms too often and wear out their welcome. At one time the citizens of Rājagaha complained about the number of monks in the city, probably because they were putting a strain on people's ability to give.[12] The Buddha counselled his monks not to inconvenience their donors in any way. "As a bee takes nectar and goes its way without damaging the colour or the fragrance of the flower, so the sage should go through the village for alms."[13] Once, while alms gathering in Sāvatthī, the Buddha paused at the house of a particular man who filled his bowl with rice. The next day he went again, and the same thing happened. Mistakenly thinking this was a sign that the donor was happy to give him a generous meal, the Buddha went on the third day, and the man gave him rice but mumbled under his breath: "This troublesome samaṇa keeps coming again and again."[14]

As with other monks, the Buddha usually ate humble fare, but when invited to a wealthy family's home, he might have fine rice with various condiments and curries set before him.[15] At Ugga's home, for example, he was served a dish flavoured with sal flowers, pork stewed with jujube fruit and fried vegetable stalks, together with the best quality rice, with the dark grains removed – obviously a sumptuous meal.[16] The more

---

11. S.II,281. Jain sūtras mention the dangers of food poisoning for monks, *Ācārāṅga Sūtra* II,1,3.

12. Vin.I,79.

13. Dhp.49. In later centuries this came to be known as the bee practice, *mādhukāra*, see Olivelle 1992, pp.198, 252.

14. S.I,174.

15. M.II,7-8.

16. A.III,49. *Sālapupphakaṃ khādanīyaṃ*: there is no evidence, ancient or modern, of *Shorea robusta* flowers being used as a food or to flavour food. However, its seeds, dried and ground into a meal, are used to make a gruel. *Sampannakolakaṃ sūkaramaṃsaṃ*: pork stewed in the slightly tart fruit of the *Ziziphus jujube*. The meaning of *nibaddhatelakaṃ nāliyāsākaṃ* is unclear; I follow Bodhi, who follows the commentary, 2012, p.1727, notes 1029 and 1030. *Sālinaṃ odano vigatakāḷako*: on *sāli* rice, see Dhammika, 2018b, p.102. Removing shrivelled, discoloured or broken grains from rice before cooking was time consuming and suggested wealth, i.e., having servants to do such work. It improved the appearance of the rice when served.

traditional *samaṇas* criticised the Buddha for eating such rich food, but he defended himself by saying: "If a monk of such virtue, such concentration or such wisdom were to eat the finest rice with various condiments and curries that would be no obstacle for him."[17] Just as controversial was the Buddha's acknowledgment that at times he would eat as much as a whole bowlful of food or more, although he wouldn't have done this out of greed, given his repeated admonishments to his monks and nuns to eat in moderation.[18] Perhaps he only did this when he had received no alms food or only a meagre amount the day before or for a few days in a row.

The Buddha once mentioned in passing that meat served with rice (*sāli maṃsodanaṃ*) was a usual part of the diet of the time and thus acceptable fare to offer to religious mendicants, something confirmed by other early Indian literature.[19] One text, for example, described a group of people preparing a feast for the Buddha and the monks with him, during which they boiled porridge and rice, made soup and cut up or minced meat (*maṃsāni koṭṭenti*).[20] While vegetarianism was yet to become a widespread practice in India, *samaṇas* such as Nanda Vaccha, Kisa Sankicca, Makkhali Gosāla and the Jains were beginning to advocate the practice.[21] The Buddha abstained from meat and fish during the time he was experimenting with self-mortification, but after his awakening he ate anything put in his bowl or served to him during a meal invitation, something the Jains publicly condemned him for if it included meat.[22] He told his monks and nuns that they should not eat a meat dish if they had seen, heard or suspected that the person serving it to them had specifically killed the animal for them. He gave no guidance to his lay disciples on the matter.[23] The only food preparation

17. M.I,38.
18. M.II, 6-8.
19. E.g., D.III,71; A.III,49; IV,187; Vin.III,208.
20. Vin.I,239.
21. M.I,238. Jain monks could eat meat if it did not have too many bones in it, *Ācārāṅga Sūtra* I,10.
22. M.I,77; A.IV,187.
23. It has been said that there is an inconsistency with the Buddha's attitude to meat eating. If it is wrong to work as a butcher, and the Buddha said it was, and if it is wrong to sell meat, which again the Buddha said it was, then one

the Buddha ever refused to eat was the milk rice (*pāyāsa*) and cakes (*pūraḷāsa*) used in certain Vedic rituals which, he said, no awakened person would eat.[24]

The Buddha abstained from eating after midday and made it a rule that his monks and nuns should follow his example. His reason for this was related to health. He said: "I do not eat in the evening, and therefore I am free from illness and affliction and enjoy health, strength and ease."[25] There may have been other reasons for this rule also. Providing alms for a monk once a day would probably be manageable for most people; showing up twice a day might be burdensome for householders. Furthermore, doing no physical labour, monks simply did not need to eat twice or three times a day.

After his morning meal it was the Buddha's habit to go to some quiet place nearby to either meditate or just sit quietly. If he decided to meditate, he would make a simple seat for himself from nearby vegetation or use a mat which he either carried or an attendant carried for him.[26] After making himself comfortable, he would pull part of his robe over his head, possibly to keep insects off his face or to shelter his eyes from the light, and sit with his legs either crossed or folded (*pallaṅkaṃ ābhujjitvā*).[27] The lotus posture (*padmāsana*), in which the legs are interlocked, is now often associated with meditation and *haṭha* yoga but is not mentioned in the Tipitaka. He also said that he would keep his body straight (*ujjuṃ kāyaṃ*), which means he kept his back upright, although probably without being rigid or forced. When he had finished meditation, he would spend some time walking up and down, no doubt to ease the stiffness in his legs and to get the blood in them moving.[28]

There are numerous references to the Buddha meditating but few about what kind of meditation he did. One of these says that during a

---

would expect it to also be wrong to purchase meat, whether the animal was slaughtered specifically for one or not.

24. Sn.480; p.15. These cakes were made of rice or barley flour, consecrated with certain mantras before being offered to the gods, and then eaten by the participants in the ceremony.

25. M.I,473.

26. E.g., A.I,136; IV,308.

27. S.I,170; Sn.p.79-80.

28. E.g.D.III,80.

three-month solitary retreat he spent much of his time doing what was called mindfulness of breathing (*ānāpāna sati*), which involves being aware of the in and out movement of the breath.[29] He described this meditation as inducing a state that was "peaceful, sublime, a deliciously pleasant way of living" (*santo ceva paṇīto asecanako sukho ca vihāro*).[30] However, a meditative state he described in detail, taught to his disciples, and very likely often spent time in himself, was called jhāna. In its pre-Buddhist usage, this word meant 'to think', 'to contemplate' or 'to ruminate', but the Buddha used it to refer to something quite different and specific.

Several meditation techniques can induce this jhānic state – for example, mindfulness of breathing, loving-kindness meditation and concentrating on a coloured object. The essential preliminaries for attaining jhāna include being ethically grounded, avoiding noise and excitement, and becoming more mindful and aware during one's everyday life. Doing this would, the Buddha said, give rise to what he called the happiness of being blameless (*anavajja sukha*), i.e., having a clear conscience, and the happiness of being untouched (*avyāseka sukha*), i.e., being undisturbed by the continual bombardment of sense stimulation. The next step was to regularly practice one or another of the techniques mentioned before until what were called the five hindrances were weakened or at least had temporarily subsided.[31] That having been achieved, a sense of relief is felt, so that "gladness arises in him (i.e., the meditator); from gladness comes joy; because of joy, his mind and body become tranquil; due to this, he feels happiness; and the mind that is happy becomes concentrated." These positive qualities open the way for attaining the first of the four levels of jhāna, each of them more refined and subtle than the previous one.

In the first jhāna, thoughts are present, although few, and the joy and happiness felt is intensified due to the absence of sensuality. The second jhāna is attained when thoughts stop completely, so that the mind becomes one-pointed, and one feels a profound physical and

---

29. S.V,326. For details of this practice see Dhammajoti pp.251-288.
30. S.V,321.
31. These are sensual desire, ill-will, sloth and torpor, restlessness and worry, and doubt.

mental tranquillity. Joy and happiness are still present, only now they are a result of the concentration. In the third jhāna, joy fades away, leaving the mind equanimous, mindful and clearly comprehending, and one's whole being is happy. In the fourth and highest jhāna, there are no feelings of either happiness or unhappiness, only a crystalline mindfulness purified by a firm and unreactive equanimity (*upekhā sati pārisuddhiṃ*). This state gives access to insights that lead to awakening.[32] The Buddha stressed the role of the jhānas in attaining awakening when he said: "Just as the river Ganges moves, slopes and inclines towards the east, so too, one who develops and enhances the four jhānas moves, slopes and inclines towards Nirvana."[33]

The Tipitaka contains little information concerning how long the Buddha would meditate for, but once, he mentioned that he would sit completely still and without uttering a word for seven days and nights. During such meditation sessions, he would experience an intense happiness.[34]

At some time in the day, probably in the morning, the Buddha would have attended to his personal hygiene, although the Tipitaka provides only scant information concerning this. There is no record of him cleaning his teeth, but, given that he commented on the benefits of doing so, it is certain that he did. He said: "There are these five benefits of using a tooth stick. It is good for the eyes, the breath does not smell, the taste buds are cleansed, bile and phlegm do not mix with the food, and one's food is appreciated."[35] In one extraordinary passage, surely unique in religious literature, he said that when he was travelling and needed to defecate or urinate, he would look up and down the road to make sure no one was coming before relieving himself.[36] There is a brief description of the Buddha standing in a bathing robe drying himself after having bathed in the Aciravatī River at the Eastern

32. This whole program of discipline and training is fully described at D.I, 62-84.

33. S.V,307-308.

34. M.I,93.

35. A.III,250. On how tooth sticks were used and the species of trees they were made from, see Dhammika 2018b, pp.20 and 120. See also Heirman and Torck, p.109 ff.

36. A.IV,344.

Bathing Ghat, just beyond the eastern ramparts of Sāvatthī.[37] This is said to have taken place in the early evening. There is another reference to him bathing, again in a river and again later in the day. When he and the group of monks who accompanied him arrived at Daṇḍakappaka after a long walk, he sat at the foot of a tree while they went into the town to see if the public hall was available for them to stay in. On their return, they all went together to the nearby river to bathe and wash off the dust and sweat of the day's traveling.[38] On the day of his final passing while in Pāvā, he suffered an attack of diarrhoea and shortly afterwards bathed in the Kakuṭṭhā River. Perhaps he had become soiled and needed to clean himself.[39]

The rest of the morning would be taken up with a variety of activities: instructing his monks and nuns, talking with visitors or going out to meet particular individuals, visiting the sick, and so on.

Like most people, the Buddha had his own little quirks and ways of doing things. When about to enter a building he would make a coughing sound or clear his throat loud enough for those inside to hear and know he was coming - a small courtesy to them. He never turned his head to look behind him but rather turned completely around. If invited to deliver a talk or come to someone's home for a meal he would indicate his acceptance by remaining silent, although this was perhaps accompanied by a particular facial expression or a slight nod of his head. Sometimes he would remain silent when expected to speak, in order to indicate that he considered something to be amiss or unacceptable. For

---

37. M.I,161. King Pasenadi commented that this river, now called the Rapti, would break its banks when it rained in the mountains to the north, M.II,117. About forty-five kilometers north of Sāvatthī, the Rapti enters Nepal and abruptly turns east into a narrow, steep-sided valley now part of the Bardia National Park. This valley acts as a catchment area flushing large amounts of rainwater into the river and causing sudden flooding downstream. The author once witnessed this phenomenon, despite there being no rain in the immediate area at the time. The mention of the river's behaviour strongly suggests that the author or authors of this passage, at least, had an intimate knowledge of this part of the country. On the river's unpredictability and danger see also Dhp-a.I,360; II,263-264.

38. A.III,402.

39. D.II,134.

example, once when he was to lead the chanting of the monastic rules by an assembly of monks he simply sat in silence while they waited for him to commence the event. After waiting patiently for several hours, and no doubt wondering what the problems was, Moggallāna approached him and asked if there was a problem and if so what it was. The Buddha replied that one of the monks in the assembly was unfit to participate because of his immorality. The monk was identified, removed, and the Buddha finally began the event.[40]

Early in the Buddha's career it became clear that fulfilling his teaching activities would leave him little time to attend to his personal needs and the numerous small tasks that had to be done, such as conveying messages, announcing an upcoming talk he was going to give, collecting alms food, and washing his robes. It was therefore arranged for him to have a personal attendant (*upaṭṭhāka*). During his career he had nine such attendants, they being Sunakkhatta, Upavāna, Cundaka, Nāgita, Nāgasamāla, Rādha, Meghiya, Sagata, and Ānanda. The first of these eventually left the monastic Saṅgha and began publicly criticising the Buddha, which, even though it must have been something of an embarrassment, was nonetheless recorded in the texts, another example of their fidelity.[41] Upavāna appears to have had some competence in medicine; he accompanied the Buddha on his last journey and was with him in his final hours.[42] For the last twenty-five years of the Buddha's life his attendant was his cousin Ānanda who, in his own words, said he "served the Lord with loving words, thoughts and deeds, and was like a shadow that never left him."[43] In dozens of discourses Ānanda is mentioned as being in the background making the Buddha's life easier in numerous small ways and occasionally contributing to the conversations taking place. One of the small services he rendered when it was hot, was positioning himself behind the Buddha and fanning him while he talked with people.[44]

40. Vin.IV,16; A. IV,204; Ud.51-52; M.II,91-92.

41. D.III,2; M.I,68.

42. S. I,174-175; D.II,139.

43. Tha.1039-1041-1043; D.I,206.

44. D.II,73. Others sometimes did this too, e.g., D.III,141; M.I,83; I,501. Apart from keeping cool, fans made of large palm leaves were used to blow away mosquitos, Vin.II,130.

At around midday the Buddha would take an afternoon nap or siesta (*divāseyyā*), although he probably only did this later in life and only during the height of the summer. The ascetic Saccaka once asked him if he slept in the afternoon, and he replied: "I acknowledge that in the last month of the hot season, after returning from alms gathering and having eaten my meal, I would fold my robe into four, spread it out, lie down and go to sleep mindfully and fully aware." Saccaka was not impressed by this and sniffed: "Some would call that abiding in delusion."[45] During such naps the Buddha would lie down in what he called the lion posture: reclining on his right side, with one foot on the other.

In the second half of the day the Buddha had no set program but might be involved in a range of activities: instructing his monks and nuns; talking with the various people who came to see him; continuing his journey if he was on a walking tour; or just sitting quietly by himself.

The Tipitaka gives the impression that the Buddha would attract large crowds wherever he went. The brahmin Soṇadaṇḍa said of him that "people come to consult him from different districts and countries... and even the heads of different sects and groups come to consult him."[46] As his reputation grew, all kinds of people would seek him out: those sincerely interested in what he had to say; the curious; a few who just wanted to argue; and the inevitable type who are only interested in being seen in the company of the famous.

While the Buddha was happy to make himself available to anyone who wanted to talk with him, there were times when dealing with the crowds could be stressful (*kilamatha*) and their continual questions irksome (*vihesā*).[47] Even while walking through the streets alms gathering or standing at a door to receive something, he would occasionally be approached by someone wanting to talk to him or ask him a question. When this occurred he would put the person off by saying that it was not the right time, although if the person persisted, and some did, he would speak with them, if only briefly.[48] When the villagers of Icchānaṅgala came to know that he and his monks had

---

45. M.I,249. This shows that, for whatever reason, the Buddha would sometimes go alms gathering and eat later in the morning.

46. D.I,115.

47. M.I,168; D.II,93.

48. E.g., S.II,19; Ud.7-8.

arrived in a nearby forest grove, they streamed out to see him, bringing offerings of food. In their enthusiasm they made a great noise, causing the Buddha to complain that they sounded like a group of fishermen hauling in nets full of fish.[49] A similar thing happened when the Buddha was staying in one of his favourite haunts on the edge of the Mahāvana north of Vesālī. A large crowd of Licchavi worthies, chariots and all, streamed out of the city to see him, chatting, laughing and making a great racket. When the monks who were with the Buddha heard the noise and realized what was soon to happen, they quickly made themselves scarce, leaving the Buddha to deal with the crowd.[50]

There were those who expected the Buddha to be on call for them no matter what he was doing at the time. Once, a group of people, including some eminent brahmins visiting from Magadha and Kosala, went to where the Buddha was staying and asked his attendant, Nāgita, where he was and if they could have an audience with him. Nāgita had been instructed by the Buddha that he was not to be disturbed, so he replied: "Now is not a good time to see the Lord, as he has retired."[51] Unused to having their requests ignored and determined to see the Buddha, the brahmins sat down, asserting that they would not leave until they had seen the famous teacher. Shortly afterwards the novice Sīha turned up, saw all the people waiting, and pointing this out to Nāgita, suggested that he inform the Buddha that there were people who wanted to see him. Nāgita replied that he would not do this but would not object if Sīha did. Sīha went into the residence and informed the Buddha that there was a crowd outside wanting to see him, and he, giving in to the inevitable, said to Sīha: "Prepare a seat for me in the shade of the building"; he then came out, took a seat and conversed with the brahmins.[52] On rare occasions, if the Buddha decided that a visitor had no real interest in Dhamma and just wanted to chat, or if his meditation had left him utterly serene and he just did not wish to talk,

---

49. A.III,30-31.
50. A.V,133.
51. *Paṭisallīna* could imply resting, meditating, in seclusion or perhaps having a nap.
52. D.I,150-52.

he would engage the visitor briefly and then bring the conversation to a close so they would leave.[53]

Given all this, it is hardly surprising that the Buddha sometimes felt the need to refresh himself with periods of solitude and silence. Occasionally he would have what he called a day's abiding (*divāvihāra*), as when he asked Ānanda to bring a sitting mat and follow him to Vesālī's Cāpāla Shrine so he could spend the day there without being bothered.[54] Another example of this is when he decided to spend the day in the forest completely alone, instructing Ānanda, who was usually always by his side, not to follow him.[55] There were times when he went for extended retreats, announcing: "I wish to spend the next half month in solitude. No one should come to me except the person who brings my food."[56] Only once is the Buddha reported to have gone off by himself without informing anyone. When a group of monks at Kosambī became involved in an argument, and the Buddha tried to arbitrate between the protagonists, they told him that he should keep out of it and let them settle the problem themselves. Disgusted with this insubordination, he went to the room where he had been lodging, tidied it, put everything in its proper place, and, without informing the monks or even his personal attendant, left for the more congenial atmosphere of the forest.[57]

When the Buddha undertook extended retreats he would do so in any nearby stretch of forest. Favourite places included the Mahāvana north of Vesālī, a royal reserve known as the Guarded Forest woodland near Kosambī, and the Gosiṅga forest near Nādikā which apparently had a park on its edge. Some monastics appreciated forests not just for the quiet and solitude they afforded but also for their sylvan beauty. Sāriputta mentioned how beautiful the Gosiṅga forest was in the moonlight when all the sal trees were in blossom and their scent wafted

53. M.III,111. The phrase *uyyojaniyapaṭisaṃyuttaṃ yeva kathaṃ* could have several different meanings, see Anālayo 2011, Vol. II, p. 692-693, note 43.c.

54. M.I,229; S.V,259.

55. A.IV,438.

56. S.V,12; V,320.

57. S.III,95. A more detailed account of the incident is at M.III,152 ff.

through the air.[58] The Buddha too was sensitive to the beauty of the forest environment. When someone asked him if he was afraid to stay alone in the forest he replied: "At the midday hour when the birds are quiet, I find the rustle of the great forest delightful."[59]

While being able to communicate his Dhamma to large numbers of people was the positive side of the Buddha's esteem, and he was able to put up with its negative side of having less time for meditation and solitude than he would have liked, he was disdainful towards celebrity itself. "Dire indeed are gains, honour and fame...they are obstacles to the highest security from bondage."[60] With typical insight he pointed out how celebrity can all too easily side-track even a sincere person when they acquire it: "There are some dangers that a monk is not prone to until he acquires fame and renown, but which he can become prone to when he acquires them."[61] Those dangers are complacency, arrogance, and an inflated sense of self.

The Buddha was not haughty but neither was he humble or self-effacing. He believed that his realizations elevated him far beyond those who had no such experience, and he accepted the regard others gave him as his due, although he did not insist upon it when it was not forthcoming. However, he did not like exaggerated marks of esteem or the adulation that went with fame, and he called the pleasure some people derived from their celebrity as on a par with excreta (*mīḷha*).[62] When the adulation towards him personally became too much, as it sometimes did, he would put his foot down, or in one particular case, literally refused to put his foot down. During a visit to Suṃsumāragira, Prince Bodhi invited him to his palace for a meal. In preparation for his arrival, the prince had a white cloth spread over the stairs leading to the palace entrance, a mark of considerable esteem equivalent to today's red-carpet treatment. When the Buddha arrived and saw the white cloth, he halted just short of it. Perplexed, the prince asked what the problem was, but the Buddha said nothing. When the prince inquired for a second and then a third time and still received no response,

58. M.I,212.
59. S.I,7.
60. S.II,226.
61. M.I,318; also I,193.
62. A.III,342.

Ānanda explained to him that the Buddha would not walk on the cloth because he was "concerned about future generations."[63] By this he meant that the Buddha wanted to set an example for monks and nuns in the future who might become too fond of the esteem shown to them by devoted lay people and fall prey to pride. Prince Bodhi had the white cloth taken up, and the Buddha entered the palace.

If the Buddha thought devotion to him was excessive or unnecessary, he could go beyond just refusing to be a party to it and resolutely, even bluntly, put a damper on it. Hearing that the monk Vakkali was seriously ill, he went to visit him. As he approached, the patient tried to rise from his bed, but the Buddha told him to desist. "Enough, Vakkali. There are seats; I will sit there." As anyone visiting a patient would do, the Buddha inquired from Vakkali about his condition and how he was feeling. Vakkali told him that, far from being stable or improving, his illness was actually getting worse. "Then are you remorseful about or do you blame yourself over anything?" the Buddha asked. Vakkali replied that he was only sorry about one thing: "For a long time I have wanted to come and see you but have been too sick to do so." "Enough, Vakkali!" the Buddha responded. "Why do you want to see this foul body of mine? One who sees the Dhamma sees me. One who sees me sees the Dhamma."[64]

There were a few incidents when devotion towards the Buddha was excessive, and yet he accepted it without comment. On one occasion King Pasenadi was on an outing in the countryside and, learning that the Buddha happened to be staying nearby, decided to visit him. When the two met, the king prostrated before the Buddha, kissed and stroked his feet and announced his name as he did so. The Buddha simply asked the king why he thought he was worthy of such gestures. Perhaps he thought it prudent to not say anything about Pasenadi's somewhat exaggerated behaviour – he was a king, after all.[65]

In general, the Buddha's disciples followed his example by avoiding excessive reverence where possible. When King Pasenadi came to visit Ānanda, he laid out an opulent elephant rug and invited Ānanda to sit on

---

63. M.II,91-92.

64. S.III, 119-20. By foul body (*pūtikāya*) he did not mean he lacked personal hygiene but rather that human bodies, including his own, produce a steady stream of unpleasant excretions requiring continual washing. See also It.91.

65. M.II,120.

it while they talked. Ānanda politely declined, saying that he had his own mat. The king was pleased with the conversation that ensued, and when it was over he offered Ānanda his own cape, which he said was sixteen hands long, eight wide and had been gifted to him by King Ajātasattu. Again Ānanda politely declined.[66] Perhaps because some disciples were aware of their proclivity to pride they deliberately cultivated humility, as for example Sāriputta, who said he tried to maintain a mind like a lowly dusting rag or like that of an outcaste child, and Mahā Kassapa who, when he was in Rājagaha and went alms gathering, preferred to do so in the weavers' street in the poor end of the city.[67]

The Buddha had once said that his monastic disciples should look upon him as a father and that he in turn would treat them as his offspring.[68] As mentioned previously, monks and nuns called themselves and were known to others as "sons of the Sakyan" or "daughters of the Sakyan." The Buddha demonstrated this paternal affection towards all his disciples, monastic and lay, by his concern for their spiritual welfare and also for their physical well-being. When he met Soṇa, who had come all the way from Avanti to Sāvatthī to see him, he asked Soṇa if he was alright. "I hope you are managing; I hope you are in good health; I hope you are not too fatigued by your journey; I hope you had few problems getting food?" Soṇa replied that all was well with him, and then the Buddha instructed Ānanda to arrange suitable accommodation for the newcomer.[69] The Buddha offered his disciples advice on how to eat healthily, on the value of exercise, the benefits of cleaning their teeth regularly, and even on what might be called toilet etiquette.[70] And when someone's health broke down he would find the time to visit them, whether they be a monk in one of the infirmaries attached to some monasteries or a lay person in their home.[71] On such occasions he would inquire about the patient's condition and encourage them with a talk on some aspect of the Dhamma. If it was required, he would even help attend to the patient's needs.

---

66. M.II,113;116.
67. A.IV,376; Ud.4.
68. Vin.I,45.
69. Ud.59.
70. A.III,250; Vin.II,222.
71. E.g., A.III,142; III,379; S.III,119-120; IV,210; IV,214; V,80-81; 344-45.

While on a visit to one particular infirmary, accompanied by Ānanda, he came across a monk with diarrhoea lying in his own excrement and uncared for by his fellows. The foul matter, the flies and the smell must have been extremely unpleasant. Nonetheless, the two men washed the patient and then carried him to a clean bed. Later the Buddha called the community of monks together and reproached them for their indifference to one of their fellows. He finished by saying: "He who would nurse me, let him nurse the sick."[72] It may have been in response to this incident or a similar one that the Buddha itemized the qualities one needed to be a compassionate and attentive nurse:

> "Having five qualities, a nurse is capable of tending to the sick. What five? He can prepare the medicine; he knows what is effective and what is not and administers the effective, not the ineffective; he nurses the sick with a mind of love, not out of hope for gain; he is unaffected by excrement and urine, vomit and spittle; and from time to time he can instruct, inspire, motivate and gladden the sick with talk on Dhamma."[73]

On another occasion, he added a significant detail to the instruction about ministering to a patient "with a mind of love" (*mettacitto gilānaṃ upaṭṭhāti*). If the physician or nurse realizes that the patient's condition is such that recovery is unlikely, they should, he said, continue their ministering nonetheless.[74] He believed that loving attentiveness should continue for as long as the patient is alive. It became well known that: "Caring for the sick is praised by the Lord" (*bhagavatā kho āvuso gilānupaṭṭhānaṃ vaṇṇitaṃ*).[75]

The Buddha was long-lived by the standards of the time, which is remarkable given that, after he became a monk, his life was a hard one: eating scraps; often sleeping in the open; and spending much of the year walking the Middle Land's dusty roads and tracks, including in the summer heat. Although he must have had a robust constitution, he did sometimes fall ill, and the Tipitaka mentions a few occasions where he was sick enough to require medical attention. Once, he is said to have suffered from wind

72. Vin.I,301-302, de Silva, p.29 ff.
73. A.III,144. See also Wujastyk 2022, pp.5-7.
74. A.I,121.
75. Vin.I,303.

(*vātehi ābādhiko*) and asked his attendant to get him hot water to drink.[76] The attendant obtained the water and some molasses, recommended him to take a hot bath, which he did, and then gave him the hot water mixed with the molasses to drink, and the Buddha's discomfort abated. More than once he had what was described as a wind problem in the stomach (*udaravātābhāda*) – probably not the wind (*vāta*) of Ayurvedic theory, as in the incident just mentioned, but intestinal gas of the type which can cause bloating, pain and flatulence. Each time this happened, he himself prepared a thin porridge of either sesame, rice or green gram mixed with what was called the three pungent ingredients, drank it and was cured.[77]

This is interesting because it suggests that the Buddha had at least some basic medical knowledge. This impression is reinforced by several lists of medicines he drew up – leaves, roots, resins, fats and minerals – and the instructions he gave on how to prepare them and store them and how long they could be kept without losing their potency. According to one leading scholar of ancient Indian medicine, these lists, although short, represent the earliest *materia medica* to survive from India.[78] Scholars have also pointed out the frequency of medical imagery in the Buddha's similes and metaphors, which suggests a familiarity with, or at least an interest in, medicine. How he could have acquired this can only be guessed at – possibly from his early education or perhaps from the samaṇa tradition he was a part of.

Another reoccurring malady the Buddha suffered from was back pain, which probably only become apparent as he aged, as it commonly does with older men.[79] Once, he stood outside Jetavana's gatehouse so as not to interrupt the talk being given inside. The talk was a long one, and when it concluded he entered the building, sat down and mentioned that his back ached as he stood outside waiting. The monk who had been

---

76. S.I,174-5. This is one of the earliest references to the Ayurvedic theory of the three humours (*tidosa vidya*), the amorphous substances that supposedly regulate the bodily state: wind (*vāta*), bile (*pitta*) and phlegm (*semhā*). These in turn were believed to interact with lymph, blood, flesh, fat, bone, marrow and semen. Disease was believed to be caused by an irregularity of these humours.

77. Vin.I,210. There are different opinions about what these three pungent ingredients are, possibly ginger, long pepper (*Piper longum*) and black pepper.

78. Zysk, p.73.

79. D.III,209; M. I,354; S.IV,184.

speaking apologised to the Buddha who, seeing that he had inadvertently embarrassed the monk, praised him for his talk and the audience for assembling to listen to it.[80] A number of other texts mention that when the Buddha was sitting in an assembly hall he would lean against a pillar, suggesting again that his back needed support. Most interesting of all such vignettes is the one describing the Buddha sitting warming his back in the late afternoon sun and Ānanda noticing this, going to him and massaging him as the two of them talked.[81]

The Tipitaka records four occasion when the Buddha was struck by more serious ailments. During one of these, he suffered from an irregularity of the bodily humours (*kāya dosābhisanna*). Ānanda consulted Jīvaka, the royal physician who treated the Saṅgha gratis, and he recommended that the Buddha be 'oiled' (*sinehetha*) for two or three days. Being oiled could mean one of several things: being massaged with medicinal oil; ingesting such oil; putting drops of it in the nose or ears; or having it administered as an enema – all treatments mentioned in early Ayurvedic texts. This course of treatment having finished, Jīvaka then prescribed a regimen of strong purging (*oḷārikaṃ virecanaṃ*) for the Buddha, which included inhaling the perfume of several bunches of blue water lilies (*uppala*) that had been treated with some type of medicine.[82] Again, how this medicine was administered is unclear; perhaps the water lilies were dusted with powdered herbs and inhaled with the perfume. After this, and again on Jīvaka's advice, the Buddha took a hot bath and ate only soup until he was back to normal.[83]

On another occasion, while staying in Rājagaha, the Buddha became "ill, unwell, stricken with a painful sickness" (*ābādhiko hoti dukkhito bāḷhagilāno*). This time, rather than taking medical advice, he asked his attendant to recite the seven factors of awakening for him, which the attendant did, and sometime later he recovered. The text implies that hearing these aspects of the Dhamma had a role in the Buddha's recovery.[84]

80. A.IV,358-9.

81. S.V,216.

82. The blue water lily, *Nymphaea nouchali*, contains apomorphine which can relieve anxiety and induce vomiting, although such affects are probably miniscule when the plant's perfume is inhaled.

83. Vin.I,279-80. Four types of soup are mentioned at M.I,245.

84. S.V,80. The Factors of Awakening (*satta bojjhaṅga*) are mindfulness,

One further passage in the Tipitaka briefly mentions that the Buddha had just recovered from an unspecified illness while he was visiting Kapilavatthu, which was probably connected to one of the incidents mentioned previously.[85] In the months before his death he was struck by two bouts of sickness which left him seriously weakened and probably hastened his demise. These episodes will be discussed in detail in Chapter 13.

The Buddha's interactions with people would slow down after sunset, giving him more opportunity to rest and relax. The Tipitaka provides little information about when and for how long the Buddha would sleep at night. He asked his monks and nuns to remain awake, either meditating or mindfully walking up and down, during the first and last watches and sleep only during the second watch, a schedule that he presumably followed as well.[86] Night was considered to start at sunset and end at sunrise, and the intervening period was divided into three watches (*yāma*), the length of each differing according to the season.[87] The Buddha is said to have sometimes spent much of the night walking up and down or giving a talk.[88] Other texts simply say that he spent the night in the open rather than in a building or under shelter, and not just in the summer but even during the winter when nights could be very cold.[89] When he was staying in a forest grove outside Āḷavī, he made a bed for himself out of leaves, which he would also sit on while meditating. He would not have plucked these leaves but collected fallen ones from the ground.[90] Two texts describe him spending the night in the open despite a light shower of rain.[91] The evidence suggests that the Buddha was in the habit of finishing his meditation and starting his day's activities shortly before dawn.

---

scrutiny of mental states, energy, joy, tranquillity, concentration and equanimity.

85. A.I,219.

86. A.I,114; also Dhp.157.

87. On early Indian chronometry and water clocks see *Vedāṅgajyotiṣa* II,5-6 and *Arthaśāstra* I,19,6.

88. S. I,107; D.II,86.

89. Vin.I,196; S.I,107; Ud.59.

90. A.I,136.

91. S.I,104; I,109.

8
On the Road

Long is a yojana for one who is exhausted.

Dhammapada 60

As continental trade in the sixth and fifth centuries BCE grew, so did the network of roads throughout the Middle Land. Their quality improved too. What had been little more than footpaths and jungle tracks gradually became proper thoroughfares. Strong centralized governments such as those of Magadha, Kosala and Vaṃsā played a part in this transformation too. Governments had a stake in encouraging trade because custom charges and tolls for the use of roads and ferries helped to fill their coffers, and troops could be dispatched quickly to troublesome outer provinces or engage invaders. Tolls for ferries and at fords were standardized, while wandering ascetics, brahmins and pregnant women were generally allowed to pass free.[1] Religion played a minor part in this transformation too. Pilgrimage was already drawing the faithful to holy sites, and the Buddha observed that people would go to bathe in sacred rivers such as the Sundarikā, Sarassatī and Bahumatī and at places such as Gayā, Payāga and elsewhere. The Buddha himself encouraged his disciples to visit at least once the places where the seminal events in his life occurred: where he was born; awakened; proclaimed the Dhamma for the first time; and where he would pass away.[2]

---

1. *Manusmṛti* 8,406-407. A legend recounted at *Lalitavistara* XXVI 18, attributes the Buddha with getting a law enacted in Magadha allowing ascetics to use ferries without payment.
2. D.II,140.

The Tipitaka mentions a variety of thoroughfares: footpaths; jungle tracks; lanes; and high roads, such as the ones that ran between Sāvatthī and Verañjā, Sāvatthī and Sāketa,[3] and the one that came from Ukkalā and passed through Uruvelā. There were also what were called chariot roads, which were probably fairly well maintained to facilitate the passage of such vehicles.[4] However, it is almost certain that even the best thoroughfares were dusty, rutted, maintained only intermittently, and perhaps impassable during the rainy season. The Buddha mentioned how a carter on a smooth-surfaced highway might take a shortcut and end up with a broken axle because of the byway's uneven surface.[5] The Jātaka tells of a civic-minded villager who mobilised his friends to help remove large stones from roads, fell roadside trees that might hit passing vehicles and break their axles, construct bridges, watering places and rest houses for the convenience of travellers. Such stories must reflect things that people actually did and encouraged others to follow their example, thereby easing the difficulties of the being on the road.[6]

The numerous rivers that run through the Middle Land were a hindrance to communication. Bridges were rare, and although there were ferries on some main arteries, fords were the main way of crossing rivers. In places where such conveniences were unavailable, travellers would have to improvise. The Tipitaka recounts how monks arrived at a river just as a cowherd was driving his cattle into the water, so they clung to the animals' tails and backs and were carried across by them.[7] Rivers in more remote areas could be crossed by improvising a raft or float from nearby tree branches, foliage and

3. Vin.IV,228 says one had to cross a river when travelling between these two cities, although no river can be seen there today. However, satellite photography shows a long chain of oxbow lakes and marshes where a large river once cut across this route, evidence that the topographical information in the Tipitaka is generally accurate.

4. *Ekapadika*, *vanapantha*, *addhānamagga*, *patha* and *rathikā*, A.II,57; IV,187; Vin.I,4. On the roads and road networks of the time see Agrawala p. 242-245.

5. S.I,57.

6. Ja,I,199.

7. Vin.I,191.

grass. An alternative to getting to one's destination overland was to go by boat. The Tipitaka mentions Ānanda embarking on a boat, probably at Pāṭaligāma, and sailing up the Ganges to Kosambī, one of the few references to long distance riverine travel in the Tipitaka.[8] Many roads ran through inhabited areas with villages and their cultivated fields, but just as many passed through jungle or semi-desert wilderness. One traveller commented: "These wilderness roads have little water and food, and it is not easy to go along them without taking provisions for the journey."[9] Such provisions would be carried in a knapsack (*puṭosena*). During the summer, even relatively short stretches of road posed a threat if water was unavailable, and thus monks would carry water pots (*karaka*) and water strainers (*parissāvana*) when going on long journeys.

Beyond this, the perennial problem of travel in India has always been banditry. The Buddha described some roads as "frightening, dangerous and along which one must go with a weapon" because of the chance of being robbed, or worse, and how travellers carrying valuables through a wilderness area would experience relief when emerging safely from it.[10] Travellers on the road between Sāvatthī and Sāketa were often robbed, and at one time a fearsome robber dubbed Aṅgulimāla, who murdered his victims, operated in forested areas in Kosala.[11] The Buddha observed that such highwaymen would strike from and then disappear back into "impenetrable grass or trees, a gully or a great forest."[12] Some of these men would capture a party of travellers and release one of them to go and try to get a ransom for the others.[13] Once, the Buddha and his attendant Nāgasamāla were travelling through Kosala when they came to a fork in the road. The Buddha said they should take one fork, while the attendant insisted

8. Vin.II,290. Vin.II,301 mentions monks embarking at Vesālī to sail up-river, *ujjaviṃsu*, to Sahajāli, now identified with Bhita near Allahabad. If this is correct, going up-river must refer to the stretch of the voyage along the Ganges and Yamuna.

9. Vin.I,270.

10. Vin.IV,63; M. I,276.

11. M. II,97; Vin. III,212.

12. A. I,153–154; M.III,158.

13. Ja IV,115.

on the other. This disagreement continued for some time until, in a huff, the attendant put the Buddha's bowl down and walked off on the way he thought correct. He hadn't gone far when he was attacked by bandits, who punched and kicked him and tore his robe.[14]

More normally, though, long distance travel was just uncomfortable, tedious and undertaken only when necessary. And yet despite these and other problems, the Buddha spent much of his time on the road in order to reach as many people as possible – such was his determination and compassion. In keeping with the rules laid down by himself and in accordance with a long established samaṇa tradition, he would spend the three months of the rainy season in one location and the rest of the year on what were called walking tours. According to a quite plausible later tradition, after the twenty-fifth year of his ministry the Buddha spent every rainy season except the last one in or around Sāvatthī, which would explain why more of his discourses are set in that city than in any other place.[15] If true, he may have decided to limit his wanderings to the region around Sāvatthī at that time due to age, as he would have been about sixty; because the Kosalan language was the same or similar to his own; and perhaps because the city was only a four or five-day walk from his hometown.

After his awakening, the Buddha set out on a long journey to find his five former companions and share his discovery with them. Equally significant was that his instruction to them and his next group of disciples was that they should wander through the countryside teaching others what he had taught them "for the welfare of the many."[16] The Buddha warned his monks and nuns against prolonged aimless wandering but also staying for too long in one place. The first would deprive them of time with learned monastics and of forming fruitful friendships with others, while the second could lead to accumulating too many things, of getting involved with lay people and all their problems, or becoming too attached to a particular location.[17]

---

14. Ud.90. Being a monk was no protection from being murdered by bandits; see Tha.705 ff and M.II,97-98. For a contemporary example of such encounters, see Ajahn Sucitto and Nick Scott's highly readable *Rude Awakening*, 2010, pp.237 ff.

15. Bv-a.4.

16. Vin.I,5.

17. A.III,257-8.

It is possible to get at least some idea about the extent of the area the Buddha travelled through during his teaching career. His movements northward were limited by what were then the trackless forests of the Himalayan foothills, although there is a single reference to him once staying in a forest hut in a part of these hills controlled by Kosala.[18] There is no evidence that he ever went into the mountains of the southern edge of the Ganges Yamuna plain – the Mizrapur Hills, the Rajmahal Hills and the Vindhyachal Range – or even approached them. The furthest east he ever went that can still be identified was Kajaṅgala and the furthest west was Madhurā. This first place corresponds to the modern towns of Kankjol in Rajmahal District, Jharkhand, and Mathurā is the modern Madhura, a hundred and fifty kilometers south of Delhi. Kankjol and Mathura are nearly a thousand kilometers from each other as the crow flies. It is uncertain how thoroughly the Buddha covered this area, but during fifty years of wayfaring, he could have easily travelled through much of it. The Tipitaka names over nine hundred places that he visited or passed through: cities; towns; villages; hills; caves; rivers; forests; and other landmarks. Thus, he may well have wandered over an area of at least 280,000 square kilometers, although a good deal of this would have taken place in the eastern part of this area, between the great cities of Sāvatthī, Rājagaha, Vesālī and Kosambī.

The Tipitaka records the itinerary of several of the Buddha's journeys, giving some idea of the distances he sometimes travelled. For example, we know that, within the first twelve months of his awakening, he went from Uruvelā to Isipatana via Gayā and Bārāṇasī, spent the three months of the rainy season there, and then made his way from there back to Gayā and then on to Lativana and Rājagaha. All these places can be identified with certainty, and thus it can be calculated that the Buddha walked at least 300 kilometers from Uruvelā to Rājagaha. During another tour he went from Verañja to Bārāṇasī via Soreyya, Saṅkassa and Kaṇṇakujja, crossing the Ganges at Payāga. Although not explicitly mentioned in the text, he probably took a boat down the Ganges from Payāga to Bārāṇasī.[19] Verañjā is the modern Atranji Khera

18. S.I,116.
19. Vin.III,1-11.

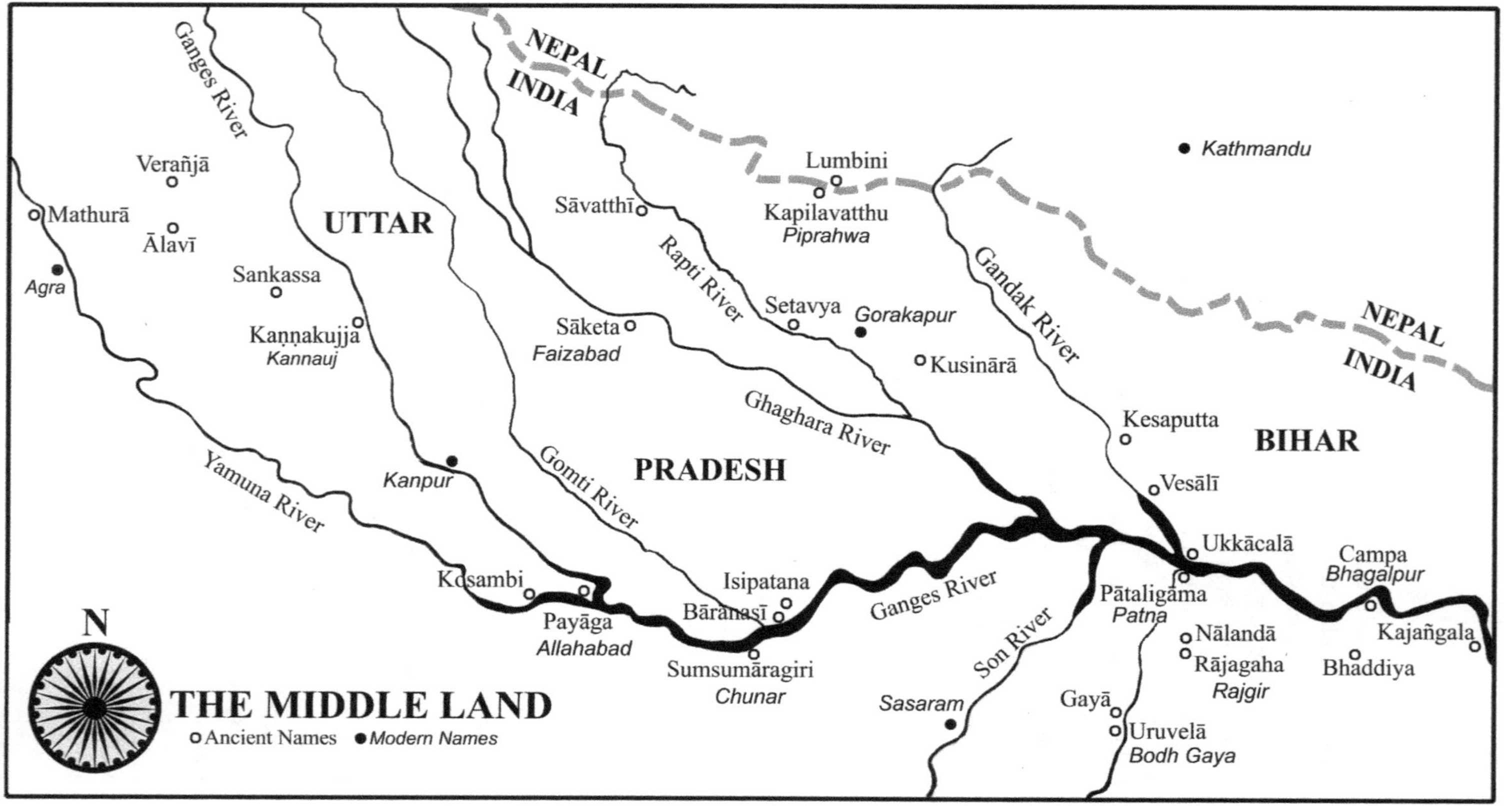

THE MIDDLE LAND
Ancient Names
Modern Names
N
NEPAL
INDIA
NEPAL
INDIA
UTTAR
PRADESH
BIHAR
Kathmandu
Lumbini
Kapilavatthu
Piprahwa
Sāvatthī
Rapti River
Setavya
Gorakapur
Kusinārā
Gandak River
Kesaputta
Vesālī
Ukkācalā
Campa
Bhagalpur
Kajañgala
Bhaddiya
Pātaligāma
Patna
Nālandā
Rājagaha
Rajgir
Gayā
Uruvelā
Bodh Gaya
Son River
Sasaram
Ganges River
Isipatana
Bāraṇasī
Sumsumāragiri
Chunar
Payāga
Allahabad
Kosambi
Kanpur
Gomti River
Ghaghara River
Sāketa
Faizabad
Yamuna River
Ganges River
Verañjā
Mathurā
Ālavī
Agra
Sankassa
Kaṇṇakujja
Kannauj

near Etah, Kaṇṇakujja is the modern Kannauj, both of them in Uttar Pradesh, and ancient Payāga is identified with Jhusi across the river from modern Allahabad.[20] This tour would have involved walking at least six hundred kilometers. In the longest single journey recorded in the Tipitaka, the Buddha went from Rājagaha to Vesālī to Sāvatthī and back to Rājagaha via Kīṭāgiri and Ālavī, the modern town of Airwa, a round trip of about 1,600 kilometers.[21] It is likely that he would have started a trip like this at the end of the rainy season and arrived back in time for the next one nine months later.

How much time the Buddha's journeys might have taken can only be guessed at, although the ancient commentary mentions that a journey he made from Rājagaha to Kapilavatthu took him two months, walking at one yojana a day. From the Mahāparinibbāna Sutta we know that he went from Rājagaha to Kusinārā via Nāḷandā, Pāṭaligāma (modern Patna), and Vesālī, a total distance of about three hundred kilometers. According to this text, he left Vesālī after the end of the rainy season (mid October) and died in Kusinārā, according to tradition, on the full moon of Vesākha (May/June). If he left Vesālī shortly after the end of the rainy season, it would mean it took seven months for the Buddha to travel about ninety-five kilometers, which seems like a very long time, even allowing for the fact that he was old and in ill health. However, at some time before leaving Vesālī, he predicted that he only had three more months to live, meaning that he would have passed away in January.[22] But it should be pointed out that we do not know when he left Vesālī - it could have been weeks or even a month or two after the end of the rainy season - and also that nowhere in the Tipitaka does it explicitly say that the Buddha died at Vesākhā.[23]

It can be conjectured that when the Buddha was on a walking tour, he would wake before sunrise and go for alms gathering to the nearest available place: a village, town or the city he was staying near. After eating his meal, he would set off while it was still cool. He might walk until the midday heat became unpleasant and then take an afternoon

20. Chakrabarti, 2001 p.263. Allahabad was recently renamed Prayagraj.
21. Vin.II,159-175.
22. D.II,106.
23. The Buddha's birth and awakening are also traditionally celebrated on Vesākhā, now widely known by its Sri Lankan contraction Vesak.

rest, or if a village on the way seemed a good place to stop and talk with the locals, he might stay there for the rest of the day or for two or three days. If he arrived at a town or village later in the afternoon, he would probably stay there until the following morning.

There are records of the Buddha sleeping in a roadside rest house, a chaff hut, a brahmin's fire hall, an old potter's shed and, when nothing else was available, in the open under a grove of trees.[24] On one of his return visits to Kapilavatthu, he could find no accommodation and had to make do in the simple hermitage of the ascetic Bharaṇḍu; and once, when he was in the Kuru country, he stayed in a small hut carpeted with grass.[25] When convenient, the Buddha would lodge at religious shrines or local sacred trees. These places often had some kind of shelter next to them which were the scene of occasional large gatherings. Others may have had nothing more than small huts adjacent – basic, but convenient for a few nights' stay.

Another option was to stay in one of the rest houses that governments, guilds or pious individuals built along some roads or in towns for the benefit of travellers. Many cities had such buildings just outside their main gates so that travellers who arrived at night after the gates were closed would have somewhere to stay.[26] There were also royal rest houses for the use of the king or government officials travelling on state business.[27] Most public travellers' rests provided shelter and little else, although in the town of Uttara, for example, the headman Pāṭaliya built and maintained one that had basic but

24. M.I,206; III,238; D.II,131; A.I,136; III,402. Chaff huts, *bhusāgāra*, were next to the threshing floor where workers would rest and the straw would later be stored.

25. A.I,276 ff; M.I,501.

26. E.g., Ja.I,115.

27. It is not clear what the difference was between *āvasathāgāra*, *āgantukāgāra*, *sabhā*, *āvasatha*, and *sālāya nivāsa*, if any; S. IV,219, Ja. I,115; 302, IV,147; Vin. IV,16. The first three were certainly open to anyone, as the Buddha mentions that even low caste travellers could lodge there, while the last one may have been some type of commercial lodge or hotel. *Santhāgāra* was a city or town assembly hall; M.I,353. In some places it was necessary to seek permission to stay in the local hall; Vin.IV,17. Some towns had alms halls, *dānasālā*, which may have doubled as public traveller's rests; e.g., Ja. I,231.

adequate furniture and fittings.[28] A few provided food for anyone who might turn up. Once, a group of monks went to a rest house for alms so often that the locals grumbled, saying: "The alms food is not prepared just for them; it's supposed to be for everyone." Anxious that his monks not get a reputation for greed, the Buddha made it a rule that monks should go for alms at such places no more than once, unless they were sick.[29] He also made it a rule that monks should not use an umbrella or a walking staff when travelling. In the case of umbrellas, this was because they were associated with power and status, and he did not want people to think his monks were putting on airs. A group of monks using umbrellas was mocked for looking like treasury officials (*gaṇakamahāmatta*).[30] Monks and nuns were allowed to use sandals, although there is no record of the Buddha having a pair or using them.

How long the Buddha stayed at a particular place would have depended on many factors: whether local people came to talk with and listen to him; whether alms and water were available; and whether the atmosphere was congenial. When staying in large population centres, his accommodation would have been reasonably comfortable, and he would have been well-provided for. When he returned to Rājagaha after his awakening, King Bimbisāra donated one of his pleasure parks, the Bamboo Grove, to the Saṅgha, a gift followed by many others in the coming decades. The first monasteries established on such properties were little more than small thatched wattle and daub huts or shelters made of leaves, foliage or grass. Only later in the Buddha's career were more permanent structures built. The Jetavana, the first large, purpose-built monastic complex, had halls, covered walkways, wells, bathrooms and other amenities.[31] This monastery flourished right up to Indian Buddhism's last days in the twelfth century.

The Buddha must have enjoyed the freedom his life of wandering gave him. He said: "The household life is full of hindrances, a path of dust. Free as the breeze is the life of one who renounces all worldly things."[32] Moving from place to place allowed him to spread his teachings,

28. S.IV.348.
29. Vin.IV,69-70.
30. Vin.II,130-131.
31. Vin.II,159.
32. D.I,62.

but there were other reasons behind it too. He was aware that some personal contact with him was important for his disciples, especially for newly ordained monks and nuns, and this was sometimes a factor in determining which districts he visited and how often.[33] During his wanderings he might visit a district, teach, make some disciples, even ordain a few monks or nuns, and then perhaps not come again for years. For lay disciples with domestic obligations, undertaking a long journey to see the Buddha would have been difficult, and so they had to wait, perhaps years, before they got to see him again. One text gives us some idea of the excitement caused in an outlying district when its inhabitants heard that the Buddha might be on his way to their village and how the excitement increased as word of his gradual approach reached them.[34] Once, a monk who had spent the rainy season with the Buddha in Sāvatthī arrived in Kapilavatthu. When people heard where he had come from, he found himself deluged with questions about the Buddha and what he had been teaching.[35]

Naturally, the Buddha could not be everywhere at once, and so monks and nuns would sometimes have to undertake long journeys for the privilege of spending time in his presence. For example, while he was residing in Catuma, a few hundred monks arrived in the city to be with him and listen to him.[36] Another example concerns the monk Sona Kutikaṇṇa who ordained under the tutorage of Mahā Kaccāna. About a year later, he developed the desire to meet the man whose teachings he had committed himself to. He said to his preceptor: "I have not yet met the Lord face to face; I have only heard about what he is like. If you give me permission, I will travel to see the Lord, the Worthy One, the fully awakened Buddha."[37] He was able to fulfil this wish.

Those wanting to know where the Buddha was in order to meet him could find they had a problem if they came from a distant region or another country. But an official in the court of King Pasenadi, who was an admirer of the Buddha, was sometimes able to know his whereabouts at any given time or where he was travelling from or

33. S.III,90.
34. S.V,348-349.
35. S.V,405;406.
36. M.I,456.
37. Ud.58.

to because of the information he received, presumably from monks, merchants or his fellow royal officers who had come from outlying districts or even other countries.[38]

There are three examples of people coming from beyond the Middle Land to meet the Buddha, evidence that his reputation had spread to adjacent regions of India. There is an account of the sixteen disciples of the ascetic Bāvari setting out from the Godavari, probably from where it flows through Maharashtra, for the Middle Land in the hope of meeting the Buddha. When they heard that he was at Sāvatthī, they headed there, going through Kosambī and Sāketa, and arrived in Sāvatthī only to learn that he had left some time previously. They followed his route through Setavya, Kapilavatthu, Kusinārā, Pāvā and Vesālī, finally catching up with him at the Pasanaka Shrine.[39] The ascetic known as Bark Blanket Bāhiya is said to have come all the way from Suppāraka to meet the Buddha.[40] This place, now called Sopara, is on the west coast of India some fifty-five kilometers north of Mumbai. That the Buddha's reputation could have reached so far and that Bāhiya could have travelled such a distance, some 1300 kilometers, is not as far-fetched as it might first seem. Suppāraka was a major seaport and the terminus of the Dakkhinapātha, the great highway that started at Kosambī, and was already a major emporium by the fifth century BCE. Merchants may well have brought news of the Buddha to Suppāraka, and Bāhiya may well have travelled to the Middle Land with a merchant caravan headed there.[41] Another story tells of the monk Soṇa, who came all the way from the kingdom of Avanti to meet the Buddha. Avanti was a kingdom to the south of the Middle Land, linked to it by the Dakkhiṇāpatha.[42] These stories indicate just how mobile the ascetics of the time could be.

---

38. S.V,349-350.

39. Sn.1014. The various places they passed through during their journey are mentioned in inscriptions from Sañchi, and most can still be identified; see Marshall, pp.299-300. On the first of these places, Patiṭṭāna, see Kennet *et al*, pp.10-11.

40. Ud.6. On ascetics' garments made of bark, see Dhammika 2018b, p.160.

41. On the Buddhist antiquities from Sopara, see Falk, 2006, p.136-138.

42. Ud.58. Bhaddā wandered through most north Indian states during her fifty years as a Jain nun, Thi.110.

There would have been as many languages and dialects spoken in the Middle Land as there are in that region today, and this would have created special problems for someone like the Buddha, who travelled widely. Theravāda tradition maintains that the Buddha spoke Pali, although there is no mention in the Tipitaka of what his mother tongue was. As with merchants, diplomats and others whose professions required frequent long-distance travel in different regions, he may well have been competent in several languages. The Buddha said that insisting on using one's own language or dialect in an area where another is spoken can only cause confusion and discord:

> "It has been said, 'One should not stake too much on the local language...' How does one do this? In different regions they might call the same thing a bowl, basin, dish, crock, vessel, tureen, concave container or rounded receptacle. But whatever they call it in one region, one uses that word, thinking, 'It seems this person is referring to that object', and one uses that word accordingly."[43]

Nor did he believe that any one language communicated his Dhamma any better than any other, saying: "I want you to learn the Buddha's words each in your own language."[44] The Buddha was equally open about regional customs. On one occasion he said:

> "I clearly remember all the assemblies of nobles, brahmins, householders, ascetics and gods...I have attended. Before I sat with them, spoke with them or joined their conversations, I adopted their expression, their speech, whatever it might be, and then I instructed them in Dhamma."[45]

This is the kind of thing one would expect of an urbane, open-minded and well-travelled individual. Whatever the Buddha was, he was not parochial, and no doubt his travels made him even more flexible and tolerant of differences.

---

43. M.III, 235.
44. Vin.II,139. For an alternative translation see Levman 2008-2009, pp.33-39. On the Buddha's attitude to language see Gombrich 2018, pp.86-90.
45. D.II,109, condensed.

9
Praise and Blame

There was not, there is not now,
and there never will be someone
who is wholly blamed or praised.

Dhammapada 228

Having been in the public arena for so long and proclaiming ideas that challenged many of the existing ones, the Buddha of course attracted opposition, criticism and sometimes even antipathy. When this happened he would attempt to justify his position by explaining himself more fully, while remaining unruffled and not striking back at his critics. Likewise, he instructed his disciples not to be provoked but remain as objective as possible when he, they, or the teaching were targets of criticism or misrepresentation or even when any of the three were praised:

"If anyone should criticise me, the Dhamma or the Saṅgha, you should not because of that be angry, resentful or upset. For if you did, that would hinder you and you would not be able to know whether what they said was right or wrong. Would you?"

"No, Lord."

"Therefore, if others criticise me, the Dhamma or the Saṅgha, simply explain what is incorrect, saying, 'That is incorrect. That is not right. That is not our way. We do not do that.' Likewise, if others should praise me, the Dhamma or the Saṅgha, you should not because of that be pleased, elated or self-satisfied. For if you were, that would hinder you. Therefore, if others praise me, the Dhamma or the Saṅgha, then simply explain what is correct, saying: 'That is correct. That is right. That is our way. That is what we do.'"[1]

Within a year of the Buddha's awakening, he had made disciples of his five former companions, the wealthy young man Yasa and his friends, and the three Kassapa brothers who were the most well-known and esteemed *samaṇas* in Magadha, together with all their followers. Shortly after this, most of the followers of another samaṇa teacher, Sañjaya Belaṭṭhiputta, some two hundred and fifty in all, abandoned him to join the Buddha's Saṅgha also. These last two events created great interest throughout Magadha and made the Buddha well-known early in his career. Soon, numerous young men were requesting to become monks, and the Buddha was happy to accept them all. But his readiness to ordain anyone who asked for it created problems. Ill-trained and unsupervised monks were soon wandering all over the place causing embarrassment. Also, with many youths and men abandoning their families, this created disquiet amongst the people affected by it and led to grumbling against the Buddha himself. People were saying: "The samaṇa Gotama proceeds by making us childless, by making us widows, by breaking up families." If the Buddha was concerned by this, he did not mention it. When informed of what people were saying about him, he dismissed it, commenting: "This noise will not last long; it will continue for seven days and then cease."[2] Only after this did he start laying down rules for vetting candidates and for ordaining and training monks. He had apparently not given sufficient thought to the proper organisation of his order before accepting large numbers of men into it.

Although the Buddha saw himself firmly within the non-Vedic samaṇa tradition, he disregarded some of its most basic assumptions, particularly the practice of rigorous austerities (*tapa*) and self-mortification (*attakilamatha*). For this he was sometimes criticised by other ascetics. When, after four or five years of undergoing such disciplines himself, he finally abandoned them and started washing and eating properly again, the five disciples who had attached themselves to him were outraged. They accused him of reverting to the life of abundance (*āvatto bahullāya*) and left him in disgust. One ascetic

1. D.I,3.
2. Vin.I,43.

dismissed him as a "shaven-headed householder" (*muṇḍagahapatika*) meaning that he was little more than a layman posing as an ascetic.[3] The ascetic Kassapa repeated to the Buddha an accusation he had heard about him: "The samaṇa Gotama disapproves of all austerities; he criticises and blames all those who live the hard life." The Buddha denied this, explaining that he praised austerities that led to understanding and liberation and criticised those that did not.[4] As will be shown below, it is probable that the real reason for Devadatta breaking with the Buddha and founding his own Saṅgha was the Buddha's de-emphasis of the value of austerity and self-mortification.

A few of the more extreme ascetics accused the Buddha of being careless with life. When the ascetic Māgandiya saw the grass spread out on the floor where the Buddha was sleeping, he commented: "It is a sorry sight indeed when we see the bed of samaṇa Gotama, that destroyer of growth."[5] It is not entirely certain what this criticism meant, but it is likely that Māgandiya accepted the belief, current at the time amongst certain *samaṇas*, that plants were sentient life, and thus to pluck or cut them was tantamount to killing, something the more scrupulous ascetic avoided. Some ascetics went so far as to carry brooms or whisks to sweep the ground before them as they walked to avoid treading on and killing tiny insects.[6] Given such scrupulousness, it is hardly surprising that the Jains, who were strict vegetarians, attacked the Buddha and his disciples for eating meat.

> "A crowd of Jains went through the town, from street to street, from one square to another, waving their arms and shouting, 'The general Sīha has this very day slaughtered a large creature to feed to the samaṇa Gotama, and he is going to eat it knowing that it was slaughtered specifically for him.'"[7]

The Buddha did not respond to the charge that accepting from a donor and then eating a meal containing meat amounted to killing.

---

3. Vin.IV,91.
4. D.I,161.
5. M.I,502.
6. S.IV,300. Today Jain monks carry brooms called *oghā* made of either peacock feathers or strands of wool for the same purpose.
7. A.IV,187.

However, he made a rule that his monks and nuns should not accept such a meal if they saw, heard or suspected that the meat was from an animal that had been slaughtered specifically for them.[8]

One interesting misgiving that some people had of the Buddha was that, despite his relative youth, he claimed to be fully awakened, while most others making such a claim were generally old. King Pasenadi asked the Buddha about this:

> "Even those samaṇas and brahmins who are the head of orders and sects, well-known teachers, famous and considered so by the general public – even they do not claim to have attained the unsurpassed perfect awakening. Therefore, how can you make such a claim when you are still so young and have so recently become a samaṇa?"

The Buddha replied that awakening had nothing to do with age, just as a young king, a newly hatched snake or a recently ignited fire could still have an impact and therefore should be taken seriously.[9]

As was shown previously, public discussions and debates on religious questions were a feature of Indian society during the Buddha's time. For some, such events were a chance to learn about the new ideas being aired, while for a few they were an opportunity to promote themselves as clever and entertaining disputants. There were "certain learned nobles who are clever, well-versed in the doctrines of others, real hair-splitters, who go about demolishing the views of others with their sharp intelligence. When they hear that the samaṇa Gotama will visit a certain village or town, they formulate a question, thinking, 'We will go and ask him this question, and if he answers like this, we will say that, and if he answers like that, we will say this and thereby refute his Dhamma.' But when they confront the samaṇa Gotama, he instructed, inspired, motivated and gladdened them with talk on Dharma, and they do not so much as ask their question, let alone refute his Dhamma."[10] As a result of the Buddha's

8. M.I,369. It is widely believed that the Buddha taught vegetarianism but this is not correct, although the practice was advocated by some Indian Buddhists in later centuries. See Dhammika 2016.

9. S.I,68-69.

10. M.I,176, condensed.

ability to disarm and impress such opponents and disputants, some people suspected him of using magical power to do so.[11]

A village headman once asked the Buddha if it were true that he used some kind of magic to convert people, and he admitted that he did, much to the headman's surprise. "Then it is true: the samaṇa Gotama is a magician!" But the Buddha then pointed out that knowing magic does not necessarily mean being a magician (*māyākāra*).[12] What he meant becomes clear from another dialogue with someone who also broached the subject of magic with him. Bhaddiya asked him if it were true that he knew magic and used it to convert the disciples of other teachers. The Buddha replied firstly by saying that one should not be guided by, amongst other things, supposed revelations, tradition, hearsay, the authority of the scriptures, or what a particular teacher might claim, and he then explained aspects of his teachings in detail. By the time he had finished, Bhaddiya was so taken by what the Buddha had said that he asked to become a disciple. The Buddha responded:

> "Now Bhaddiya, did I say to you, 'Become my disciple, and I will be your teacher'?"
>
> "No sir."
>
> "Although I declare and proclaim my teaching in the manner I just gave to you, some samaṇas and brahmins dishonestly and falsely, unfairly and inaccurately misrepresent me by saying that I use magic to lure away the disciples of other teachers."
>
> "An excellent and wonderful thing is this magic of yours! If only my beloved kin and the members of my family could be converted by this magic, it would be for their welfare and happiness for a long time."[13]

---

11. M.I,375.
12. S.IV,340-341.
13. A.II,190-194. Since ancient times in India, magic (*māyā*) and conjuring (*indrajāla*) have been associated with gods and saints and at the same time with impostors and charlatans. "Nature is a magic trick and the Lord is the magician; the things of the world are but elements of Him," *Śvetāśvatāra Upaniṣad* 4,9-10. "Through cunning in the art of magic and conjuring, the false is given the impression of being true," *Vikramacarita* 114-15. The Buddha's comments on magicians at S.III,142 explain why he would not have liked to be thought of as one. On the use of magic to win debates see Bronkhorst 2011,

Another criticism of the Buddha, and, interestingly, one that continues to be made even today, was that his concept of Nirvana and his doctrine of Not-self (*anatta*) amounted to a form of nihilism (*uccedhavāda*). When accused of teaching this, he responded: "There is a way of speaking truthfully that one could say I teach a doctrine of annihilation and train my disciples in it. I teach the annihilation of greed, hatred and delusion, I teach the annihilation of all the many evil and wrong states of mind."[14]

At the end of a discussion with the Buddha, an interlocutor would often express his or her satisfaction with what the Buddha had said, but not always. While on a visit to Kapilavatthu, the Buddha met his mother's brother Daṇḍapāni, who asked him to explain his Dhamma. After listening without comment until the Buddha had finished, the old man "shook his head, wagged his tongue, raised his eyebrows so that three wrinkles formed on his forehead, and then walked off, leaning on his stick."[15] After giving a talk to a group of his own monks at Ukkaṭṭhā, we are told that they were far from delighted by what he had said.[16] Once, during a talk with a brahmin, the Buddha compared brahmins who so confidently explained what the ancient sages taught, while admitting that they themselves did not share their attainments, to a string of blind men. "The first one does not see, the middle one does not see and neither does the last." At this, the brahmin became extremely angry and threatened the Buddha, saying: "The samaṇa Gotama will be disgraced!"[17] In this case, there was a rapprochement, the discussion continued and eventually the brahmin developed some respect for the Buddha.

The Tipitaka also records a few examples where some of the Buddha's disciples abandoned him. Throughout the texts, people who had been

---

pp.185-187. Lee Siegel's otherwise excellent history of Indian magic fails to make clear the Buddha's distinction between psychic powers and magic, *Net of Magic, Wonders and Deceptions in India*,1991. Interestingly, some of the earliest Christian apologists had to defend Jesus against the charge that he was only a magician, e.g., Tertullian's *Apologeticus* 21.17; 23.7,12 and Justin Martyr's *Dialogue with Trypho* 69.7.

14. Vin. I, 234-235.
15. M.I,108.
16. M.I,6.
17. M.II,200.

conversing with the Buddha typically express their appreciation for what he had said and announce that they wish to become one of his disciples "for as long as life lasts." While such sentiments are usually couched in a stereotyped form, there is no reason to doubt that many people did say something like this. However, this does not mean that they meant what they said: some were probably just being polite, while others may have meant what they said, but after their initial enthusiasm wore off, they may have returned to their old beliefs or just lost interest in the Dhamma. A few may have momentarily wanted to become a disciple but then had second thoughts. After listening to the Buddha, the ascetic teacher Sakuludāyin expressed the wish to become a disciple, until his dismayed followers pleaded with him: "Master, don't become a monk under samaṇa Gotama! Having been a teacher don't become a student! It would be as if a large jug should become a small mug." The thought of losing his status made Sakuludāyin change his mind[18]

A close reading of the Tipitaka reveals that there were people who had been Buddhists, and even monks, and later left. Once, some thirty monks being trained by Ānanda disrobed en masse, although it is not certain whether they were dissatisfied with Ānanda's tutelage, realized that the monastic life was not for them, or were no longer convinced about the Dhamma.[19] On another occasion, the Buddha gave a long talk to a group of monks in which he told them that they should use the basic requirements for life given to them by devotees with great care and strive resolutely for their own benefit while at the same time considering the good of others. Some sixty of the monks became extremely angry, perhaps thinking that the Buddha was indirectly reproaching them, and another sixty told him: "That is difficult to do Lord, very difficult" and then announced that they had decided to disrobe.[20] Sunakkhatta had once served as the Buddha's attendant. After seeing ascetics who had taken rigorous vows, such as restricting their movements to very small areas or practicing bizarre austerities such as going naked and imitating the behaviour of dogs or cows, he developed an admiration for them.

---

18. M.II,39. *Maṇika* and *uddekanika*, water pots or receptacles for water of some kind, one apparently larger than the other.

19. S.II,217.

20. A.IV,134.

Compared with such attention-grabbing practices, the disciplines and lifestyles taught by the Buddha seemed rather tame. Eventually, he went to the Buddha and announced: "Sir, I am leaving you. I am no longer living by your guidance." The Buddha responded to this declaration by questioning Sunakkhatta:

> "Did I ever say to you, 'Come, live by my guidance?'"
> "No sir."
> "Then did you ever say to me, 'I wish to live by your guidance?'"
> "No sir."
> "So if I never made such a promise to you and you never gave such a condition to me, who are you to be giving up anything, you foolish man?"
> "But sir, you never performed any super-human wonders, any psychic powers or any miracles for me."
> "Did I ever say to you, 'Come, live by my guidance and I will perform such things for you?'"
> "No sir."

The Buddha then explained his position on miracles and psychic powers, saying that they were one thing and overcoming suffering was another and that he was primarily interested in this latter goal. These words did not placate Sunakkhatta, and he left the Saṅgha. Subsequently, he let it be widely known that he no longer had any confidence in or respect for the Buddha.

> "The samaṇa Gotama has no extraordinary powers or any special knowledge or vision one would expect of a true worthy one. What he teaches has been hammered out by reason and according to his own notions. When he teaches his Dhamma to someone, it only leads them to the ending of suffering."

When the Buddha heard what Sunakkhatta had been telling everyone, he said of him: "He is an angry and foolish man and speaks out of anger."[21]

At that time, switching from one religion to another was called 'going over to the discipleship' (*sāvakattaṃ upagaccheyya*) of whatever

21. D.III,2-4 condensed; M.I,68.

sect or teaching one had newly adopted. When lay people decided to become Buddhists, they would often choose to distinguish themselves by wearing white clothes and were usually known as "lay people dressed in white." When an ascetic or monk of another sect converted to Buddhism, they would almost always abandon the accoutrements and practices of their former religion, ordain, and don the tawny-coloured robe distinct to Buddhist monastics and abide by the rules of the Vinaya. But apparently, this was not always the case.

The wandering ascetic Sarabha identified himself as a disciple of the Buddha while remaining within his own sect, at least outwardly. After some time, he decided that he was no longer a Buddhist and told anyone he met or who would listen to him that he now rejected the Dhamma precisely because he understood it. The Buddha would not let such a claim pass without being challenged, and he went to see Sarabha and questioned him: "Is it true that you have been saying that you left the Dhamma and training of the samaṇas who are sons of the Sakyan because you understand it?" Sarabha was silent. The Buddha continued: "Then explain to me your understanding of this Dhamma and training. If you have not learned it completely, I will complete it for you, and if you have learned it completely, I will be happy to hear you explain it." Again Sarabha did not answer, but the Buddha persisted for a second and a third time, until it was clear that the hapless Sarabha either would not, or more likely could not, give an answer. After explaining to the others who had witnessed this encounter why he had interrogated Sarabha the way he did, the Buddha got up and left.[22]

Those who dropped out of the monastic Saṅgha nonetheless sometimes maintained their commitment to the Dhamma.

> "Even those who leave the monkhood and return to the lay life still praise the Buddha, the Dhamma and the Saṅgha. It is themselves that they blame, saying, 'We were unlucky, we had scant merit, for although we ordained in such a well-proclaimed Dhamma, we were unable to live the perfect and pure spiritual life for our whole lives.' Having become monastery attendants or lay disciples, they take and observe the Five Precepts."[23]

22. A.I,185.
23. M.II,5. According to *Śāṭyāyanīya Upaniṣad* 329-330, an ascetic who

One of the most disturbing events in the whole of the Buddha's career happened during one of his sojourns in Vesālī. He had given a talk to an assembly of monks about a meditation called *asubha bhāvanā*. This practice involved contemplating the unpleasant aspects of the body – the discharges that are revolting in themselves or which soon become so without regular washing. The purpose of this practice was to encourage detachment towards the body, to cool sexual impulses, and to act as a counterbalance to the usual over-emphasis on physical attractiveness. After his talk, the Buddha announced that he wanted to go into a solitary retreat for half a month. While he was away, the monks did this contemplation, with tragic results for some of them. The Tipitaka recounts that some thirty monks became so repelled and disgusted with their bodies that they committed suicide. When the Buddha returned from his retreat and noticed some familiar faces missing, he asked where they were and was told what had happened. The Tipitaka records that he then gave a talk on mindfulness of breathing meditation, emphasising its ability to evoke tranquillity and calm, but it records nothing he had to say about this tragedy.[24] It is also silent about comments others may have made about this event, although one could well imagine that some people would have been as deeply shocked by it as most would be if it happened today. It is often claimed that the Buddha was able to read a person's mind, or at least sense their abilities and inclinations, and present the Dhamma to them in such a way that it would resonate specifically with them. This incident is evidence that he could not always do this.

As mentioned previously, Brahminism during the Buddha's time was being re-evaluated and reinterpreted as it struggled to maintain its relevance in a rapidly changing world and tried to compete with the samaṇa tradition. Consequently, there were brahmins who expressed an interest in and appreciation for some of the things the Buddha was teaching, or at least were prepared to listen to what he had to say. Others, the more orthodox and traditional, saw him as a serious threat and never missed an opportunity to vent their hostility towards him,

---

reverted to the lay life committed one of the gravest of all sins, and for *Yājñavalkya Dharmasūtra* 1.152 it warranted the death penalty.

24. S.V, 321-322.

his monks and his nuns. This hostility rarely took the form of criticism of what the Buddha was teaching but was usually expressed in terms of his supposed inferiority and ritual impurity. On one occasion, while alms gathering, the Buddha approached the house of a brahmin just as he was doing his morning rituals. Seeing him coming and not wanting his presence to make the ritual impure, the brahmin called out: "Stop there, you shaveling, you miserable ascetic, you outcaste!"[25] On another occasion, when a particular brahmin found out that a member of his clan had joined the Buddhist Saṅgha, he went to the Buddha in a rage and insulted him.[26] However, there are incidents indicating divided opinions amongst brahmins about the Buddha, with some despising him and others having regard for him and his followers – sometimes great regard.

It seems that the brahmini Dhānañjānī was devoted to the Buddha, and once, as she tripped and nearly fell, she exclaimed three times: "Praise to the Lord, the Worthy One, the fully awakened Buddha!" The brahmin Sangārava happened to be nearby, and, hearing this, he said in disgust: "This Dhānañjānī should be disgraced and degraded! In the presence of brahmins she praises that shaven-headed samaṇa."[27] Once, some nuns on a journey arrived in a village and, having nowhere to stay, they approached the house of a certain brahmini and asked her if they could stay there overnight. She asked them to wait until her husband returned, so they went inside, spread out their mats and sat down while they waited. The brahmin return after nightfall and, seeing the nuns, asked his wife who the strangers were. She replied: "They are nuns." He demanded angrily: "Throw the shaven-headed whores out!"[28] In these two stories at least, brahmin women are depicted as being more accepting of Buddhists than the men were. Other stories show that hostility could change

---

25. Sn. p.21. On 'shaveling', *muṇḍaka*, here see Levman 2011, pp.45 ff.
26. S.I,161-162.
27. M.II,209-210. Sangārava was probably advocating that Dhānañjānī lose her caste, which would mean social death for her. Several *Dharmasūtras* stipulate loss of caste for joining a samaṇa sect. The rite of excommunication is briefly described at D.I,98, and *Manusmṛti* 11,183-189 and *Baudhāyana Dharmasūtra* 2.1.36 stipulate how it was conducted at a later period.
28. Vin.IV,274.

to tolerance and even respect when personal contact created an opportunity for the Buddha's Dhamma to be explained.

The senior monk Mahā Kaccāna happened to be staying in the forest when some young brahmin students out collecting firewood came across his hut.[29] Realizing that there was a Buddhist monk inside, they circled the hut, making a great commotion, while saying loudly that the only people who respected monks were ignorant bumpkins. Deciding not to let this rudeness pass, Kaccāna came out and told the students that, while the brahmins of old led pure simple lives, their successors today had unguarded senses and a preoccupation with chanting hymns, meaningless rituals and outward show. Unused to being spoken to like this, the indignant youngsters marched back to their teacher, Lohicca, and told him that a Buddhist monk had insulted the Vedas. He was very angry and resolved to go and confront Kaccāna but thought it best to hear his account of the incident first. When he arrived at the hut, his students following behind, he greeted Kaccāna politely and, after the usual small talk, asked him if he had said what his students had reported to him. Kaccāna confirmed that he had indeed said such things. A few moments of uneasy silence must have followed. But then, rather than scold Kaccāna as he had intended, Lohicca asked him what he had meant by unguarded senses. Kaccāna took the opportunity to describe the meditation practice of being aware of sensory impingement, the value of remaining detached from it, and the insights that would result. Lohicca was quite impressed by this and told Kaccāna that any time he came to his house for alms, he would be given food with every mark of respect, including from his students.[30]

Despite the criticisms and negative assessments of some, the Buddha was the most respected teacher of his time, along with the Jain leader Mahāvīra, who was senior to him by about a decade. Someone who had attended a talk by the Buddha noticed that when it was finished, the audience got up and left reluctantly, keeping their eyes on

29. The initiation ritual into Vedic studentship included approaching the teacher holding a piece of firewood, and collecting firewood daily was an important part of a student's duties to his teacher, see e.g., *Chāndogya Upaniṣad* 5.4,8; 5.11,6; and *Muṇḍaka Upaniṣad* 1.2,12.

30. S.IV,117-121.

him as they did so.[31] This interesting observation, and several similar ones, confirm the impression that the Buddha had great personal charisma and, for some people at least, that it was his good looks and commanding presence that initially attracted them to the Dhamma.

The Tipitaka provides a great deal of information about the Buddha's physical appearance. We are told that he was four finger-breadths taller than his handsome and younger half-brother Nanda, who could be mistaken for him from a distance.[32] According to the Buddha's own comment, before his renunciation he had black hair, probably long, and a beard.[33] Although statues of the Buddha always show him with tightly curled hair, this is an iconographic convention without any historical basis. After his renunciation, he cut off his hair and beard and ever after regularly shaved his scalp and face, as did other monks. He said of himself: "Dressed in my robe, homeless do I wander and with my head shaved" (*Saṅghātivāsī agiho carāmi nivuttakeso*).[34] When disapproving brahmins would encounter him they would often express their disdain by calling him "bald-headed" or "shaven-headed" (*muṇḍa*).

All sources agree that the Buddha was particularly good-looking. Sonadaṇḍa described him as "handsome, of fine appearance, pleasant to see, with a good complexion and a beautiful form and countenance."[35] To Doṇa he appeared "beautiful, inspiring confidence, calm, composed, with the dignity and presence of a perfectly tamed elephant."[36] These natural good looks were indicative of his deep inner calm, as another observer noted: "It is wonderful, truly marvellous how serene is the good Gotama's presence, how clear and radiant his complexion. As a yellow jujube fruit in the autumn is clear and bright, or a palm fruit just plucked from its stalk is clear and bright, so too is the good Gotama's complexion."[37] The ancient Indian notion of a desirable and attractive

---

31. M.II,140.
32. Vin.IV,173. Srinivasan gives a finger-breadth, *aṅguli*, as about 2.54 cms, pp.9-11.
33. M.I,163.
34. Sn.456.
35. D.I,115.
36. A.II,38.
37. A.I,181. The fruit of the *Ziziphus jujube* is yellow when ripe, gradually turning rusty-brown. The palm fruit mentioned is that of *Borassus flabellifer*,

complexion was that it was "not too dark and not too fair," and as the Buddha was frequently praised for his fine complexion, presumably his skin tone was like that.[38] He himself said that those who live in the present moment tend to have a beautiful complexion (*vaṇṇo pasīdati*).[39] Saccaka noticed that during a debate, when the Buddha was verbally attacked, his features seemed to change: "It is wonderful, truly marvellous that when good Gotama is continually berated and subjected to rude, impolite language, his complexion becomes beautiful and his face bright, which is just as one would expect of a worthy one, one who is fully awakened."[40]

Enhancing the Buddha's physical attractiveness was the way he spoke, i.e., one person who had attended several of his talks described the tone and timbre of his voice, as "clear and distinct, silvery and audible, orotund, sonorous, deep and resonant."[41]

The Buddha observed that old age brought with it "brokenness of teeth, greyness of hair, wrinkling of skin, decline of vigour and the failing of the sense faculties," and there is no reason to doubt that he too exhibited some of these characteristics as he aged.[42] Ānanda said this of him towards the end of his life: "The Lord's complexion is no longer pure and bright, his limbs are flabby and wrinkled, his body stooped, and his sense faculties have deteriorated."[43] In the months before his death, he said of himself: "I am now old, aged, worn out, having traversed life's path, approaching the end of my life, being about eighty. Just as an old cart can only be kept going by being strapped together, so too, my body can only be kept going by being strapped together."[44]

---

which has a greyish-brown skin and is golden yellow inside.

38. M.I,88.

39. S.I,5.

40. M.I,250.

41. M.II,140; *visaṭṭha, viññeyya, mañju, savanīya, bindu, avisārī, gambhīra, ninnadī.*

42. S.II,2.

43. S.V,216.

44. D.II,100. The phrase here translated as "being strapped together," *vagha missakena*, is obscure. For an alternative reading and translation, see Gombrich,1987 and Levman, 2020, pp.81-82.

Images of the Buddha from the earliest time onwards always show him with elongated and partly slit earlobes, an iconographic convention which may well have had its origins in an authentic memory of the Buddha's physical features. Ancient Indian males wore earplugs (*kaṇṇālankāra*) of crystal, lacquer, agate, ivory, clay or shell, which when removed, and Gotama would have done this on becoming an ascetic, caused the stretched earlobes to hang down.[45]

Some passages in the Tipitaka assert that the Buddha's body exhibited thirty-two auspicious marks (*mahāpurisa lakkhaṇa*), the most curious and perplexing innovation in the early Buddhist texts – curious because the marks are so strange, perplexing because they are contradicted by other texts.[46] When King Ajātasattu went to meet the Buddha, he was unable to distinguish him from the surrounding monks, which he would have been able to do immediately if the Buddha had these marks.[47] The young man Pukkusāti sat talking to the Buddha for hours before realizing who he was. If the Buddha had any of the marks, Pukkusāti would have immediately noticed it and known that he was in the presence of someone quite unusual.[48] And as mentioned before, when Upaka encountered the Buddha walking along the road from Uruvelā to Gayā, the thing that caught his attention was not the Buddha's unusual body but his serene and radiant complexion.[49] More importantly, the Buddha rejected the notion that physical attributes made one special, saying rather that it was having a liberated mind (*vimutticitta*) that qualified one to be called 'a great man.'[50]

The Buddha's penetrating wisdom and the persuasiveness with which he explained his Dhamma are mentioned time and again as among his most impressive abilities. The Tipitaka records this conversation between two brahmins:

---

45. Postel, pp.9-10 and Banerjee pp.220-225.
46. The texts attribute the notion to Brahminism, although it is not specifically mentioned in any Vedic texts. See Levman 2013 pp.163-165.
47. D.I,50.
48. M.III,238.
49. M.I,170.
50. S. V,158; A.II, 35 ff.

"At that time, the brahmin Kāranapāli was constructing a building for the Licchavis. On seeing his fellow brahmin Pingiyānī coming in the distance, he approached him and asked: 'How now! From where is your honour Pingiyāni coming so early in the day?'

'I come from the presence of the samaṇa Gotama.'

'Well, what do you think of his clarity of wisdom? Do you think he is a wise man?'

'But what am I compared to him? Who am I to judge his clarity? Only one like him could judge his clarity of wisdom.'

'High indeed is the praise that you give the samaṇa Gotama.'

'But what am I compared to him? Who am I to praise the ascetic Gotama? Truly he is praised by the praised. He is the highest amongst gods and humans.'"[51]

Once, the Buddha was talking with Nandaka, a senior member of the Licchavi ruling council. Just as the talk finished, Nandaka's servant, apparently anxious to get away, whispered to him that it was time for his bath, to which Nandaka replied: "Enough of that outer washing my good man! Being washed inwardly by confidence in the Lord is sufficient for me."[52] Such was the Buddha's Dhamma and the way he presented it that it could even have a noticeable effect on a person's physical features. When Sāriputta met Nakulapitā and noticed how composed he looked, he said to him: "I assume that today you have had a face to face talk with the Lord?" Nakulapitā replied: "How could it be otherwise, Sir? I have just now been sprinkled with the nectar of the Lord's Dhamma."[53]

People often expressed surprise at what was seen as the Buddha's magnanimity and openness, particularly concerning religious matters. Once, on meeting a party of ascetics, their leader asked him to explain his Dhamma. He replied: "It is hard for you, having different opinions, inclinations and biases, and who follow a different teacher, to understand the doctrine I teach. Therefore, let us discuss your teaching." The ascetics were astonished by this: "It is wonderful, truly

51. A.III, 237.
52. S.V,390.
53. S.III,2.

marvellous, how great are the powers of the samaṇa Gotama in that he holds back his own teaching and invites others to discuss theirs!"[54]

Some teachers would tell their disciples or admirers not to help those of other religions, an attitude not entirely absent amongst some religious partisans even today. While the Buddha could be critical of other doctrines, he said of himself: "I analyse things first. I do not speak categorically" (*vibhajjavādo nāhaṁ ettha ekaṃsavādo*).[55] He refrained from making sweeping generalisations about other beliefs but would examine them and acknowledge any truths they might contain, while also pointing out their weaknesses. Likewise, he was able to acknowledge that the followers of other religions might well be sincerely striving for truth and thus be worthy of encouragement and support. When Upāli, who had been a Jain, decided to become a Buddhist instead, the Buddha said to him: "For a long time your family has supported the Jains, so you should consider still giving them alms when they come to your house."[56] On another occasion someone said to the Buddha:

> "I have heard it said that you, good Gotama, teach that charity should only be given to you, not to others, to your disciples, not to the disciples of other teachers. Are those who say this representing your opinion without distorting it? Do they speak according to your teaching? In truth, good Gotama, I am anxious not to misrepresent you."

The Buddha replied:

> "Those who say this are not of my opinion; they misrepresent me and say something false. One who discourages another from giving charity hinders in three ways: he hinders the giver from receiving merit, he hinders the receiver from receiving the charity, and he has already ruined himself through his stinginess."[57]

There is no record of what people thought of the Buddha's openness towards and respect for others' beliefs, but it is likely that

54. D.III,40.
55. M.II,197.
56. M.I,378-379.
57. A.I,161, condensed.

they considered it to be a welcome departure from the more common jealousy and competitiveness between many other sects of the time. And that he practised what he preached was certainly one thing people noticed about him. One of his admirers once asserted that: "The Lord speaks as he acts, and he acts as he speaks. Other than him, we find no teacher as consistent as this, whether we survey the past or the present."[58]

People also noticed and admired the Buddha's love of silence. He said: "Learn this from rivers: those that flow through clefts and chasms gush loudly, but great rivers flow silently. Empty things make a noise, but the full is always quiet. The fool is like a half-filled pot, while the wise person is like a deep still lake."[59] He praised, in particular, the maintenance of a dignified silence in the face of insults and false accusations: "Not to respond to anger with angry words is to win a battle hard to win. It is to act for one's own and the other's welfare, although those who do not know the Dhamma will think you are a fool."[60]

Despite the numerous accounts of the Buddha giving talks and engaging in dialogues and debates, he nonetheless would sometimes meditate all through the night, go into solitary retreats or just sit in silence. It was said of him that he "seeks lodgings in the forest, in the depth of the jungle, in quiet places with little noise, places far from the crowd, undisturbed by people and well suited for solitude."[61] Once, a group of ascetics were sitting noisily talking and arguing when they saw the Buddha coming in the distance. One of them said to the others: "Quiet, sirs, make no noise. That samaṇa Gotama is coming, and he likes silence and speaks in praise of it. If he sees that our group is quiet, he might come and visit us."[62] He did just that, and a discussion ensued.

Even people who met and listened to the Buddha without necessarily becoming a disciple would sometimes express their admiration for him. A good example of this is this comment by the leading brahmin Soṇadaṇḍa:

---

58. D.II,224.
59. Sn.720-721.
60. S.I,162.
61. D.III,38.
62. D.I,179.

"The samaṇa Gotama is well-born on both his mother's and father's sides, of pure and unbroken descent for at least seven generations, not a stain on him as far as his birth is concerned. He renounced a large family and gave up much gold and grain both below and above ground. He has the virtue of a worthy one, a skillful virtue, fully endowed with such virtue. His voice and his conversation are beautiful, polite, clear, not at all rough and in discussion he makes his meaning clear. He is the teacher of many and has given up sensuality and vanity. He teaches action and the results of action and respects the brahmin traditions that are blameless. He is a samaṇa of high birth, coming from a leading warrior caste family, one with great wealth and riches. People come from foreign kingdoms and lands to consult him. Many gods and humans are devoted to him, and if he stays in a particular town or village, that place is not troubled by malevolent spirits. He is polite, genial and agreeable, not at all stern, clear-mouthed and first to open the conversation. He has a crowd of followers, he is a teacher of teachers, and even the heads of various sects come to discuss matters with him. Unlike some ascetics and brahmins, his fame is based on his genuine attainment of the highest knowledge and conduct. Even King Bimbisāra of Magadha has become his disciple, as has his son and wife, his courtiers and ministers. So has King Pasenadi of Kosala and the brahmin Pokkharasāti too."[63]

Soṇadaṇḍa's accolade reveals something about the concerns and interests of the brahmin class of the time and what they considered admirable, but at the same time it reveals something about the Buddha.

63. D.I,115-116, condensed.

10
Monastic and Lay Disciples

The monk or the nun, the layman or the laywoman who lives by the Dhamma and perfectly fulfils it: it is they who honour me with the highest reverence.

Dīgha Nikāya II,138.

After the Buddha's awakening, he saw the need for some kind of community, bound together by shared values and norms, which would provide the optimal environment for awakening and could disseminate the Dhamma as widely as possible. Thus what came to be known as the four-fold community (*catu parisā*) evolved, its four parts being monks and nuns (*bhikkhu* and *bhikkhunī*) and lay men and women (*upāsaka* and *upāsikā*).[1] He envisaged the parts of this community being mutually dependent (*aññamaññaṃ*) on each other – monastics on the laity for their basic needs and the laity on monastics for knowledge of the Dhamma. Furthermore, because the Buddha considered his Dhamma to be distinct from other teachings, it was only right that he would want his disciples to be distinct too – most importantly in their probity but also in their dress. The ascetics of other sects tended to wear whatever clothes they could find or were given and in any style they liked, but the Buddha wanted his monastics to all use the same type of robe dyed a similar colour so that they could be immediately distinguished from other ascetics. The colour was called *kasāva*, which probably referred to a tawny-yellowish hue.[2] Although

1. See Anālayo 2018, pp.9-17.

2. Vin. I,306 gives a range of colours that monastics' robes should not be, including red, yellow and orange. Buddhist monks today are often said to wear 'saffron' robe, and indeed the colour of their robes sometimes resembles the

the Buddha never required it be done, lay disciples dressed in white (*gihī odātavasana*) as an alternative to more ostentatious, brightly coloured and embroidered wear and perhaps because it was thought to suggest purity and simplicity.

At the beginning of the Buddha's career, people expressed their intention to become a disciple, whether monastic or lay, by taking what were called the Three Refuges (*tisaraṇa*) – a refuge being a place offering security from a threatening or dangerous situation. The Buddha was considered such a refuge because his awakening demonstrated that the continual process of birth, death and rebirth could be transcended; the Dhamma was a refuge because it provided the means by which this could be achieved; and the Saṅgha was a refuge by offering the guidance and encouragement, example and support needed to transcend conditioned existence. The word *saṅgha* means a group or assembly and is generally used for the monastic orders, i.e., monks and nuns, although in the Three Refuge avowal it does not usually refer to monks or nuns but to anyone who has realized either a stage at which awakening becomes irreversible and inevitable or awakening itself. To this day, those who decide to become Buddhist recite three times a simple formula – I take refuge in the Buddha; I take refuge in the Dhamma; I take refuge in the Saṅgha – by which they affirm their confidence in and commitment to Buddhism.

The Buddha's first move in developing a community of disciples was to establish a monastic Saṅgha. An order of monks unencumbered by familial ties and social obligations would provide the best opportunity to develop the spiritual qualities needed to attain awakening. Furthermore, such monks would be in a good position to disseminate the Dhamma. In the beginning, joining the monastic community required approaching the Buddha and requesting to become a monk, but as time went by the Buddha saw the need for a more formal and structured organization, which the monastic Saṅgha eventually became. Some years after the first monks were ordained, a group of women expressed a desire to become nuns, and a nun's Saṅgha was founded.

---

bright orange of saffron. But the saffron plant was unknown in fifth century BCE India and even later was never used as a dye because of its expense and poor fixing properties.

The Buddha never conceived of his monks and nuns as having the sacerdotal role that brahmins had, nor were they meant to be leaders of the community, as Christian pastors and Jewish rabbis are. They were simply individuals who had a deep desire to reach a state of complete awakening and who had turned their backs on society and its demands in order to focus completely on achieving that goal. And, while doing this, they were encouraged to share with others how they understood the Dhamma and how it should be practiced.

Sāriputta and Moggallāna were the Buddha's two chief disciples, who as childhood friends had both become ascetics together under the teacher Sañjaya Belaṭṭhiputta.[3] Eventually, they became disillusioned with him and his philosophy, left, split up and went their separate ways looking for a better teacher. One day, Sāriputta heard about the Buddha's Dhamma, converted and straight away went in search of his friend to tell him of the wonderful teaching he had discovered. When they met again and Moggallāna heard the Dhamma, he too was won over, and then the friends went to find the Buddha so they could become monks under him.[4] They took to the monastic life with ease, and in time, the Buddha came to look upon them as his most accomplished and trusted disciples and heirs.

Sāriputta's forte was his ability to understand the more abstruse aspects of the Dhamma and expound them in a clear and comprehensible manner, so much so that the Buddha gave him the title of General of the Dhamma. Psychic powers came easily to Moggallāna, and, being a diligent meditator, they manifested within him to a high degree. The Buddha recommended the two to other monks in these words:

> "Cultivate the friendship of Sāriputta and Moggallāna; associate with them, for they are wise and helpful to their companions in the spiritual life. Sāriputta is like a mother, and Moggallāna is like a foster-mother. Sāriputta trains others to attain the first stage leading to awakening, while Moggallāna trains them to attain the highest goal. Sāriputta is able to

3. The Sānṭiputta mentioned at *Isibhāsiyāiṃ* 38, Schubring p.88, would seem to be this Sāriputta, see *Brill's Encyclopedia of Buddhism*, Vol. II. 2019. p.411.

4. Vin.I,38 ff.

announce, teach, describe, establish, reveal, expound and exhibit the Four Noble Truths."[5]

One of Moggallāna's psychic powers was clairvoyance. Once, he and Sāriputta were staying together in a hut in Rājagaha's Bamboo Grove. Moggallāna had spent the day in secluded meditation, and when the two came together towards evening, Sāriputta noticed his friend's serene smiling countenance and asked him about it. Moggallāna replied that he had been conversing with the Buddha, who happened to be in Sāvatthī at the time, many yojanas away. Aware of this, Sāriputta inquired: "Did the Lord come to you by using the power of levitation, or did you go to him by means of yours?" Moggallāna replied: "Neither. The Lord purified his powers of clairvoyance and clairaudience and used them to communicate with me, and I purified mine and used them to communicate with him."[6] The Buddha is sometimes depicted as being able to read other peoples' minds and to see events happening or hear conversations taking place at distances beyond normal sight and hearing. In most religions, such abilities are attributed to either divine favour or the divinity of the person having them. The Buddha taught that psychic abilities were awakened when ordinary consciousness was developed and purified and were available to anyone who managed to do this. Thus most of the powers attributed to the Buddha were not different from those of some of his disciples, as in the previous incident, or even the *samaṇa*s of other sects.

The Tipitaka includes dozens of talks by Sāriputta and Moggallāna with the Buddha, with their fellow monks, ascetics of other sects and lay disciples. These talks cover a range of subjects and issues and confirm the two men's profound grasp of the Dhamma and skill in explaining it. There are also occasional brief glimpses of the human side of the two men. When a desperately ill monk talked of killing himself, Sāriputta

---

5. M.III,248.

6. S.II,275-276. The words for these two powers are *dibbacakkhu* and *dibbasota*. *Dibba* means wondrous, divine or heavenly, but here the modern terms are used for them. Apparently, such abilities need to be cleared or purified (*visujjhi*), before being usable, suggesting that they are latent and more likely to manifest after some preparation. It should be pointed out that there is meagre scientific evidence for any extrasensory perception.

implored him not to do so: "Do not kill yourself Channa. Live! I want you to live. If you do not have suitable food or medicine, I will get it for you. If you do not have suitable care, I will take care of you. Do not kill yourself. Live! I want you to live."[7]

Moggallāna and Sāriputta both predeceased the Buddha, although only scant details of the circumstances surrounding the latter's death are given in the Tipitaka.[8] There are accounts of the activities of other leading disciples in the decades after the Buddha's demise, those such as Ānanda, Anuruddha and Hatthaka, Khemā, Mahā Kassapa and Upāli, but no records of how, where or when they died.

The second branch of the four-fold community was that of the nuns (*bhikkhunī*). Early in the Buddha's career he happened to be visiting Kapilavatthu, and while there his stepmother Mahāpajāpatī asked him to allow her to become a nun, a request he refused. Shortly afterwards, when he left for Vesālī, Mahāpajāpatī and a number of other women who aspired to become nuns decided to follow him. When they arrived, Ānanda saw Mahāpajāpatī, "her feet swollen, her limbs covered with dust and her face stained with tears" and decided to speak to the Buddha on her and the other women's behalf. Again the Buddha refused to ordain the women. Finally, Ānanda asked him whether or not women were able to attain awakening, like men, and he replied: "Having renounced their home, women too are able to become worthy ones," i.e., awakened. Finally relenting, the Buddha gave permission for the establishment of a nun's order.[9] This story leaves one with the impression that he did this somewhat reluctantly, but also with the impression that Mahāpajāpatī Gotamī was a strong woman determined to get her way.

Women responded enthusiastically to the founding of an order of nuns, seeing the life of renunciation as an opportunity to be free from husbands, children and housework, but more importantly as a means for attaining complete awakening. On one occasion Mahāpajāpatī Gotamī together with five hundred nuns came to visit the Buddha, and once he mentioned that more than five hundred

---

7. M.III,264.
8. S.V,164.
9. Vin.II,253.

nuns had attained awakening.[10] Although this number need not be taken literally, it does point to there being many nuns.

A nun was usually addressed by monks, lay people and her fellows by the respectful title 'lady' (*ayyā*) or the more informal 'sister' (*bhaginī*).

One nun who distinguished herself by mastering the teachings and being able to explain it with great clarity, was Dhammadinnā whom the Buddha praised as "foremost of those who can talk about the Dhamma" (*dhammakathikānaṃ*).[11] There is a record of her and a certain layman engaging in a long back-and-forth in which the protagonist's intelligent questions elicited well-informed and precise answers from Dhammadinnā.[12] Another distinguished nun was Khemā, who had knowledge and confidence enough to explain the Dhamma to the most powerful man in the land. King Pasenadi was travelling from Sāketa to Sāvatthī and had stopped for the night in the royal rest house before proceeding the next morning. On inquiring if there were any *samaṇa*s or brahmins around who would be worth visiting, he was informed that one of the Buddha's disciples, the nun Khemā, was lodging nearby and that she had a reputation of being "wise and emphatic, intelligent and learned, an elegant and confident speaker." Impressed by this, the king went to meet Khemā and she gave him informed answers to some of the questions he asked.[13]

Unfortunately, information in the Tipitaka about the lives and achievements of the first Buddhist nuns is scant when compared to that of monks; there is even evidence that much of what may have existed was later neglected and thus lost. For example, there are no discourses between the Buddha and a nun and yet five nuns – Vāsiṭṭhī, Anopamā, Cālā, Upacālā, and Sisupacālā – specifically mention the Buddha instructing them in Dhamma (*So me dhammamadesesi, anukampāya gotamo*).[14] Perhaps telling also is that despite Dhammadinnā and Khemā being lauded by the Buddha himself as outstanding teachers, the Tipitaka preserves only one discourse by each of them.

10. M.III,270; I,490.
11. A.I,25.
12. M.I,299 ff.
13. S.IV,374-379.
14. Thi.136, 155, 185, 192, 201.

There is also evidence of disapproval or a degree of jealousy or perhaps even hostility by some monks towards nuns. Bakkula said to one of his friends that in the decades since becoming a monk he had never once shared the Dhamma with a nun or a lay woman.[15] During the First Council convened shortly after the Buddha's passing, some senior monks reproached Ānanda for his well-known support for women and particularly for nuns. They blamed him for encouraging the Buddha to allow women to ordain which, they insisted, was "a wrongdoing" (*dukkaṭa*) on his part – a wrongdoing being an infraction of a monastic rule.[16] Ānanda insisted that he did not believe what he had done amounted to a wrongdoing, but perhaps thinking it best not to defend himself and have an argument ensue, he nonetheless accepted their judgment.

He could have easily marshalled statements by the Buddha to defend himself. The Buddha had said: "For the disciple who had faith in the Teacher's instruction and who lives trying to understand it, he should think, 'The Teacher is the lord and I am the disciple. The Teacher knows, I do not know.'"[17] It was a presumption on the part of the senior monks to consider that the Buddha did not know what he was doing when he founded the nun's order, and that they knew better than him. He had affirmed that women were as capable of awakening as men, and more than once he made it clear that he considered nuns to be an integral part of his spiritual community.[18] Further, Ānanda was quite correct when he said that he did not believe his action was an infringement of the rules, because there is no such rule in the Vinaya.

The Buddha would occasionally ordained a nun, and presumably teach her the Dhamma beforehand or afterwards, although as mentioned before, what he may have imparted to such nuns is nowhere recorded.[19] Ānanda was always happy to share the Dhamma with the nuns but when they failed to receive the encouragement and support they deserved, they relied upon each other. Uttamā for example, Soṇā, Candā, Subhā and Isidāsī were all instructed in the Dhamma by their

15. M.III,126.
16. See Upasak, p.114.
17. M.I,480.
18. A. II,8: D.II,105;138; III, 123-124.
19. Thi.108-109.

sister nuns and most attained awakening as a result.[20] And for those who thought it too difficult for women to reach the spiritual heights because of their supposed 'two inch intelligence' (*dvaṅgulapaññāyā*), the nun Somā had a ready reply. "What does femininity matter in a mind well concentrated, with growing knowledge and insight, fully understanding the Dhamma? Whoever thinks, 'I am a woman' or 'I am a man' or 'I am this or that', Māra can speak to them."[21]

It is interesting to note that the Buddha's first disciples were two laymen, the merchants Tapussa and Bhallika, who encountered him in Uruvelā just after his awakening. It is perhaps also significant that several months later, when the Buddha tried to convince his five former companions that he was fully awakened, he met with an initial scepticism, while Tapussa and Bhallika immediately recognized his profound spiritual accomplishment and needed no convincing to become his disciples. In the decades after that, many thousands of ordinary men and women, from the humblest levels in society to the most exalted, followed these two men's example and became disciples.

The Buddha said that what was required to be a virtuous lay Buddhist was to take the Three Refuges "with a pure heart" (*pasanna citto*) and to sincerely adheres to the Five Precepts (*pañca sīla*), the foundational ethical principles of the Buddha's philosophy.[22] These Precepts are to abstain from harming or killing any living being, from stealing, sexual misconduct, lying, and from consuming alcohol. Put another way, this requires having respect for the lives of others, for their possessions, their dignity and right to choose, and respect for their right to be spoken to honestly. The fifth Precept concerns self-respect by maintaining one's mind in its natural state. The Precepts are, of course, the bare minimum; the Buddha expected the highest ethical, intellectual and spiritual aspirations from all of his disciples. "Whether in a householder or a monastic, I praise right practice. And whether they are a householder or a monastic, if they practise in the right way, then because of their right practice, they will attain the method, the truth, the skilful."[23]

20. Thi. 42; 102; 122; 338; 400.
21. S.I,129.
22. D.I,145; A.IV.222.
23. S.V,19.

If there were no lay disciples accomplished in the Dhamma, then the holy life would be incomplete. "Just as the Ganges moves, slopes and inclines toward the ocean and merges with it, like that the good Gotama's monastic and lay disciples move, slope and incline toward Nirvana."[24] In later centuries, a sharp division emerged between the monastics and the laity, where monks came to be seen as the sole preservers, teachers and interpreters of the Dhamma, and lay people were relegated to the role of being providers of the monks' material needs, a situation that has persisted to a large degree up to the present. Such a baneful division does not accord with the Buddha's vision and did not exist for the first generations of Buddhists. He encouraged all his disciples to be well-versed in the Dhamma so that they could help to preserve it, teach it to others, and benefit from it:

> "I will not pass away until the monks and the nuns, the lay men and the lay women are learned and well-trained, skilled and competent, erudite in the Dhamma and walk the path of the Dhamma; not until they, with confidence in the teachings, can pass on to others what they have learned from the Teacher, explain it and establish it, expound it, analyse it and make it clear; not until they can use it to thoroughly refute false teachings that have appeared and proclaim the Dhamma in all its wonder."[25]

And he said it was because of these disciples – monks and nuns, lay men and women, whether celibate or not - that his Dhamma "prospers, flourishes and spreads, is popular, known far and wide and well-proclaimed amongst gods and humans" (*iddañ ca phitañ ca vitthārikaṃ bāhujaññaṃ puthu bhūtaṃ yava devamanussehi suppakāsitaṃ*).[26]

The Tipitaka mentions the lay woman Nandamātā who would rise before dawn and chant some of the Buddha's discourses and another woman named Kāḷī who chanted passages from a discourse to a monk and then asked him to explain their meaning to her. Some lay people had a good enough grasp of the Dhamma that they could explain it

24. M.I,493.
25. D.II,104.
26. D.III,124-126 condensed.

to others and correct misunderstandings or misrepresentations of it. The Buddha praised Vajjiyamāhita for being good at this.[27] He also mentioned a hypothetical situation in which a monk might go to a layman's home to learn from him a discourse that he, the monk, did not know. This suggests that, in at least some locales, there could be lay people who had committed to memory discourses that monks in the same area had not.[28] According to the tradition, it was the servant woman Khujjuttarā who remembered and thus transmitted many of the sermons the Buddha gave in Kosambī.[29]

The Tipitaka also records several examples of lay disciples teaching the Dhamma and even of monks learning from them. Citta and Hatthaka were the model Buddhist laymen whose learning and behaviour the Buddha encouraged others to emulate. On one occasion, the Buddha said: "Should a devoted mother wish to encourage her beloved and only son in a proper way, she should say to him: 'Try to become like the disciple Citta and the disciple Hatthaka of Āḷavī.'" Citta was a rich merchant and landowner in the town of Macchikāsaṇḍa, not far from Sāvatthī. He seems to have heard the Dhamma for the first time from the monk Mahānāma, after which he offered the monastic Saṅgha a park he owned and built a spacious monastery on it. After that, any monks or nuns coming to Macchikasanda were always assured of a warm welcome and adequate support. The Buddha considered Citta to be the most learned and erudite of all the lay Dhamma teachers. After accepting the Dhamma, Citta explained it to the other citizens of the town, converting hundreds of them, and on one occasion took all of these new converts to Sāvatthī to meet the Buddha. The discourses in the Tipitaka preached to and by Citta indicate his good grasp of the subtlest aspects of the Dhamma, and indeed later he attained the third stage leading to awakening.

---

27. A.IV,63; V.46;191.

28. Vin.I,140-141. Lay expertise in the sacred text continued for some centuries. Amongst the inscriptions from Sañchi dating from the 2nd and 1st centuries BCE, some lay donors describe themselves as "versed in the suttas," "who can chant [a text]," "a woman who knows a sutta." See Rhys Davids 1903, pp.167-169 and Marshall, pp.298 ff.

29. Ud-a.32.

Once, a group of monks were sitting discussing the Dhamma in a pavilion in the monastery that Citta had built. Some were saying that it is the sense objects that fetter the mind, while others maintained that it is the sense organs that cause the problem. Citta arrived at the monastery and, seeing the monks, asked what they were discussing. When they told him, he gave his opinion on the matter:

> "Sirs, these two things – sense objects and sense organs – are different. I will use a simile so that you can understand what I mean. Imagine that a black ox and a white ox were tied together with a yoke or a rope. Now would it be right to say that the black ox is the fetter of the white ox or that the white ox is the fetter of the black ox?"
>
> "Certainly not. The black ox is not fettered to the white ox nor is the white ox fettered to the black one. They are both fettered by the yoke or rope."
>
> "Well, sirs, in the same way, the eye is not the fetter of visual objects nor are visual objects the fetter of the eye. Rather, the fetter is the desire that arises from the meeting of the two. And it is the same with the other sense organs and their objects."

The monks were pleased with Citta's lucidity in explaining and answering the question.

On another occasion, the monk Kāmabhū, perplexed by one of the Buddha's more unusual and cryptic sayings, asked Citta if he could give his explanation as to what it might mean. The saying was: "Pure-limbed, white-canopied, one-wheeled, the chariot rolls on. Look at he who is coming in it – he is a faultless stream-cutter, he is boundless." Citta explained the verse with considerable originality and insight, saying:

> "Pure-limbed means virtue, white-canopied means freedom, one-wheeled means mindfulness, and rolling on refers to coming and going. The chariot means the body, he who is coming is a term for the enlightened one, stream means craving, and faultless, stream-cutter and boundless all refer to one who has destroyed the defilements."

Citta's ability to give a spiritual interpretation to what appeared to be merely a beautiful verse surprised and satisfied Kāmabhū.

Citta was not just able to teach the Dhamma, but he was also able to demonstrate its superiority over other doctrines. Once, Mahāvīra arrived in Macchikāsaṇḍa with a large number of his disciples. Citta went to meet Mahāvīra, who, knowing that he was a disciple of the Buddha, asked him if he believed, as the Buddha taught, that it is possible to attain a meditative state in which the thinking process ceases. "No," answered Citta, "The Buddha teaches that but I do not believe it." Surprised and pleased that Citta seemed to be expressing doubts about some of the Buddha's teaching, Mahāvīra looked around at all his disciples, saying as he did: "See what a straightforward and intelligent person Citta is. Anyone who could believe in a meditative state where all thinking stops might just as well believe that the wind can be caught in a net or that one could stop the Ganges flowing using the hand." When he had finished, Citta asked him: "What is better, venerable sir, to know or to believe?" "Knowledge is far better than belief," replied Mahāvīra. "Well, I can attain that meditative state where all my thought ceases. So why should I believe what the Buddha says is true when I know it is true?" Annoyed at being caught out, Mahāvīra again looked around at his disciples and said: "See what a sneaky, deceitful and crooked person this Citta is?" Remaining unruffled by this reproach, Citta said: "If your first statement is true, then your second one must be false, and if your second statement is true, then your first one must be false," and, having said this, he rose from his seat and departed, leaving an irritated Mahāvīra struggling for a reply.[30]

The other eminent lay disciple praised by the Buddha was Hatthaka, a son of the chief of Āḷavī. Hatthaka first met the Buddha as he was out walking late one winter's afternoon. Surprised to see this lone ascetic in just one thin robe, and who had obviously been sleeping on a bed of leaves, Hatthaka asked the Buddha whether he was happy. The Buddha replied: "Yes, young man, I am happy." "But sir," Hatthaka inquired further, "It is the time of frost, the ground has been trampled hard by the cattle, the foliage on the trees is sparse, your robe is thin and a cold wind is blowing. How could you be happy?" The Buddha asked if it were possible that a man living in a cozy house with a comfortable bed could be unhappy because he was tormented by greed, hatred or

30. S.IV,281-283; 291-192; 298-299.

delusion, and Hatthaka conceded that it was possible. "Well," said the Buddha, "I have got rid of all greed, hatred and delusion, so wherever I sleep I am happy; I am always happy."[31]

Hatthaka was not so much known for his knowledge of Dhamma as for his ability to attract people to the Buddhist community. Once, he brought several hundred people to Sāvatthī to see the Buddha, who asked him how he was able to interest so many of his fellow townsfolk in the Dhamma. He replied:

> "Lord, I do it by using the four bases of community which you yourself taught me.[32] When I know that someone can be attracted by generosity, I am generous. When I know that they can be attracted by kind words, I speak to them kindly. When I know that they can be attracted by doing them a good turn, I do them a good turn, and when I know they can be attracted by treating them equally, I treat them with equality."

It seems that when people attended talks on Dhamma organized by Hatthaka, they always received a warm personal welcome that made them feel liked and respected, and so they would come again, gradually becoming interested in the Dhamma. The Buddha praised Hatthaka for his skill: "Well done, Hatthaka, well done! This is the way to attract people." After Hatthaka had left, the Buddha said to the monks: "You can take it as true that Hatthaka of Āḷavī has eight marvellous and wonderful qualities. He has faith and virtue, conscientiousness and fear of blame, he is learned, generous, wise and modest."[33]

The Buddha is often depicted as explaining aspects of his Dhamma to lay women, and they are occasionally depicted questioning him about it. But rarely are they shown taking the initiative in anything beyond providing monks with their basic requirements. Nonetheless,

---

31. A.I,136-137.

32. *Catu saṅghavatthu.* The meaning of this term is difficult to convey in English. It has been translated as "the four bases of gathering" and "the four bases of sympathy." Bodhi 2012, p.1684 note 687, gives "the four means of sustaining a favourable relationship" and has useful comments on the term. According to the Buddha, the four help the world turn smoothly like a well-secured chariot wheel, D.III,192.

33. A.IV,219-220.

when they were independent actors they could have an impact, and an example of this concerns the lady Visākhā, who was described as being "wise, intelligent and smart" (*paṇḍitāya viyattāya medhāviniyā*).[34] At one time, the monastic community in Sāvatthī made a rule not to conduct ordinations during the three months of the rainy season. It happened that one of Visākhā's grandsons wanted to become a monk, but the monks at Sāvatthī refused him, telling him it was not a good time and to come back after the rainy season was over. When it had ended, the monks informed him that they would now ordain him, but he told them he was no longer interested – it seems he had taken offence to their earlier refusal. Hearing about the rule and her nephew's response to it, Visākhā remarked: "When is it not a good time to go to the Dhamma?" The Buddha came to hear of this incident and what Visākhā had said about it – that there is no time when the Dhamma cannot or should not be practiced – and it affected him enough to tell the monks that they had been wrong to make such a rule, and he then rescinded it.[35] Visākhā's remark fitted well with the Buddha's idea about holy days, that to the pure, every day is, or should be considered, a holy day.[36]

The Buddha did not expound a set of moral principles and philosophical ideas and leave it at that. His Dhamma was meant to be a program of personal training and transformation. The whole of this Dhamma was encapsulated into what he called the Four Noble Truths (*cattāri ariyasaccāni*): suffering; the cause of suffering; the freedom from suffering; and the way to become free from suffering. The word usually translated as suffering is *dukkha* and means more than just physical and psychological pain. It includes the incompleteness, inadequate and jarring nature of ordinary life, the fact that even our pleasant experiences are never fully satisfying or lasting, and of course that death is waiting for us – if not now, then some way further down the road.

The first three Noble Truths encapsulated how the Buddha understood and explained the world, while the fourth was what he taught his disciples to do about it. He called this fourth one the Noble

34. Vin.I,291.
35. Vin.I,153.
36. M.I,39.

Eightfold Path (*ariya aṭṭhaṅgika magga*): a "path" because one journeys along it from a point of departure (ordinary conditioned existence) to a terminus (unconditioned peace and freedom). Having traversed this path himself, the Buddha was the unrivalled guide and teacher for those who had embarked on it. But being such a teacher required a range of skills: tact and discernment; empathy; patience; and, at times, firmness – all traits the Buddha exhibited in his dealings with his disciples. The Tipitaka is replete with examples of the Buddha as "an unsurpassed guide for those to be trained" (*anuttaro purisa damma sārathi satthā*).

Once, a monk found an animal caught in a trap and, feeling compassion for the poor creature, released it. Conventional opinion was that such an animal would be the property of the person who set the trap, and when some other monks came to know what this monk had done, they accused him of theft. When consulted on this matter, the Buddha opined that, as the monk had acted out of compassion, he could not be accused of stealing.[37] In a related incident, the monk Pilindavaccha used his psychic powers to rescue two children who had been kidnapped by bandits and returned them safely to their parents. The more rigid and literal-minded monks accused him of breaking the rule against displaying any psychic powers one might develop, but again the Buddha exonerated Pilindavaccha because he had acted out of compassion and possibly saved the lives of two little children.[38]

Impressed with how the Buddha explained his Dhamma, the senior and learned brahmin Soṇadaṇḍa expressed his desire to become a disciple, and the Buddha accepted him. Then he confided in the Buddha that becoming one of his disciples raised a potential problem for him. If in public he was to give the conventional marks of respect to the Buddha that a disciple would normally give to one's teacher, his brahmin colleagues would spurn him, his reputation amongst them would suffer, and, as Soṇadaṇḍa admitted, "if a man's reputation suffers, his income suffers also." He therefore asked if it would be acceptable that, rather than standing up when the Buddha entered an assembly, he would just give the añjali salute and consider it as equivalent as if he had stood up. Always gracious and probably

37. Vin.III,62.
38. Vin.III,66.

with an understanding of and sympathy for Soṇadaṇḍa's predicament, the Buddha found this arrangement quite acceptable.[39]

The monk Tissa, one of the Buddha's kinsmen, had the irritating habit of dispensing advice to others while getting annoyed if he was given advice. This made him unpopular with his fellow, and the continual taunts and chiding they directed towards him eventually brought him to tears. He tried hard to change but without success, and he grew despondent, started to doubt the effectiveness of the Dhamma and even think of leaving the Saṅgha. Informed of this, the Buddha asked him some questions about the Dhamma, saying "Good, good, Tissa! That is correct!" to each of his replies as an encouragement. Then he told Tissa that it was his attitude that had caused his problems, and thus it was up to him to change. He finished by promising Tissa his personal help and guidance: "Be of good cheer, Tissa, be of good cheer. I am here to encourage, I am here to help, I am here to instruct!"[40] These words renewed Tissa's commitment to keep trying, and eventually he attained awakening.

It is interesting to compare this with how the Buddha helped the monk Soṇa, whose problem was not doubt or lack of drive but too much energy. Determined to attain awakening, Soṇa over-exerted himself and ended up exhausted and frustrated. Knowing that he had been an accomplished musician in his lay life, the Buddha asked him:

> "Tell me, Soṇa—before you left your home, is it not so that you were skilled in playing the veena?"
>
> "Yes sir."
>
> "What do you think? When its strings were too tight or too loose, was your veena well-tuned and easy to play?"
>
> "No sir."

---

39. D.I,125-126. Soṇadaṇḍa was not his personal name but a moniker indicating that he used a staff made of wood from the soṇa tree, *Oroxylum indicum*. Amongst brahmins, staffs had great ritual significance and had to be made from very specific types of wood, mainly *palāsa*, *bilva* and *udumbara*, see Dhammika 2018b. However, I have found no references to soṇa wood being used. On the rules pertaining to making and using staffs in Brahminism, see *Śāṅkhāyana Gṛhyasūtra* 2.1.18-24 and *Gautama Dharmasūtra* 1. 22-26.

40. S.III,106-109.

> "Then when the strings were neither too tight nor too loose but tightened in a balanced way, was the veena then playable?"
>
> "Yes sir."
>
> "So too, if energy is excessive it leads to restlessness and if deficient it leads to weariness. Therefore, Soṇa, let your energy be balanced, your sense organs be unperturbed and maintain that place in the middle."[41]

The popular image of the Buddha as someone who never challenged or contradicted anyone or remonstrated with them does not accord with the portrait of him in the Tipitaka. He compared himself to a horse trainer who uses a combination of gentle and hard methods (*saṇha* and *pharusa*) to bring out the best in his charges.[42] By "hard" he did not of course mean corporal punishment but verbal chastisement and, as a last resort for monks and nuns, expulsion from the monastic Saṅgha. When once asked if he could ever say anything that might upset someone, the Buddha acknowledged that he could but added that, if he had to, his motive would always be compassion for the person, and he would pick the right time to say it.[43]

The monk Ariṭṭha somehow got it into his head that free indulgence in sensual pleasures would not be a hindrance to spiritual progress, despite what the Buddha had taught on this matter. When this came to the Buddha's notice, he called for Ariṭṭha to come and see him and then straightened him out in no uncertain terms:

> "Stupid man! Have you ever known me to teach something like that? Stupid man! In many talks have I not explained that blockages lead to much suffering and distress for a long time for one who indulges in them? ...But you, stupid man that you are, have misrepresented me by your wrong grasp of things and thereby have harmed yourself and stored up much demerit."[44]

Sāriputta and Moggallāna once arrived at the outskirts of the Sakyan town of Cātumā leading a large group of recently ordained

41. A.III,374-375.
42. A.II,112.
43. M.I,393.
44. M.I,132.

young monks. The Buddha happened to be in the town too and was alerted to the new arrivals by the loud noise they were making. He sent someone with a message asking the monks to come before him, and when they came he asked them: "Monks, why are you being so loud and noisy? You sound like fishermen hauling in nets full of fish." The monks explained that they were arranging their accommodation and chatting with the monks already in town – an explanation that did not satisfy the Buddha – and he said: "Be gone, monks! I dismiss you. You cannot stay with me." The thoroughly chastened youngsters took their gear and departed. It happened that the elders of Cātumā were gathered in their assembly hall and, seeing the monks leaving, asked them why. Hearing what had happened and feeling sorry for them, the elders went to see the Buddha to speak to him on the monks' behalf:

> "Sir, let the Lord be pleased with, welcoming to and indulgent towards the Saṅgha as he used to be. They are young, recently ordained, newly come to the Dhamma and the training. If they do not get to see the Lord, they may change and fall away, as a seedling will if it does not get water or a calf if it does not see its mother."

These sentiments mollified the Buddha, and with his permission the monks went back to their accommodation, no doubt much quieter this time.[45]

There were four offences for which a monk would be expelled from the Saṅgha and never be readmitted: sexual intercourse; theft; murder or abetment to murder; and falsely claiming to have attained an exalted spiritual state.[46] Only rarely did the Buddha give up on a disciple and expel him or her for some lesser offence or behaviour. Once, some monks were reproving one of their number for an offence he had committed but adamantly refused to admit to. When questioned, he evaded answering, became annoyed and persistently maintained his innocence despite the evidence. The Buddha happened to walk in

45. M.I,457-459.

46. There were an extra four offences for nuns: allowing a male to fondle her anywhere from the shoulder to the knee; concealing the most serious offence of another nun; becoming the follower of a monk who has been suspended; and engaging in eight types of flirtatious activities.

while this inquiry was taking place and, after watching it for a while and deciding the monk was not genuinely interested in learning or changing, said sharply: "Monks! Remove this person, throw him out, expel him! Why should you let other people annoy you?"[47]

It should not be taken from this that monks and nuns were always breaking the rules or that the Buddha was constantly watching and checking up on them. Once, he told his senior monks that they should not discipline newcomers for every minor disciplinary infraction, especially if their faith and goodwill were not yet fully developed. To do so would only dishearten them, destroy the good qualities they already had and drive them away. Rather, the seniors should treat the novices the way the loved ones of a man with one eye would behave towards him, doing everything they could to ensure that his remaining eye was protected and did not deteriorate.[48] When miscreants admitted their wrongdoing, showed genuine contrition and asked to be pardoned, the Buddha would overlook their foolishness or bad behaviour, saying to them:

> "Truly you have done wrong, foolish, confused and inept as you are. But since you acknowledge your mistake for what it is and make amends for it in accordance with the Dhamma, I forgive you for it. To see a mistake for what it is, to make amends for it and to try to refrain from it in the future is considered progress in the training of the noble ones."[49]

47. A.IV,169.
48. M.I,444.
49. S. II,128 also S.II,205, condensed.

11
The Buddha on Worldly Matters

It was mentioned in the Introduction that most biographies of the Buddha devote more space to describing his teaching than they do to recounting his personal characteristics and the events in his life. But even then, of his teachings, more emphasis is given to what might be called the deeper and more philosophical ones. This is only to be expected, as such teachings form the central focus of his understanding of reality. Nonetheless, it also means that other things the Buddha taught receive little or no attention, and as a result, he is often perceived as a profound thinker but one who promulgated a rarefied philosophy exclusively focused on liberation, directed to a small elite and which had little impact on or relevance to the wider society. The Buddha said that he taught *only*[1] suffering and the ending of suffering. But while the cause and cure of suffering is the *raison d'être* of the Dhamma, even a brief perusal of his discourses will reveal that the Buddha actually commented on, expressed opinions about and recommended a wide range of attitudes and behaviours relevant to anybody, whether monastic or lay, whether living in India in the fifth century BCE or in twenty-first century Europe, Australasia or America.

There were two characteristics of the Buddha's Dhamma that he emphasised repeatedly. The first is that he meant it to be "for the welfare of the many" (*bahujana hitāya*), not just for monastics but for anyone trying to navigate their way through the confusion, pitfalls and temptations of ordinary life. The second was that he saw his teaching as being "a gradual training, a gradual doing, a gradual path" (*anupubba sikkhā, anupubba kiriyā, anupubba paṭipadā*).[2] He was sensitive to the

1. M.I,140. *Eva* here could also be 'just' or 'simply'.
2. M.I,479.

fact that people have different levels of understanding and different abilities, and thus the Dhamma should include initial goals which could serve as a preparation for the highest and ultimate goal – the peace and freedom of Nirvana. The concept of a gradual path also became more meaningful in the light of his concept of rebirth. In theistic faiths, if one has not done what is necessary for salvation before dying, the portals of heaven are closed forever. The reality of rebirth by contrast, means that if full awakening, or even some of the higher spiritual states, have not been realized in the present life, there always remains the opportunity of doing so in the next life or in the one after that.

The Buddha's preliminary teachings are important in themselves but also because they offer further insight into his persona and his attitudes to and outlook on a variety of matters. What follows will be a look at a selection of these. The Buddha may have acquired some of these attitudes and outlooks from his upbringing, others from the society in which he lived, and still others may have been formed from the insights that were a result of his awakening experience.

Because the Buddha made suffering the starting point of his whole philosophy, some have taken this to mean that he regarded human life as characterised by disappointment and misery, in which happiness was virtually unattainable. This rather naïve view could only be the result of a superficial understanding of the Buddha's Dhamma. The Buddha was a more insightful thinker than some of his critics give him credit for, and he readily acknowledged the positive in the world. For him, physical and psychological dissatisfaction, stress and suffering were an inevitable part of ordinary life, a view that any realistic and aware person would have to agree with. He noticed that, in trying to avoid or mitigate this suffering, humans scramble to experience as much pleasure and happiness as possible, often only aggravating their own suffering or inflicting it on others in the process – thus, the primacy of his analysis of suffering, its causes, and the consequences of craving for pleasure.

But this emphasis on suffering did not blind the Buddha to the many opportunities that life offers for happiness and fulfilment and the importance of such occasions. "If there was no satisfaction in the world, beings would not fall in love with it."[3] And again: "I set out to

3. A.I,260.

find the satisfaction offered by the world, and I found it. But having clearly seen it with wisdom, I also know its limitations in the world."[4] The word here translated as satisfaction is *assāda*, which can mean enjoyment, fulfilment, gratification, even sweetness. Accepting that many people were going to live 'in the world', at least in their present lives, the Buddha took this into account in his Dhamma and offered sound, practical and realistic advice on how to do so righteously and in ways that delivered happiness without disadvantaging others.

The advice the Buddha gave concerning material wealth is a good example of this. Among the types of happiness he considered to be worthwhile and legitimate were the happiness of ownership (*atthisukha*), the happiness of wealth (*bhogasukha*), and the happiness of being free from debt (*anaṇasukha*):

> "The person who accumulates wealth lawfully and without harming others and, in doing so, makes himself happy and fulfilled, shares it with others, does good works, makes use of it without greed or infatuation, aware of its limitations and keeping in mind his own spiritual growth, is praiseworthy on all these counts."[5]

Thus wealthy individuals can be praiseworthy (*pāsaṁsa*) according to how they have made their wealth, how they utilize it, and the attitude they have towards it. His disciples should, he recommended, acquire wealth "by hard work, by strength of arm and sweat of brow, honestly and lawfully," i.e., by moral means, within the limits of the law (*dhammena*), and in ways that do not exploit or disadvantage others (*asāhasena*).[6] Secondly, they should use their wealth meaningfully, so that it gives them, their families, and friends and associates some level of enjoyment (*attānaṁ sukheti pīṇeti*).[7] Doing good works, the third of these criteria, involved giving alms to ascetics and religious teachers but also to "the disadvantaged, the poor, the homeless and beggars" (*kapaṇaddhika-vaṇibbaka-yācakānaṃ*).[8] Included in good works also,

4. A.I,259.
5. A.V,181, condensed.
6. A.V,181.
7. A.III,45.
8. It.65.

the Buddha said, were projects for the general good, such as planting trees, digging wells and constructing bridges and wayside rest houses.[9]

The Buddha recommended that a prudent disciple should try to maintain a balance in life (*samaṃ jīvikaṃ*), so that his or her expenditure did not exceed income, and avoid both extravagance and tight-fisted frugality.[10] He also counselled dividing one's income into four and using one part for basic needs, two parts for work, by either investing it or putting it back into one's business, and keeping one part aside for future eventualities.[11]

One of the negative sides of wealth that the Buddha noticed and cautioned against was its tendency to make the people who had it proud and complacent, especially if they have acquired it suddenly or with little effort. He observed: "Few are the people in the world who, when they acquire great wealth, do not get carried away by it, become negligent, chase after sensual pleasures and mistreat others."[12] Thus he warned the comfortably well-off to reflect on the limitations of their wealth (*ādīnavadassāvī*). They should, he said, keep in mind that while money can give so much in some areas, it cannot deliver some of the most important things in life, and this should encourage them to see their wealth as a means to an end rather than an end in itself. They should also consider that there are other types of wealth, of greater value and accessible to everyone, that can never be stolen or lost and that can be taken into the next life: "There are these five types of wealth. What five? The wealth of faith, the wealth of virtue, the wealth of learning, the wealth of generosity and the wealth of wisdom."[13] Whoever is rich in these and other kinds of spiritual treasures, he said, "whether they be a man or a woman, they are not poor and neither are their lives empty."[14]

Another type of happiness the Buddha frequently gave attention to was that associated with family life, the basis of which is marriage.

---

9. S.I,33.
10. A.IV,282.
11. D.III,188. Ja. I,277 gives an alternative four; one part for food, one held in reserve, one to invest in one's business and one for charity and good works.
12. S.I,74.
13. A.III,53.
14. A.IV,5.

Amongst higher castes at the time, arranging with a girl's parents to marry her off without consulting her, and even buying a wife, was not unusual. The Buddha criticised brahmins for doing this rather than the couple "coming together out of love for each other and abiding in harmony" (*sampiyenan'eva saṃvāsaṃ saṃaggatthāya sampavattenti*), which he obviously considered to be a far better motive for marriage.[15]

He believed that if a husband and wife loved each other deeply and had similar kamma, they may be able to renew their relationship in the next life.[16] The ideal Buddhist couple would be Nakulapitā and Nakulamātā, who were devoted disciples of the Buddha and who had been happily married for many years. Once, Nakulapitā said to the Buddha in his wife's presence: "Lord, ever since Nakulamātā was brought to my home when I was a mere boy and she a mere girl, I have never been unfaithful to her, not even in thought, let alone in body."[17] On another occasion, his wife Nakulamātā devotedly nursed him through a long illness, encouraging and reassuring him all the while. When the Buddha came to know of this, he said to Nakulapitā: "You have benefitted, good sir, you have greatly benefitted in having Nakulamātā, full of compassion for you, full of love for you, as your mentor and teacher."[18] From the Buddha's perspective, these qualities would be the recipe for an enduring and enriching relationship: faithfulness; mutual love; compassion; and learning the Dhamma together.

Apart from the bonds of love and affection, the Buddha offered advice on other matters that make for a successful marriage. A couple who are following the Dhamma should, he said, "speak loving words to each other" (*aññamaññaṃ piyaṃvādā*).[19] The husband, for his part, should honour and respect his wife, never disparage her, be faithful to her, give her authority in the household, and provide for her financially. The wife should do her work properly, manage the servants, be faithful to her husband, protect the family income, and be skilled and diligent in household management.[20]

15. A.III,222.
16. A.II,61-2.
17. A.II,61.
18. A.III,295-8.
19. A.II,59.
20. D.III,190.

When discussing parents and children, the Buddha again recognized the central role of love and the happiness it brings with it: "Love of one's mother and love of one's father is true happiness in the world."[21] He said that children should love, respect and honour their parents "because mothers and fathers do much for their children: they bring them up, nourish them, and introduce them to the world."[22] The minds of parents thus honoured and cherished will have "beautiful thoughts and compassion towards their children and will wish them well, saying, 'May you live long!', so that they shall not decline but flourish."[23] Apart from loving and caring for their offspring, the Buddha said that loving parents will "restrain their children from wrong, encourage them to do good, give them an education, provide them with a suitable marriage partner and leave them an inheritance."[24]As if to emphasize the blessing of gratitude, he asserted that it is impossible for children to repay their parents for all they have done for them. Then he added this proviso: "But whoever encourages their unbelieving parents to believe, their immoral parents to become moral or their ignorant parents to become wise, such a one, by so doing, does repay, does more than repay, their parents."[25]

Other than the names of his mother, stepmother and father and a few other minor details, we know nothing about Gotama's upbringing, what his relationship with his parents and kin was like and, later, whether or not his marriage was a successful one. His renunciation cannot be taken as evidence that his home life was unfulfilling, as some have claimed. Rather, it was motivated by a deep desire to soar upwards from the mundane to the spiritual, something even the happiest individuals are sometimes inspired to do, even if it means leaving their family. The Buddha's comments on and advice about conjugal, parental and filial love point to him coming from a home in which love and affection were strong.

As can be seen from above, the Buddha wanted his lay disciples to participate in and benefit from the good and wholesome things that

---

21. Dhp.332; Sn.262; 404; S.I,181-182.
22. A.II,70.
23. A.III,76-77.
24. D.III,189.
25. A.I,61.

the world had to offer. But at the same time, he encouraged them to stand back from the trivialities, distractions and the pitfalls common to many social activities. He had a definite prudish side to his nature, although without being judgmental and self-righteous. He counselled his disciples to avoid idle chatter, joking, drinking and gambling, laziness, getting up late, being out late, and various forms of light entertainment. This was especially true for monks and nuns:

> "Monks, in the training of the worthy ones, singing is wailing, dancing is derangement, and laughing so much that it shows the teeth is infantile. Therefore, do away with singing and dancing, although it is acceptable to give a smile if the Dhamma makes you glad."[26]

Once, he told his son Rāhula never to say anything untrue, even as a joke.[27] These words make sense given that the monastic vocation is a serious one dedicated to attaining a state beyond the inadequacies and limitations of conditioned existence in the present life: "Why this laughter and delight when the world is on fire? Shrouded in darkness, will you not seek the light?"[28] There may have also been practical reasons for such recommendations. The Buddha was anxious that lay people's estimation of his monks remained high so as to attract support, and monastics who gave the impression of being earnest, grave and uninterested in social events would be more likely to foster this. During Rājagaha's annual Hilltop Festival, some people noticed a group of monks watching the festivities and commented that they were little different from ordinary lay people. When these comments were reported back to the Buddha, he made it a rule that monks should avoid festivals and fairs.[29]

The Buddha had a similar message for lay people, although for different reasons. He considered alcohol to be so negative that he made abstaining from it one of the Five Precepts. The reasons he gave for this were that drinking wastes money; leads to arguments, sickness, a bad reputation, public humiliation (falling down and exposing

---

26. A.I,261; Sn.328; 926.
27. M.I,415.
28. Dhp.146.
29. Vin.II,107.

one's genitals); and impaired cognitive abilities.[30] He also disparaged games of chance, although he did not include betting in the Precepts. With a sharp eye for the social realities of gambling, the Buddha laid out the problems associated with it: the winner is resented; the loser bemoans his loss; it results in financial problems; gamblers are considered untrustworthy; friends avoid gamblers because they are always asking to borrow money; and no parents will allow their child to marry a gambler.[31] It should be noted that in ancient India the negative consequences of compulsive gambling went far beyond such problems. Men could and sometimes did wager their wives, children and even themselves, and if they lost, they or their family would be enslaved until the debt was paid.[32] The Buddha's assessment of excessive drinking and compulsive gambling highlights his concern about their impact on individuals and on the society in general. Nearly all the negative consequences he mentioned would be familiar to modern social scientists, psychologists and criminologists, and one would not have to be a killjoy to disapprove of such activities.

However, the Buddha also had a poor opinion of what many might consider innocent entertainment. "There are six disadvantages of frequenting festivals. One is always thinking, 'Where's the dancing and the singing? Where's the music and the recitals? Where's the hand-clapping and the drums?'"[33] He observed that rowdy entertainment (*visūkadassana*) was counterproductive for anyone wishing to prepare their mind for meditation.[34] Perhaps he also thought that serious and sincere lay disciples could spend their time better than attending such events. On the other hand, his disapproval may have been because some of the things that took place at such gatherings included animal fights, ribald shows, heavy drinking, over-eating and flirting. The manager of a theatrical troupe mentioned to the Buddha that he had been told that old thespians go to the heaven of the mirthful gods when they die, and he asked the Buddha what he thought of this. The Buddha tried to avoid answering, but when the manager kept pressing him, he

30. D.III,182-183.
31. D.III,183; A.I,212.
32. M.III,170.
33. D.III,183.
34. A.V,134.

finally did. He said that the emotions actors evoke in audiences – lust, anger, titillation, outrage, sadness, excitement, etc. – and which they themselves try to absorb themselves in as they act, meant that they were more likely to go to the purgatory of mirth after death. At this, the poor manager burst into tears.[35]

One thing that set the Buddha apart from the majority of his contemporaries was his attitude to the ubiquitous popular superstitious beliefs and practices of the time. In one discourse he catalogued a large number of what he called "animal arts" (*tiracchāna vijjā*), saying that he would never be involved with such things and neither should his monastics. Some of these included palmistry; predicting good or bad rainfall; selecting lucky sites for buildings; reading the future by means of the movement of the heavenly bodies or eclipses; practicing black magic and quack medicine; casting spells; and calling on various gods for favours, especially Śri, the goddess of good luck.[36] When he said that his disciples should not chant magic charms, interpret dreams and signs, or practice astrology, he was probably addressing his monks and nuns.[37] But he warned his lay followers off such things too, saying that those who made a living by fortune telling would join executioners, butchers, slanderers and corrupt judges in being reborn in very unenviable circumstances.[38] A person who practiced such things would be, he said, "the outcast, the stain, the dregs of the lay community."[39] When once asked what the most efficacious lucky sign, auspicious omen or blessing ceremony (*maṅgala*) would be, he replied by recounting a long list of good deeds, wholesome attitudes and enriching relationships. This is yet another example of him giving a new, usually ethical, meaning to old beliefs and practices.[40]

---

35. S.IV,306-307. The Buddha's low opinion of the theatre and actors put him in very good company. See Jonas Barish's *The Anti-theatrical Prejudice*,1981.
36. D.I,8-11. See also Sn.927 and S.III,238-239. The rule against practicing such things is at Vin.II,139.
37. Sn.927. Magic charms here is *āthabbaṇa*, which refers to the spells and sorcery of the *Atharvaveda*.
38. S.II,255-266.
39. A.III,206.
40. Sn.258-267.

The Buddha even discouraged what might be considered harmless superstitions and folk beliefs. Once, while giving a sermon, he sneezed, and a loud chorus of 'Live long!' (*jīvatu*) rose from the audience to which the usual response was 'Same to you!' (*paṭijīva*). Ever the rationalist, he momentarily deviated from the gist of his sermon and asked whether a person's lifespan is lengthened by saying 'Live long!' when they sneeze. The audience admitted that it does not, and so he asked them to refrain from doing such a thing in the future.[41]

The Buddha's disapproval of popular beliefs, customs and superstitions was probably because, in one way or another, they contradict or claim to be able to circumvent kamma, the idea that a person's state in the present and destiny in the future is conditioned by the moral quality of their intentional actions – physical, verbal and psychological. He must have also been aware of the cheating and charlatanism associated with such practices.

In ancient India there was a good deal of overlap between popular superstitions and psychic abilities, and while the Buddha had an unambiguous dislike of the former, his attitude towards the latter was one of cautious acceptance. Before examining the reason for this, it is necessary to clarify a few things. Miracles (*pāṭihāriya*) are usually thought of as being caused by or connected in some way with supernatural beings – gods or spirits of different kinds, either benign or malign. However, some of what many people then took to be miraculous the Buddha understood to be an outcome or a by-product of mental development, particularly intense meditation. Thus in the Buddhist context it is more appropriate to speak of psychic powers (*iddhi*) than miracles. The Buddha freely acknowledged that some of the ascetics of his time possessed psychic powers as a result of spiritual discipline. They might well have misinterpreted the significance of such powers or drawn wrong conclusions from them, but he rejected the claim that the person manifesting them had been blessed by some god or was being used by the forces of evil. Nonetheless, he was generally cool towards all claims of superhuman abilities.

Someone once asked him to get one of his monks to "demonstrate a superhuman ability, a psychic feat or a miracle, so that even more

41. Vin.II,140; Ja.II,15.

people will have faith in you." He replied that there were such powers which thoughtful or skeptical people would have legitimate doubts about. There was, however, one such power that everyone could have confidence in: what he called the psychic power or miracle of instruction (*anusāsana*). This consisted, he said, of encouraging others to be observant, to think and behave in certain ways, and to persist in doing it over a period of time.[42]

On another occasion, a wealthy merchant had a valuable sandalwood bowl placed on the top of a bamboo pole, which was then erected in the centre of the town. He then had a proclamation made to the effect that anyone who could rise to the top of the pole through psychic power could have the bowl. The monk Piṇḍola heard of this and, having manifested the ability to levitate, he took up the challenge and retrieved the bowl. When the Buddha came to know of this, he rebuked the monk in the strongest terms: "You are like a prostitute who lifts her dress for the sake of a miserable coin." Then he made it an offence for monks or nuns to display any psychic abilities they might develop. What happened subsequent to Piṇḍola's spectacular demonstration helps to explain the Buddha's reaction to it: "Noisy, excited crowds began following Piṇḍola around."[43] The Buddha wanted people to respect him and his monks and nuns because of their virtue and wisdom, not because they were mesmerized by what they took to be unusual or miraculous powers.

Another problem associated with the demonstrating of superhuman abilities is the broadcasting of extravagant claims, and even lies, that ultimately cannot be substantiated. A naked ascetic named Pāṭikaputta, who had a reputation for possessing miraculous powers and received generous patronage because of it, threw down this challenge at an assembly in Vesālī:

> "The samaṇa Gotama claims to be a man of wisdom, and I make this same claim. It is only right that a man of wisdom should prove it by performing a psychic wonder. If he comes half way, I will come the other half, and having met, we can both perform a wonder. If he performs one, I will perform two; if he performs two, I will perform four; and if he performs four, I will perform

42. D.I,211 ff.
43. Vin.II,110-111.

> eight. No matter how many psychic wonders the samaṇa Gotama performs, I will perform double that."[44]

In the end, Pāṭikaputta failed to turn up at the appointed time, and nothing came of his challenge.

The Buddhist tradition has long pointed out that miraculous powers should not be taken as evidence of spiritual or even moral accomplishments. As far as the Buddha was concerned, miracles were one thing, and the Dhamma was something else entirely. He said: "Whether superhuman abilities, psychic feats or miracles are performed or not, my purpose in teaching the Dhamma is to lead whoever practices it to the complete freedom from suffering. In which case, what is the point of performing miracles?"[45]

The Buddha's attitude to caste (*vaṇṇa*) was another area which put him at odds with many in his society, although other samaṇa sects, particularly Jainism, shared his view of the matter. The caste system as it existed in the sixth and fifth century BCE was not as rigid or all-embracing as it later became, but it created a sense of superiority and entitlement in one group and oppressed another in numerous ways. The Vedas teach that humans were created by the god Pajāpati as four distinct types according to which parts of his body he made them from, but a few centuries before the Buddha, a new god, Brahmā, was being credited with having done this. The young Vedic scholar Assalāyana gave orthodox Brahminism's view on caste during a discussion he had with the Buddha: "Brahmins are the superior caste, other castes are low; they are fair, other castes are dark; they are pure, other castes are impure. Brahmins are the offspring of Brahmā, born of his mouth, created by Brahmā and the heirs of Brahmā."[46] Concurrent with this was the doctrine that each caste had a divinely ordained position and role in society. The brahmin Esukārī explained it like this:

> "We brahmins assert that a brahmin can serve a brahmin, a noble can serve a brahmin, a merchant can serve a brahmin and a menial can serve a brahmin. A noble can serve a noble, a merchant can and a menial can. A merchant can serve a

44. D.III,12-17.
45. D.III, 4.
46. M.II,149.

merchant and a menial can too. But only a menial can serve a menial, for who else could?"[47]

In short, brahmins are superior to all other castes, and menials are inferior to all other castes.

The only significant social division the Buddha accepted was that of householders (*gahapati*) and home leavers (*pabbajita*), i.e., monastics. Neither of these states were determined by any supposed divine design or innate quality but by one's lifestyle and life goal, and rather than being fixed, as caste was, a person could choose to move from one to another. The Buddha was sometimes said by others to have been of the warrior caste, which technically he was, but after his awakening, he did not identify himself as such. When once asked what his background was, he replied: "I am not a brahmin, a warrior or a merchant, for indeed I am not anything."[48] As far as he was concerned, talk about who was or was not worthy, their birth, clan or status (*jāti*, *gotta*, *māna*), might be taken into account when selecting a marriage partner, but would be irrelevant when it came to things that really mattered, i.e., attaining the highest knowledge and conduct (*anuttara vijjā caraṇa*).[49]

The Buddha criticized the caste system on a number of grounds. The claim that it was ordained by a supreme being is nothing but a myth. When the Buddha was told by a brahmin that brahmins were born from Brahmā's mouth, he quipped that it was an observable fact that they were born from their mother's womb just like everyone else.[50] He pointed out that, in Yona, Kamboja and adjacent lands, there was no caste and thus that it is a regional custom rather than a universal and natural reality.[51] The claim that different castes have innate abilities and

47. M.II,177-178. *Manusmṛti* 8,413-414 says: "The menial was created by the Self-Existent One only to labour as a slave for the brahmin. Even if he is manumitted by his master, a menial is still a slave, for that is his nature, and no one can change that."

48. Sn.455.

49. D.I,99.

50. M.II,148. See Malalasekera and Jayatilleke, pp.40 ff.

51. M.II,149. Yona was the Indian name for Greece and for Greeks who had migrated to Gandhāra in India's north-western border regions. A few such immigrants may well have gone further east of this too. The Buddha's mention of Yona has been taken as proof that the discourse in which he used the word

personalities is not borne out by experience and is thus invalid.[52] The Buddha acknowledged that the menial caste and outcastes may be dirty because they are compelled to do dirty jobs, but they could wash the dirt off and be as clean as anyone else.[53] At the same time, he said that the brahmin assertion to be 'pure' did not accord with the known fact that some brahmins had mixed-caste ancestors. The Buddha further observed that the supposed divine origin of caste was even contradicted by practical, economic and political realities. A king wanting to beef up his defence capabilities would recruit soldiers according to their skill and strength, whatever their caste. An outcaste who managed to become wealthy could employ a desperately poor brahmin and compel him to wait on him, serve him, and do his bidding. Further, even an eminent brahmin would only be granted an audience with a king if he was separated from the royal presence by a curtain.[54]

From the Buddha's perspective, if differences were made between people, it should be based on their ethically significant behaviour and the depth of their wisdom, not on arbitrary societal or theological categories which were only man-made:

> "I will explain to you, in the proper order and according to fact, the distinction between beings, because there are many different species. Of the grass and the trees, insects, quadrupeds large and small, reptiles, fish and birds, there are many different

---

must date from after Alexander's invasion of India in 326 BCE. But that there were Greeks in Gandhāra before Alexander is almost certain. The Achaemenid Empire stretched from Asia Minor to western India, and Greeks in the service of the empire and intrepid merchants moved freely through it. The first Greek known to have visited India was *Skylax* of Karyanda who, in 520 BCE, led a naval expedition from Punjab to the mouth of the Indus. Hekataios of Miletos (549–486 BCE) and Herodotus (484-425 BCE) both wrote about India and probably got some of their information from Greeks who had first-hand knowledge of the country. It is also likely that Indians from the Middle Land travelled to Gandhāra and brought back stories about Greeks and their customs and that their attitude to caste became a talking point and came to the notice of the Buddha. See Anālayo 2011, p.551-552.

52. M.II,150; Sn.116.
53. M.II,151.
54. S.I,100; M.II,85; D.I,103.

species. The characteristics that distinguish one species from another are many, but amongst humans there is no difference in their characteristics. Not in hair, head, ears or eyes, not in neck, shoulders, belly, back, buttocks or breast, not in genitals male or female, not in hands, feet, fingers or nails, not in calves, thighs, colour or voice is there any difference as there is in other beings. Although separate [in some ways], the bodies of humans are the same. The differences that are spoken of are only conventional."[55]

Some who have commented on the Buddha's attitude to caste have pointed out that he was not a reformer who tried to abolish it, and this is quite correct. He had neither the power nor the means to initiate such a reform. But where he did have influence, within his monastic Saṅgha, he made it clear that caste had no place. This did not mean that entrenched prejudices simply disappeared when someone donned the tawny robe. Incidents of monks sniggering about and disparaging their fellows because of their caste, clan or family background sometimes happened and required the Buddha to enact a rule forbidding it.[56] But his arguments against caste were widely known and must have had some effect. One observer commented:

"Just as great rivers such as the Ganges and Yamuna, Aciravatī, Sarabhū and the Mahī lose their names and identities when they reach the great ocean and become just 'great ocean', like that, on leaving their homes and entering the Dhamma and training taught by the Tathāgata, warriors, brahmins, merchants and menials lose their names and identities and become just 'sons of the Sakyan.'"[57]

So the Buddha's rejection of and criticism of caste undermined its legitimacy and, for several centuries at least, weakened its influence. In India today, marginalized castes and untouchables are inspired by the Buddha's teachings to agitate for equality and justice.

---

55. Sn.600-611, condensed. The word translated here as 'conventional' is *samaññā* which the *Pali English Dictionary* gives as designation, name, common appellation, popular expression.

56. Vin.IV,4.

57. Ud.55. Mahī was probably the old name for the Gandak, see Hoey pp.44-46.

Slavery was as common and accepted in India during the Buddha's time as it was almost everywhere else, and it overlapped with the caste system. There were a variety of ways a person could become enslaved: being born to an enslaved mother; being purchased; being captured in war; and becoming enslaved voluntarily, e.g., to escape famine.[58] The Buddha was quite aware of the cruelty associated with slavery, apart from the slave's loss of freedom. He mentioned an incident he had heard about where a woman who was usually placid and gentle beat her slave girl for getting up late, and he was sensitive to the feeling of relief and joy a slave would feel on being manumitted.[59] He said a man should look after his employees and slaves, by not working them beyond their capacity and providing them with sufficient food and proper medical care when sick.[60] Whether such exhortations made any difference to the slaves' lot is hard to say. He considered it inappropriate for his monks and nuns to accept gifts of slaves, and it is likely that he took into consideration the problems and complications of having slaves – the coercion required to get them to work, retrieving them when they ran away, etc. – when he gave this teaching.[61] Nevertheless, the moral flaws of slavery must have been a factor too, as is clear from him calling trade in human beings a wrong means of livelihood, along with selling weapons, meat, poisons and alcohol.[62] The Buddha's prohibition of monastics owning slaves and his discouragement of lay disciples being involved in the slave trade are the earliest known repudiations of this awful institution.

At a time when famines were a recurring phenomenon in India, obtaining food was a serious matter for itinerant ascetics, such as the Buddha, who depended entirely on others for their sustenance. When people hardly had enough food for themselves, they were unlikely to give to others, and so wandering ascetics would typically be the first victims of a famine. The Buddha was well aware of this problem and mentioned those times when "there is a famine, a poor harvest, a time

---

58. Ja.VI, 285; Vin. IV,224.

59. M.I,125; D.I,72-73.

60. D.III,191.

61. D.I,5.

62. A.III,208. Several centuries later, the *Mahāvastu* warned that those who enslave the helpless, put them in manacles, beat them and force them to work will be reborn in a very unpleasant purgatory, Mvu.I, pp.18,22.

when alms food is hard to get, and it is difficult to keep going, even on gleanings."[63] But apart from such concerns, the Buddha was interested in the physical, psychological and social aspects of food – how it was obtained, consumed, and its effects on health.

Extended fasting was a significant aspect of the austerities ascetics would undergo and one that Gotama tried during the time he was searching for the truth. After his awakening, there is no record of him fasting or recommending his disciples to do so. Monks and nuns were expected to abstain from food from noon to sunrise the next day, but this is too short a period to qualify as a fast. Lay disciples were encouraged to do the same twice a month on new and full moon days, the ancient Indian equivalent to the Sabbath. For monastics, at least, the rationale for this rule was health. The Buddha attributed his good health to his practice of not eating in the afternoon or evening.[64]

The Buddha was acutely aware that even sincere monks and nuns could become preoccupied with food and slip into gluttony, which was not a problem unique to monastics either. He even thought that the problem might get out of hand in the future and undermine the integrity of the Saṅgha: "In the future, monks will become obsessed with sumptuous food, savouring the finest delicacies with the tips of their tongues."[65] His discourses are peppered with warnings against a preoccupation with food: "Without filling your stomach, be moderate in food, and have little desire for it."[66] He asked his disciples to quietly recite these words before eating:

> "We will eat in moderation. Reflecting wisely, we will not eat for fun, for amusement or for physical attractiveness but only for the maintenance and continuance of this body, for allaying the pangs of hunger, for assisting in living the holy life and with the thought, 'I will end the old desires and not encourage new ones and thus be healthy, blameless and live comfortably.'"[67]

---

63. A.III,66.
64. M.I,473.
65. A.III,109.
66. Sn.707.
67. M.I,273.

Once, King Pasenadi came to the Buddha bloated and breathing in a laboured manner as a result of having eaten yet another enormous meal. Seeing this, the Buddha commented: "When a person is mindful and thus knows moderation in eating, his ailments diminish, he ages gently, and he protects his life." The king took the hint and asked his nephew to repeat these words to him whenever he was taking his meals. As a result, the king gradually reduced his food intake, lost weight and regained his slim figure.[68] The Buddha's advice to the king, to eat mindfully (*sati*), is only beginning to be recognized by dieticians and weight-loss experts. Eating mindfully helps turn a habituated behaviour into a conscious one, where the possibility of choice is increased. It allows one to pause for a moment, to think about and be aware of what one is about to do and why, and often this is enough to bring about a change in behaviour. Mindfulness can also allow one to notice the urge to eat as it arises and then just watch it with detachment rather than giving in to it.

It is also significant that the Buddha chose to motivate King Pasenadi with a positive rather than a negative message. Instead of regaling him with an account of the problems of obesity, he emphasised the benefits of losing weight: a reduction of bodily ailments (*tanu tassa bhavanti vedanā*); a slowing of the ageing process (*saṇikaṃ jīrati*); and a general enhancement of life (*āyu pālayaṃ*) – all benefits of a healthy weight and diet. The Buddha seems to have known that positive reinforcement can sometimes be more effective in motivating people.

As mentioned previously, the Buddha made suffering (*dukkha*) the central concern of his philosophy – identifying its causes, explaining the means to overcome them, and finally, encouraging the application of those means to one's life. He added to this by saying that suffering could be either physical or psychological, and of the first of these there were eight types, one of them being sickness.[69] It has been claimed that the Buddha taught the notion that anything experienced by individuals, pleasant or unpleasant, is caused by something they did in the past, i.e., their kamma. If true, this would mean that being sick has its origin in some past moral failing. In fact, the Buddha taught no such thing. He

68. S.I,81-82.

69. S.III,1; V,421.

coupled this notion with the equally false one that everything is caused by or under the control of a supreme being, saying that it goes "beyond personal experience and what the world generally holds to be true" (*yaṃ ca sāmaṃ ñātaṃ taṃ ca atidhāvanti yaṃ ca loke saccasammataṃ taṃ ca atidāvanti*), that it is the result of "muddled mindedness" (*muṭṭhassati*), and to refute those who asserted such a notion would be fully justified (*sahadhammika niggaha*).[70] The Buddha recognised a range of things that can cause illness, only one of which was kamma. Some of the others were an imbalance in the bodily humours, changes in the weather, carelessness, accidents, a poor diet and overeating. He also mentioned that certain maladies are specific to certain seasons (*sāradikena abadhena phuṭṭhānaṃ*).[71] Nāgasena summed up the Buddhist position on kamma well when he said: "What happens as a result of kamma is much less than what happens as a result of other causes. The fool goes too far in saying that everything is a result of kamma."[72]

Recognizing sickness as a source of pain and suffering, the Buddha encouraged his disciples to cherish their health and take steps to maintain it. He described being healthy as "having well-being, an even digestion, not overly cold or overly hot but balanced and conducive to striving," and he lauded being healthy as a good fortune (*sampadā*), as something desirables (*kanta*), a great gain (*paramā lābhā*), and a wonderful opportunity to practice the Dhamma.[73] He also saw physical well-being as having an important role in spiritual progress and identified one of the five factors of striving as "being free from illness and affliction."[74] His emphasis on the value of good health meant that from an early period, and for many centuries after, Buddhist monks had a close involvement in medicine and healing.[75]

---

70. A. I,173-174; S.IV,230.
71. S.I,81-82, IV,230; M.I,473; Vin.I,199.
72. Mil. 135-136.
73. A.III,103; 135; V,134; Dhp.204; D.III,235.
74. M.II,95; A.III,65.
75. See Wujastyk 2022 pp.5-7, 18-21, Zysk and Tatz.

12
A Time of Crisis

> There is one thing which when it is present in the world is for the welfare and happiness, the good and the benefit of gods and humans. What is that one thing? It is unity in the Saṅgha.
>
> Itivuttaka 11-12

By the time the Buddha was seventy-five, he had been teaching the Dhamma and guiding the monastic Saṅgha for forty years. He certainly continued teaching until his last days – in fact, until his final hours – but he had probably withdrawn from direct involvement in the monastic Saṅgha, relegating that job to experienced and trusted elder monks. The early decades of his efforts to spread his philosophy had been highly successful: he claimed at one time that he had one thousand two hundred and fifty monk disciples and at another time mentioned that he had many thousands of disciples, monastic and lay.[1] But as is sometimes the case, success brought with it less desirable effects. The Tipitaka contains a noticeably large number of discourses in which the Buddha deplored laxity amongst monks, personal quarrels between them, and most serious of all, disagreements about how his Dhamma should be interpreted. Disagreements about the monastic rules would be, he said, a minor matter (*appamattaka*), but quarrels about the Dhamma would be disastrous.[2] Although it is not possible to know when such problems started to become apparent, one suspects that they did so in the later years of the Buddha's ministry, perhaps during its final decade.

1. D.II, 52; M. I,490 ff.
2. M.II,245.

Early on, the Buddha had the prescience to see that something like this might happen. At one time, he warned of what he called the five dangers that had not yet arisen but which will arise in the future and asked his monks to be alert to them and nip them in the bud before they ruined the Saṅgha. Unsuitable monks, he said, will ordain unsuitable candidates who would gradually corrupt the whole Saṅgha; there will be a general indiscipline, misunderstanding of and confusion about the Dhamma; and monks will become more interested in trivial matters than in spiritual ones and lose their enthusiasm for personal spiritual development.[3]

On one occasion, the Buddha said to Mahā Kassapa: "Either you exhort the monks and teach them the Dhamma, or I will," giving the impression that there were problems which had to be dealt with but which he was reluctant to do himself and hoped that Kassapa would. Somewhat surprisingly, Kassapa declined to help, saying: "At present, the monks are difficult to instruct; they have an attitude that makes them difficult to instruct. They are intransigent and do not accept advice respectfully."[4] The Buddha agreed with this assessment and proceeded to list a range of problems besetting the Saṅgha. From what he said, it would seem that the commitment to the life of simplicity and austerity of the early days had waned amongst some.[5] This was probably not widespread, but it was clearly a noticeable and perhaps growing trend.

The general laxity and misbehaviour required more and more rules to counter them, until there were over two hundred, almost all couched in a negative form, i.e., forbidding monks from doing certain things rather than requiring them to do certain things. Mahā Kassapa had noticed this trend and asked the Buddha why it was that, in the past, there were fewer rules and more worthy ones (*arahants*), whereas now, there were more rules and fewer worthy ones. The Buddha replied: "That is just the way it is, Kassapa. When beings are [morally] declining, and the true Dhamma is disappearing, there

3. A.III,106-108.

4. This was not the only time Kassapa refused a request made by the Buddha, albeit politely, S.II,203-204. There are no other examples of a disciple ever having done this.

5. S.II,208-210.

are more training rules and fewer awakened monks."[6] It is difficult to imagine the Buddha saying this without feelings of sorrow, disappointment or perhaps resignation. There are also comments by older and more senior monks bemoaning the fact that the quality of monks was not as good as it used to be. As will be seen later, shortly after the Buddha died, one monk was actually bold enough to say that his death should not be a cause for sorrow because now he and the others could do what they wanted.[7]

What was responsible for this deplorable decline even before the Buddha had passed away? Paradoxically, one of the reasons may have been the respect that the Buddha and most of his disciples, particularly monks and nuns, had earned from the general public. King Pasenadi mentioned some of the things he noticed about monks that had led him to have such admiration for and confidence in them. They lived together in concord and mutual regard, and they seemed to listen to the Buddha's talks with such attentiveness. They even looked more appealing than some other ascetics:

> "I have gone from one park and garden to another, and some of the samaṇas and brahmins I see look so morose, wretched and thin, their skin ugly and sallow and with protruding veins all over their bodies.[8] Seeing this, I think to myself, 'Either they must be discontented with the life of renunciation, or they are suppressing some evil they did in the past.' They look so wretched and ugly that you would not want to see them again. Once, I asked some of them why they looked like that, and they said, 'It's a sickness that runs in the family.' Then I see the Lord's disciples, and they are happy and cheerful, elated and relaxed, their sense facilities clear, at ease and unruffled, content with what they have and with minds like forest deer."[9]

Such admiration brought with it donations, at first in sufficient amounts, then in abundance, and finally of the best that was available:

---

6. S.II,224.
7. D.II,162.
8. Interestingly, appearing gaunt and having protruding veins were some of the very things the Buddha praised monks for, Dhp.395.
9. M.II,120-121.

robes of silk rather than cast-off rags; comfortable purpose-built accommodations instead of huts of leaves and straw; sumptuous fare, as opposed to scraps collected by alms gathering. There were incidents when the laity "did not take food, hard and soft, or drinks themselves, they did not give it to their parents, spouse or children, not to their slaves, servants or friends, and not to their colleagues or relatives, but they did give it to the monks, who, as a result, were handsome, plump, and with radiant complexions and clear skin."[10]

The Vinaya contains more than a few stories of men ordaining for reasons entirely unrelated to the monastic Saṅgha's true purpose, including getting a free meal. One of these tells of the son of a noble family, now fallen on hard times, noticing that monks, "having eaten good meals, lie down to sleep on beds sheltered from the wind." He then decided to become a monk so as to enjoy such benefits.[11] Another story relates how a certain farmer stopped off at the local monastery on the way home after a hard morning's toil in the fields. One of the monks gave him a helping of delicious food from his own bowl and, never having eaten so well before, the man decided that the monk's life had definite advantages that the farmer's did not, and so he joined the Saṅgha.[12] There were incidences of men ordaining to escape having to pay their debts, to avoid their obligations to the king or because they were physically disabled, which would otherwise have forced them to beg in the streets. King Ajātasattu mentioned to the Buddha that, if one of his slaves absconded and it was later discovered that he had become a monk, he, the king, would not have him arrested and returned to bondage – almost an inducement for slaves to run away and join the Saṅgha.[13] The Buddha eventually had to make rules forbidding such individuals being ordained, but that this became necessary gives some idea of the types who were being attracted to the monkhood and the need for thorough vetting of candidates before accepting them.

The generous support monks received led some of them to develop a distinctly blasé attitude towards the things they were provided with.

---

10. Vin.III,88.
11. Vin.I,86.
12. Ja. I,311. For other reasons some men ordained see e.g., M.I,463 and II,66.
13. D.I,60-61.

Once, the members of a certain guild offered a group of monks a large amount of cooked rice, a good deal of which ended up on the floor of the refectory due to the monks' carelessness. Understandably annoyed by this, the donors said to each other: "How can these samaṇas, these sons of the Sakyan, accept this food so carelessly? Each mess of rice is the result of a hundred [days] of hard work."[14] When another group of monks turned up in Kapilavatthu, the town's potter told them that should one of them need a bowl, he would make it for him. Suddenly, he was deluged with requests from monks who, despite already having perfectly adequate bowls, wanted a better one, a smaller one or a bigger one. Turning out all these bowls left him with no time to make the items he earned his living from, and he found himself struggling to feed his family. The Buddha came to know of this and scolded the monks for "having no sense of moderation."[15] His frequent reminders to monastics to be sparing in what they asked for, to use what they received with care, and to be thoughtful towards the lay community, suggests that such admonishments were not always taken to heart.

Something else that became a problem as time moved on was conflict between one monk and another and between factions of monks, a problem not confined to monastics alone but common whenever people come together in groups. Some of these arguments were due to temperamental differences of the individuals involved, others to petty jealousies, and a few were about different interpretations of the Dhamma.

The first serious incident of this kind broke out in the great city of Kosambī. There are three accounts of the conflict, each similar in outline while differing slightly in detail and perhaps confused in parts. The monk Bāhiya was responsible for starting the dispute, although details are not given, and because senior monks such as Ānanda and Anuruddha were initially reluctant to get involved, things quickly got out of hand.[16] The account of the conflict runs thus. A disagreement over some matter ended up involving most of the other monks in

14. Vin.II,131-132.
15. Vin.III,244-245.
16. A.II,239.

the city. "They acted disgracefully towards each other with gestures, words and even blows." Having come to know of this, the Buddha called the disputing parties together and asked them:

> "Is it true that you are arguing, quarrelling, disputing and stabbing each other with the weapon of words; that you can neither convince nor persuade the others or be convinced or persuaded by them?"
>
> They admitted that it was true, and the Buddha said:
>
> "What do you think? When you are doing this, are you relating to your companions in the spiritual life with love through body, speech and mind, in public and in private?"
>
> "No, Lord."
>
> "You foolish men! Can you not understand or see that this will be to your detriment and suffering for a long time?"

Having rebuked the monks for their behaviour, the Buddha then made an appeal to their better natures. They should, he urged, express love in body, in speech and in mind towards each other. Whatever they received properly and according to the rules, even if it be the contents of their alms bowl, they should share it with their fellows. Whatever virtues they knew to be wholesome and commendable they should live by them. And finally, they should accept and live by whatever views will lead to their liberation.[17]

This seemed to have soothed the tension between the various factions for a while, but sometime later – although exactly when is not clear – it erupted again. This time, when the Buddha again tried to bring about a reconciliation, the monks told him, in effect, to mind his own business, such was their insolence. "Lord, Dhamma master, hold on a minute! Don't worry yourself about this. You spend your time in peace, and we will take care of the arguing and quarrelling." With this, the Buddha had enough. The next morning, he went alms gathering in Kosambī, ate the food he had received, tidied his lodging and left the city without informing anyone.[18] It may have been in reference to this

17. M.I,321-322.

18. M.III,153; Vin.I,341. There are hints of other serious divisions within the Saṅgha which seem to have been resolved before getting out of hand; e.g., A.II,239.

situation that he said: "Wherever monks are arguing and quarrelling, I do not even like to think about that place, let alone actually go there."[19] One account of the Kosambī crisis has him adding these words to his rebuke of the monks as he left them: "Those who break bones, take life, steal cattle, horses, wealth and who plunder the country, even they can get along with each other, so why can't you?"[20]

The Buddha was not the only one disgusted with the monks' behaviour – so were Kosambī's lay disciples, and they withdrew their support from them, no longer giving them food when they came alms gathering.[21] This very soon brought the disputants to their senses, and they went in a group to Sāvatthī, where the Buddha had gone, to beg for his forgiveness. Word of the dispute had already reached the city and caused uncertainty amongst the lay disciples there. When they heard that the troublemakers were soon to arrive, they asked the Buddha how they should react to them. He told them they should give the monks alms and even listen to their side of the story so they could make up their own minds about where blame lay for the uproar and trouble. "Give alms to both parties and listen to the details from both and, having done this, accept the opinion, the group, the view, the standpoint of the monks who speak according to fact."[22] Such advice was typical of the Buddha – not imposing his opinion on others but suggesting an objective examination of the evidence and letting the facts speak for themselves. Unfortunately, the Tipitaka does not say how or even if the trouble at Kosambī was ever resolved, leaving us in the dark about what eventually happened.

After leaving Kosambī, and before proceeding to Sāvatthī, the Buddha first made his way to the forest near the village of Bālakaloṇakāra, where Anuruddha and two other monks were staying on an extended retreat. The three welcomed him, took his bowl and extra robe, arranged a seat for him, and gave him a pot of water so he

19. A.I,275, condensed.

20. M.III,154.

21. Vin.I,353. Ud.41-42 suggests he went to Pārileyya forest where he was ministered to by an elephant. On the interaction between Buddhist monks and forest animals in Pali literature see Dhammika 2018b pp.32-35.

22. Vin.I,355, condensed. For more the Buddha had to say about making judgments and assessing claims see A.II,71; Dhp. 256-257.

could wash his feet, the proper way of showing hospitality to a visitor. He asked them how their retreat was going, and they replied that they were living together in perfect harmony. Asking further how they were able to do this, Anuruddha described for him the trio's relationship with each other and their daily routine:

> "I always consider what a blessing it is, a real blessing, that I live with such companions in the spiritual life. I think like this: "Why don't I put aside my own wishes and do what the others want?' Then I do that, and so we are different in body but one in mind. Whoever returns first from alms gathering in the village gets the seats ready, puts out the drinking water, the washing water and the refuse bowl. The last to return may eat any of the leftovers or, if he has enough, they are thrown away. Then he puts away the seats, the water and refuse bowls and sweeps the refectory. Whoever notices that the bowls for drinking or washing are empty fills them, and if he cannot do this himself, he signals with his hands to one of the others to help him; without breaking his silence. Then, every fifth day, we sit through the night discussing the Dhamma. This is how we live—diligent, ardent and resolute."[23]

It must have pleased the Buddha to know that there were still monks being true to the spirit of the lifestyle he had always taught: simplicity; mutual respect; learning; and periods of solitude and silence.

The conflict in Kosambī, as recounted in different parts of the Tipitaka, is confused in parts and may not be the whole story either. The Tipitaka mentions a monastery founded in the city during the Buddha's lifetime by the wealthy merchant Ghosita and named after him.[24] The ruins of this establishment were unearthed by archaeologists in 1950, and its identity was verified by inscriptions found at the site.[25] The ancient commentary mentions two other monasteries in Kosambī as well – one founded by Kukkuṭa and the other by Pāvārika, who it claims were friends and business associates of Ghosita. But strangely, while

---

23. M.III,156, condensed.
24. S.IV,113-114.
25. Ghosh 1963, pp.14-16.

the commentaries mention these two men and their monasteries, the Tipitaka does not, raising the question of why this should be so. That later commentators should have invented these individuals and the circumstances surrounding the founding of their monasteries seems unlikely, but why should the Tipitaka be silent about them? Could it have been that the conflict in Kosambī broke out at and involved the monks of Kukkuṭa's and Pāvarika's monasteries, and the distaste caused by the whole affair prompted the monks who compiled the Tipitaka to refuse even to mention them?

While the conflict at Kosambī would have been a cause for serious concern for the Buddha and a shock for the more disciplined monks, it was only the precursor of an even worse problem to come. When the Buddha made his first return visit to Kapilavatthu shortly after his awakening, a group of Sakyan men, including some members of his extended family, decided to join his Saṅgha. One of these was Devadatta, the son of the Buddha's maternal uncle Suppabuddha. The records show that Devadatta was a good monk, although he only gets an occasional mention in the texts. In two or three places he is praised, and the Buddha included him together with ten other monks who he considered good and worthy disciples.[26] But this same Devadatta was to instigate the greatest crisis in the Buddha's career and fracture the Buddhist community, although not irrevocably. It can be calculated that this happened sometime during the Buddha's final years and when King Ajātasattu was on the throne of Magadha. The *Mahāvaṃsa*, the ancient chronicle of Sri Lanka, which includes some material based on earlier Indian sources, states that Ajātasattu came to the throne eight years before the Buddha's death, although there is no corroborating evidence for this in the Tipitaka.[27]

The whole affair as recounted in the Tipitaka seems to be dramatized and may even be exaggerated in part, the better to vilify Devadatta. It includes regicide, assassination attempts, a rampaging elephant, a message from a divine being, bribery, lies and intrigue. The sequence in which the events unfolded as laid out in the Vinaya is also confused in part. For example, in one place it has the Buddha mildly

---

26. A.IV,402 ff; Ud.3-4.
27. Mhv. II,32.

reprimanding Devadatta for infringing a minor rule about food while saying nothing about his four recent attempts to murder him.[28] Despite these problems, it is possible to discern elements of fact in the story and construct what might have actually happened.

That there was a schism within the monastic Saṅgha during the Buddha's last years and that it was instigated by Devadatta seems certain, but its cause can be best explained by certain demands Devadatta made concerning the Saṅgha, not by the claim that he was greedy, hungry for power or just intent on making trouble. The demands Devadatta made were reforms in how monks lived. These were: monks should reside in the forest, far from habitation; they should get their food only by going alms gathering and never accept an invitation to someone's home for a meal; they should use only robes made of rags and never accept ones made of new cloth; they should live at the foot of a tree, without any man-made shelter over them; and they should abstain from eating meat or fish.[29]

For some time, Devadatta must have been quietly sowing dissent and doubt and accusing the Buddha of betraying the true ascetic ideal, and he had managed to get some monks to agree with him. Even a few within the lay community sided with him. There had been disagreements before about which lifestyle was most appropriate for monastics. Those who spent much of their time in solitude and practiced rigorous self-denial had a tendency to look down on those who did not, and sensitive to this, the Buddha had counselled mutual respect between the two groups.[30]

Eventually Devadatta went to the Buddha, recommending, with just a hint of insistence in his voice, that his five austere practices be made incumbent on all monks. But the Buddha had long maintained that while physically strenuous self-denial and prolonged isolation in the forest could be helpful, they were not suitable for everyone and did not necessarily lead to inner transformation. He had noticed and pointed out that a monk could live in the forest and still be restless, proud, vain, and talkative and have little meditational

---

28. Vin.II,196.
29. Vin.II,197.
30. M.I,469.

development.[31] He also saw the value in monks and nuns having contact with the lay community and so acting as a conduit for the Dhamma to become known and accepted within society, where it could have a positive influence on everyone, not just monastics. So he declined to make Devadatta's recommendations compulsory, although, in a spirit of compromise, he said that a monk could undertake such practices if he wished.

This was not enough for Devadatta, but while he did not press the issue, he continued to promote his ideas amongst the monks, gradually increasing his support. Arguing for rules that the Buddha did not make or endorse was divisive enough, but soon Devadatta went beyond this, first insinuating and then actually saying that it might be better if he replaced the Buddha as the head of the Saṅgha. He may have thought that being a close relative of the Buddha put him in a good position to take over from him if and when he stepped aside. Indeed, that someone of the Gotama clan, or at least a Sakyan, should have the prerogative to lead the Saṅgha would have been quite in keeping with the thinking of the time, despite being repugnant to the Buddha.

It seems that word of what Devadatta had been saying got back to the Buddha, because he discussed the matter with some of his trusted disciples but neither confronted Devadatta about it nor took action against him, perhaps hoping that the problem would blow over. But a showdown could not be avoided, and finally it came to a head. One day, while the Buddha was giving a talk to a large gathering, Devadatta came out of the audience, ostentatiously bowed before the Buddha and, in a loud voice that everyone could hear, said: "Lord, you are now old, aged, worn out, having traversed life's path and approaching the end of your life. Content yourself now to live devoted to meditating and abiding in ease. Hand over the monastic Saṅgha to me, and I will lead it." The Buddha refused, Devadatta repeated his request, and once more the Buddha refused. When Devadatta insisted for a third time, the Buddha said to him: "Devadatta, I would not hand over the Saṅgha even to Sāriputta or Moggallāna, let alone to a wretch like you who should be spat out like phlegm." The acerbic tone of the Buddha's

31. A.III,391. See also A.III,355.

words must have shocked the audience, and being publicly rebuffed so strongly certainly would have humiliated Devadatta. Nonetheless, he kept his feelings well under control and, with a forced smile on his face, he once again bowed to the Buddha and left the assembly.

The Buddha now decided that enough was enough and resolved to take action against Devadatta. He instructed Sāriputta to assemble a number of senior monks and, in accordance with ecclesiastical procedure, censure him and then make a public announcement in Rājagaha to that effect.[32] Undeterred by this and determined to get his way, Devadatta soon announced that he was forming his own sect. This caused confusion everywhere, with some monks announcing that they were with Devadatta and others proclaiming that they strongly disapproved of his action. The lay disciples were split between supporters, opponents, and those who were unsure who was right and who wrong. It looked like a spiritual community that the Buddha had guided for over four decades, and which had earned the support and respect of thousands, was about to end the way the Jain Saṅgha had when its leader died: with division, recrimination and confusion. And the Buddha had not even passed from the scene! The Tipitaka refrains from saying what the Buddha thought about this, but it must have been of deep concern and disappointment to him.

Followed by his supporters, Devadatta left for Gayā, but before going he had managed to convince a group of newly ordained Vajjian monks that he, and not the Buddha, was upholding the authentic samaṇa tradition, and they joined him. The Buddha asked Sāriputta and Moggallāna to go to Gayā and reason with the schismatics, especially with the young and impressionable Vajjians, who concerned him most. The two arrived in Gayā and managed to address the monks without Devadatta being present. According to the Vinaya account, what they said was so convincing that it made every one of the monks reconsider what they had done, although one suspects that changing their minds would have actually taken time, arguments and pleading.[33]

---

32. In canon law this procedure is called *pakāsanīya kamma* and would be done after another one called *ñatticatuttha kamma*. During the Buddha's life, this was the only time this procedure was ever used. For details see Upasak pp.101 and 126.

33. Vin.II,200.

When Sāriputta and Moggallāna had finished, they announced that they were leaving and that anyone who approved of what they had said could come with them. Again, according to the Vinaya, every one of the monks rose and accompanied Sāriputta and Moggallāna back to Rājagaha and to the Buddha. The schism was over. The Tipitaka also says that when Devadatta realized that his followers had all abandoned him, hot blood spurted from his mouth, a term traditionally interpreted to mean that a person has died but which is probably a colourful expression for being infuriated.[34]

Although the austerities Devadatta demanded were extreme, they would have been uncontroversial within many samaṇa sects. They were, however, quite at odds with the Buddha's ideas. He had always rejected austerity for its own sake, insisting that deliberately self-imposed hardship and deprivation were pointless. There is enough hardship one has to endure in life, dealing with which can help one to spiritually grow, without deliberately creating it. From the beginning of the Buddha's career, this had put him at odds with the general understanding amongst other *samaṇas*, and many of them criticised him for it. It would seem, therefore, that Devadatta's demands and the subsequent schism they caused actually represented a clash between a traditionalist who insisted on doing what *samaṇas* had always done and someone with more psychologically sound insights who was not averse to breaking with the past. The Buddha was also prepared to be flexible about these demands, whereas Devadatta insisted that only one approach was valid and suitable for everyone.

---

34. Vin.II, 184 ff, also at A.IV,135.

13
The Last Days

There was trembling and hair standing on end when the Buddha of great virtues attained final Nirvana.

Dīgha Nikāya II,157

Nearly half a century had passed since the young Gotama had been so moved by human suffering that he abandoned his home and family in the hope of finding a way beyond this predicament. But time was moving on and one by one the people he had known – his patrons, helpers and disciples – were passing from the scene. The ancient commentaries say that the Buddha's two chief disciples Sāriputta and Moggallāna predeceased him a year or two before he himself died, although the Tipitaka gives only brief details concerning Sāriputta's passing. It seems Sāriputta had been staying in his hometown of Nālakagāma, more commonly known as Nāḷandā, about fifteen kilometers north of Rājagaha. He would have been quite old at the time and may have returned there in order to spend his final days near his kin. At some point he became critically ill and died. The monk Cunda had been looking after him and thought it proper to go to Sāvatthī where the Buddha was, inform him of what had happened and give him Sāriputta's bowl and robe. The Buddha heard the news without comment but Ānanda, who was with the Buddha at the time, was deeply affected by it. He said:

"Venerable Sāriputta was an advisor and mentor to me, he instructed, inspired, motivated and gladdened me, and never tired of explaining the Dhamma. He was a benefactor to his companions in the spiritual life and I [will always] remember the essence, the riches, and the help of the Dhamma Sāriputta gave."[1]

Later, when the Buddha stopped in Ukkācelā during his final journey, he expressed the sense of loss he felt by the absence of his long-term friends. "Monks, this assembly seems empty to me now that Moggallāna and Sāriputta have attained final Nirvana. It did not seem empty before, and I had no concern about what was happening wherever they were staying."[2]

The last months of the Buddha's life are recounted in the Mahāparinibbāna Sutta, the longest discourse in the Tipitaka. It is also one of the few sections of the Tipitaka in which the inner feelings and emotions of the characters concerned are expressed. It opens with the Buddha residing on the Gijjakūṭa, a small rocky hillock on the side of the much higher hill now called Chatha, a little beyond the east gate of Rājagaha. Vassakāra, the chief minister of Magadha, came to visit the Buddha and informed him that King Ajātasattu was planning to attack his northern neighbours, the Vajjians, and destroy them. The Buddha turned to Ānanda, who was standing directly behind him, fanning him, and asked him about the Vajjians: "Do they hold regular and frequent assemblies?" Ānanda affirmed that they did. Then the Buddha continued, asking whether the Vajjian assemblies met, conducted business and adjourned in concord, whether they authorised nothing or abolished nothing that has been decided upon and followed long-standing precedent, whether they appreciated and respected the clan elders and followed their advice, whether they had ceased abducting women and forcing them to live with them, whether they respected and maintained their shrines, and whether they supported the worthy ascetics who live among them. Ānanda replied in the affirmative to all these inquiries, and the Buddha said that, for as long as the Vajjians continued to do such things, it was likely that they would be able to fend off attacks and maintain their independence. Whether the Buddha was speaking so that Vassakāra could hear it or was speaking to Ānanda in private is not stated in the text – both scenarios are possible.[3]

---

1. S.V,161-162.
2. S.V,164.
3. Singh, p.254 interprets this incident to mean that the Buddha was

After this, the Buddha and his party left Rājagaha and headed north, passing through Ambalaṭṭhikā and Nāḷandā and a few days later finally arriving in Pāṭaligāma in the early evening. Welcomed by the lay community, they were invited to stay in the local rest house. The Buddha having accepted the invitation, the villagers prepared the rest house by filling the water pots, arranging seats, and putting oil in the lamps. When all was ready, the Buddha washed his feet at the entrance,[4] went inside and sat down against the central pillar, facing the east, while the lay people sat facing him.[5] He then gave a talk that went through much of the night.[6]

On rising early, as was his habit, he was informed that Vassakāra, assisted by another minister, was supervising the construction of fortifications as part of Magadha's planned confrontation with the Vajjians. The Buddha told Ānanda that he could see thousands of earth spirits moving into the area where the construction was taking place, trying to influence the minds of the officials to build near or over their abodes. Why the Buddha would bother to share this curious piece of information with Ānanda is not explained. Sometime later, the Buddha and those accompanying him crossed the Ganges, passed through Koṭigāma, and eventually arrived in the small village of Nādikā on the southern outskirts of Vesālī, where they stayed in the travellers' rest known as Giñjakāvasatha.[7]

---

indirectly telling Vassakāra how to undermine the Vajjians. I read it to say the opposite, that he wanted Vassakāra to know that with the Vajjians being strong and united, it would be difficult to overcome them.

4. Also at M.I,206; I.414; III,155; D.III,208, etc. In later centuries the Buddha came to be seen as so exalted that it would have been unthinkable for him to do something so mundane and low as wash his own feet.

5. The *Upaniṣads*, the *Dharmasūtras*, etc., give the east various auspicious and mystical significance, probably originating from Vedic sun worship; e.g., *Bṛhadāraṇyaka* 2.7,5 and 3.9.20. By sitting facing the east, the Buddha was probably following the convention of the time expected of an honoured guest.

6. D.II,84-6.

7. The name means 'the brick house' and suggests that construction of this material was unusual. Archaeology has shown that baked bricks were rare in India before the Mauryan period.

The next day, the party moved to a nearby mango orchard owned by the well-known courtesan Ambapālī.[8] Hearing of this, she drove her carriage out to the orchard, met the Buddha, and after listening to a talk by him, invited him and the monks for a meal to her house the next day, which he accepted. As it happened, a group of young Licchavis also came to know of the Buddha's arrival and, mounting their chariots, they too drove out to meet him, encountering Ambapālī on the way. She told them of the invitation and they, wanting the honour of being the first in Vesālī to offer hospitality to the Buddha, said that if she would transfer the invitation to them, they would pay her handsomely. She refused and drove off home to prepare the meal. Not to be outdone, the young men raced to the mango orchard and, seeing them as they approached, with their different coloured makeup matching their attire, the Buddha commented to Ānanda that they looked like gods.[9] When the Licchavis arrived, the Buddha gave them a talk, and when finished, they extended an invitation to him for a meal the next day, which he politely refused, saying that he had already accepted Ambapālī's invitation. Irritated by this, they snapped their fingers, saying: "We have been beaten, upstaged, by this mango of a woman!"[10]

The next morning, the Buddha and his monks went to Ambapālī's house and were served a sumptuous meal, and afterwards, she announced that she was going to donate her mango orchard to the Saṅgha. Ambapālī later became a nun, and in her old age composed a poem comparing her beauty when in her prime with how she looked in old age, one of the earliest literary works by a woman from India.[11]

---

8. The Chinese pilgrim Faxian, who visited the orchard in the fifth century, said it was three *li* south of Vesālī on the west side of the road, i.e., the main north/south road, so it must have been somewhere near Nādikā.

9. For centuries it was the norm for upper class Indian males to wear makeup. The Buddha's half-brother Nanda used to paint his eyes, S.II,281. On male grooming in ancient India, see *Kāmasūtra* I, 4, 5-6 and Ali, p.63. In the 11th century, Alberuni found Indian men distinctly dandified and effeminate compared to what he was used to: "The men wear articles of female dress; they use cosmetics, wear earrings, arm-rings, golden seal-rings on the ring-finger as well as on their toes," Edward Sachau's *Alberuni's India*, 1910, Vol.I p.181.

10. This is a word play on Ambapālī's name, which means 'mango guardian.'

11. Thi.252-270.

The Buddha's acceptance of Ambapālī's invitation has been likened to Jesus' forgiveness of 'the sinful woman' who anointed his feet with expensive oil, probably a prostitute and traditionally identified as Mary Magdalene. The similarity is tenuous. In first-century Israel, prostitutes were despised social outcasts, and Jesus was being compassionate towards the woman, expressing his loving acceptance of the rejected, a central theme of his gospel. In India, courtesans (*nagarasobhinī* or *gaṇikā*) such as Ambapālī, Aḍḍhakāsī, Sālavatī and Sulasā, as opposed to common prostitutes (*vesiyā*), were held in high regard. They were often independent, wealthy women, literate and cultured, skilled in the so-called sixty-four arts, and sometimes had influence with or even sat on their city's governing councils.[12] The Buddha accepted Ambapālī's invitation and turned down the young Licchavis' simply because she had asked him first.

Shortly after the Buddha arrived in Vesālī, the rainy season began, and in accordance with samaṇa tradition, he and his party found places to reside for the next three months. The Buddha and Ānanda took up lodgings in the small village of Beluva, one of the outer suburbs of the city. While there, at some point he "was attacked by a severe sickness, with sharp and death-like pain, but he endured it mindfully, fully aware and without complaint." After recovering, he came out from his dwelling and sat in the shade of the porch. Ānanda went up to him, bowed and said:

> "Lord, it is wonderful that you are comfortable and well again. When you were sick, my body felt as if it was drugged, I was disorientated and things were not clear to me. But I was consoled by the thought that you will not pass away without making some statement regarding the monastic Saṅgha."[13]

Apparently surprised by this, the Buddha replied:

> "But what does the Saṅgha expect from me, Ānanda? I have proclaimed the Dhamma without making any distinction between secret and open teachings. I do not have the teacher's fist, which holds some teachings back. If anyone thinks, 'I will take charge of the Saṅgha' or 'The Saṅgha should follow me', then let them make

---

12. See Vin.I,268 and *Kāmasūtra* 1.3,16-22. On the less glamorous side of the courtesan's life, see Kaul, p.146 ff.

13. D.II,99.

such a statement. But the Tathāgata does not think like that, so why should he make some such statement regarding the Saṅgha"?

Then he reiterated his appeal for self-reliance in spiritual matters:

"Ānanda, be an island unto yourself; be your own refuge, with the Dhamma as your island and refuge, with no other refuge. Whether now or after I have passed away, anyone who lives as their own island, their own refuge, will attain the highest, if they have the desire to learn."[14]

As clearly as he could, the Buddha was reaffirming that his was a path of self-realization, of self-awakening. A teacher such as he could and did inspire and encourage, prod and explain, but ultimately, it was up to individuals to make the effort and to understand for themselves.

After the rainy season had finished, the party set off again, heading north, crossing the Gandak River and then turning north-west and passing through Bhaṇḍagāma, Hatthigāma (Hathikhala near Hathua), Ambagāma (Amaya near Tamkuhi), Jambugāma, and Bhoganagara, they eventually arrived at Pāvā, where they stayed in a mango orchard owned by Cunda, a blacksmith.[15] Cunda welcomed the party and invited them to a meal the next day. During the meal the Buddha was served and ate a dish called *sūkaramaddava*, after which "he was attacked by a severe sickness with bloody diarrhoea and sharp and death-like pain."[16]

This turned out to be his last meal, and as a result, there has been much speculation and controversy surrounding the identity of this dish, much of it uninformed. Theories include that the meal caused the Buddha's death, that he had accidentally been served poisonous mushrooms, or even that he was deliberately poisoned.[17]

---

14. D.II,100-101. *Dīpa* here could mean either island or lamp.

15. Where they would have crossed the Gandak is impossible to know, as the river's constantly changing course has long since washed away any evidence of an ancient ford.

16. D.II,127.

17. Armstrong posits the poisoning theory as possible and then adds: "The Pāli texts however, do not even consider this appalling possibility," pp.179-180.

Sūkaramaddava literally means 'pig's softness', so it might have been a pork preparation of some kind, e.g., tender pork, but not necessarily. Then, as now, culinary preparations could have names entirely unrelated to their ingredients. The fact that the tradition preserved the name of the dish may be because it was an expensive, rare or unusual one.[18]

That the Buddha's main symptoms were exudative diarrhoea (*lohita pakkhandika*) and sharp pain (*pabāḷha vedanā*), probably in the abdomen, suggests that he suffered from bacterial gastroenteritis. It usually takes at least twenty-four, sometimes forty-eight or even seventy-two hours for gastroenteritis symptoms to become apparent, which is why people mistakenly attribute the last thing they ate to any stomach problem they have. Thus it may not have been *sūkaramaddava* that was responsible for the Buddha's sickness but something he ate the day before or even several days before arriving in Pāvā. Further, there is no reason to assume that food was the problem. The Buddha would have been regularly rehydrating, and thus it is not at all improbable that he had drunk contaminated water before he arrived in Pāvā.

The Pali texts do not consider it because it has no basis in fact. Armstrong's book is marred by many such flights of fancy and factual errors.

18. D.II,127. For some of the theories on the identity of *sūkaramaddava* and its possible role in the Buddha's death, see Mettananda and Hinüber, Wasson and O'Flaherty, Ireland, and Masefield and Revire. Dhammapāla (5th cent. CE) gave the opinions of various ancient authorities on the identity of *sūkaramaddava* – that it was pork, bamboo shoots, a type of mushroom, or some kind of elixir – indicating that what the original was had been lost by his time. One of the most widespread and persistent theories today is that it was truffles, a theory first put forward by western scholars in the nineteenth century. The Indian truffle, *Tuber indicum*, grows mainly in parts of the Tibetan and Indian Himalayas and would have been unknown in the Ganges and Yamuna valley where the Buddha lived, and there is no evidence that they were ever eaten in India, or even harvested, until the 1980s. Indian truffles lack the pleasant fragrance of European varieties, have little of their distinctive taste, and are used today mainly as a cheap substitute for them. Nor was *sūkaramaddava* mushrooms as some maintain, a food that Indians have, along with garlic, always shunned as impure; see *Manusmṛti* 5,5; 11,156; *Āpastamba Dharmasūtra* I.17,28; *Vasiṣṭha Dharmasūtra* 14,33, etc.

Given that the Buddha had been sick while staying in Vesālī, that he had mentioned the only time he had a degree of physical comfort was when he went into deep meditation, and that he was around eighty, it seems most likely that his death was due to a continuation of this earlier sickness, whatever it was, and gastroenteritis exacerbated by exhaustion and old age, rather than being entirely due to the last thing he ate. This conclusion is similar to the one current at the turn of the first millennium: "It was not from food that the Lord became sick. It was because of the natural weakness of his body and the completion of his lifespan that his sickness grew worse."[19]

Having recovered somewhat, the Buddha and his party continued on their way the next day, but he grew increasingly frail and had to stop again. He asked Ānanda to fold a robe into four so he could sit on it while resting at the foot of a tree. Soon afterwards, the party was approached by a man named Pukkusa, who, it turned out, had been a disciple of the Buddha's old teacher, Āḷāra Kālāma. Pukkusa offered the Buddha two sets of cloth of gold robes, which the Buddha accepted, asking Pukkusa to drape one over him and the other over Ānanda.[20] When Pukkusa left, the Buddha was transfigured, becoming radiant and glowing, so much so that the cloth of gold robe appeared dull. When Ānanda expressed his astonishment at this, the Buddha said that this phenomenon had only happened to him once before, on the night he attained awakening. The account of this first transfiguration mentions that rays (*raṁsi*) of blue, yellow, red, white and orange light emanated from his body.

After resting for a while, the party moved on to the Kakuṭṭhā River, where they all drank and bathed.[21] The Buddha then asked Cundaka,

---

19. Mil.175.

20. *Siṅgivaṇṇaṃ*, Sanskrit *hiraṇya*, and after the Muslim period *kimkhawād*, was made of silk or cotton thread wrapped in thin strips of gold. This is possibly the oldest reference to this type of fabric from India.

21. Now called the Khanua River, it is about ten kilometers east from Kusinārā, seemingly a long way for the weak and ailing Buddha to walk in the time he had remaining. However, the Khanua has a very meandering course, as do most rivers in the region, and may well have been closer to Kusinārā at the time. The commentary gives the distance between Pāvā and Kusinārā as three *gāvutas*, which Rhys Davids calculated at a little less than two miles,

one of the monks travelling with him, to put a folded robe on the ground so he could lie down and rest again. Cundaka did this and then sat watch beside the Buddha to attend to anything he might need. He had been attentive to the Buddha's needs in the past as well. Once, when the Buddha was sick, he had visited him, and the two of them talked about the Dhamma. The texts suggest that, on that occasion, the Buddha's illness eased as a result of Cundaka's caring presence.[22]

As the Buddha was resting, it occurred to him that, as the blacksmith Cunda had provided him with his last meal, the poor man might think he was somehow responsible for causing the Buddha's death and be tormented by remorse. To forestall this, he asked Ānanda to return to Pāvā and tell Cunda that he had heard this from the Buddha's own lips: that to provide a Buddha with a meal just before he attains awakening and just before he attains final Nirvana are the most auspicious and meritorious of all almsgivings. It is indicative of the Buddha's compassion that, despite exhaustion and discomfort and being near death, he was thinking of others.[23]

Setting off again, the party eventually crossed the Hiraññavatī River[24] and arrived at a grove of trees on the outskirts of the Mallas' main town, Kusinārā, just as the light was fading. The Buddha asked Ānanda to prepare a bed for him between two large sal trees. As he lay down, the two trees spontaneously burst into blossom, and flower petals showered down over his body.[25] Ānanda expressed his astonishment at this, and the Buddha took the opportunity to make an important point:

> "These sal trees have burst into blossom out of season. Never before has the Tathāgata been so honoured and revered, respected, esteemed and saluted. But the monk or the nun,

---

see Srinivasan, pp. 18, 23, 25. Unfortunately, we do not know exactly where Pāvā was in relation to the Kukuṭṭhā at that time, or to Kusinārā, nor is their certainty about how long a *gāvuta* was.

22. S.V,81.

23. D.II,135-136.

24. Until recently the Chota Gandak, now renamed Hiraññavatī for the benefit of pilgrims.

25. The sal has fragrant-smelling pale yellow flowers, see Dhammika 2018b, pp. 179-181.

the lay man or lay woman disciple who lives practising the Dhamma fully and perfectly fulfils the path of the Dhamma, it is they who truly honour the Tathāgata, revere, respect and worship him in the highest way."[26]

This is yet another example of the Buddha giving miracles a secondary place, after living in accordance with the Dhamma, and of stating that the Dhamma is for everyone – monastic and lay, men and women.

Realising that the end was drawing near, the Buddha gave some final advice and instructions. He encouraged every disciple to visit four sites at least once in their life: where he was born, where he awakened, where he proclaimed the Dhamma for the first time, and where he passed away. He warned monks not to become too familiar with women, gave instructions about how his remains were to be disposed of, advised that the errant monk Channa be disciplined, and granted permission for any of the minor monastic rules to be changed as new situations arose.

Unable to restrain his tears, Ānanda had quietly gone to a nearby building and leant against the door post, sobbing: "Alas, I am still a learner with much to do, and the Teacher, he who is so compassionate, is about to pass away." Noticing Ānanda's absence, the Buddha called for him to come, and seeing him so upset, comforted him and thanked him for his many years of selfless giving: "For a long time, Ānanda, you have been in the Tathāgata's presence, showing bodily acts of love, showing verbal acts of love, showing mental acts of love, beneficially and whole-heartedly, happily, and unstintingly. You have created much good, Ānanda. Make an effort, and in a short time, you will be free from the defilements." Ānanda's tears and the Buddha's expression of gratitude and thanks are testament to the close bond between the two men, one that went beyond their kin relationship.

After this, the Buddha asked Ānanda to go into Kusinārā and inform the Mallas of his arrival in their town and his impending demise. The Mallas were gathered in their assembly hall, and when Ānanda delivered his message, there was shock and consternation. The crowd followed him out to the sal grove, and he introduced each family to the Buddha as he

26. D.II,137-138.

lay there. Although it is not mentioned in the text, the Mallas must have brought torches or lamps with them, which would have illuminated the whole grove in flickering light. Amongst this large gathering was a wandering ascetic named Subhadda, who happened to be in Kusinārā. Knowing of the great teacher but never having met him, he approached Ānanda and asked if he could talk to the Buddha. Ānanda refused, saying that the Buddha was weary, but Subhadda persisted. Overhearing this exchange, the Buddha asked Ānanda to let the ascetic come forward. After a brief conversation between the two, Subhadda requested ordination. This was done, and according to the text, he attained awakening soon afterwards, although how soon is not stipulated.[27]

Some years before this, the Buddha had said that he would always be available to answer questions from inquirers who wanted to know about the Dhamma and that he would be capable of doing so:

> "Even if you have to carry me around on a stretcher, there will be no change in the clarity of my wisdom. If anyone were to speak rightly of me, they could say that a being not liable to delusion has appeared in the world, for the good of the many, out of compassion for the world, for the good and happiness of gods and humans."[28]

His exchanges with Subhadda, even as he was breathing his last, show that he was true to his word.

As a final encouragement, the Buddha addressed these words to Ānanda and the others: "Ānanda, it may be that you think, 'The Teacher's guidance has ceased, and now we have no teacher.' But this is not how you should see it. Let the Dhamma and the training I have taught you be your teacher after I am gone."

Now the end had come. With the monks who had accompanied him during his final journey, Subhadda and others, gathered around, the Buddha uttered his final words: "Now, monks, I declare to you: all conditioned things are impermanent. Strive on with awareness" (*Handa dāni bhikkhave āmantayāmi vo, vayadhammā saṅkhārā. Appamādena sampādetha*).[29]

---

27. D.II,149-152.
28. M.I,83.
29. D.II,156.

The Buddha entered and proceeded through the jhānas and continued on into even more subtle and exalted states of consciousness; he then descended through the jhānas, ascended back up to the fourth jhāna, and then finally passed away.

There was a shocked silence for a while, which was soon broken by sobbing. Some of those present cried out through their tears: "Too soon has the Lord passed away, too soon has the Happy One passed away, too soon has the Eye of the World gone!" Others, understanding the nature of ordinary conditioned existence, remained calm and spent the rest of the night in silent meditation. The atmosphere under the sal trees that night must have been sombre as the monks absorbed the fact that their guide, inspiration, mentor and long-time friend was no more. His sudden absence must have created a sense of uncertainty and required time to accept.

14
Aftermath

I will go from town to town, from city to city, praising the Buddha and the Dhamma so excellently taught by him.

Sutta Nipāta 192

While the Buddha's passing evokes sadness and a sense of loss, such feelings are tempered by knowing that it came at the end of a long and fruitful life and that it was in keeping with the natural course of things. When the sun came up the next morning, Anuruddha asked Ānanda to go into Kusinārā and inform the Mallas what had happened. Many of them were once again gathered in their assembly hall, and when they heard the news, there was profound sorrow. With the monks' agreement, they started to prepare for an elaborate funeral and commemorative ceremony, which was to last for a week.

As these preparations were being made, a large group of monks led by Mahā Kassapa happened to be going along the main road to Kusinārā when they met an Ājīvaka ascetic who was coming from the town. Kassapa asked him if he knew his and his party's teacher, the Buddha, to which the Ājīvaka replied that he did know of him, and he had passed away in Kusinārā only a few days ago. This news caused dismay, confusion and grief amongst the monks. One monk, however, Subhadda by name, who had ordained late in life, reacted quite differently, saying: "Enough weeping and wailing, friends. We are well rid of the great samaṇa. We were continually bothered by him saying, 'It would be good if you did this. It would not be good if you did that.' Now we can do or not do what we want." Such sentiments expressed at this time must have compounded the shock the other monks had just experienced, but no one said anything to rebut it.[1]

1. D.II,162-163.

The fact that Kassapa and his companions were on this road and heading in the direction they were is intriguing. A look at a map will show that the ancient road would have passed through Kusinārā and continued all the way to Sāvatthī and that at some point beyond Kusinārā, it would have branched off to Kapilavatthu. It would not be unreasonable to conjecture that, when the Buddha set off from Rājagaha on his final journey, his destination was Kapilavatthu, where he hoped to spend his last days. If so, before departing he would have asked some monks to spread word to senior disciples that they should meet him in Kapilavatthu for final instructions and goodbyes, but as it happened, he died in Kusinārā before reaching his planned destination. If this conjecture is correct, it would also explain why Mahā Kassapa, one of the Buddha foremost disciples and one who preferred to live alone in the forest, was where he was when he heard of the Buddha's passing – he had been on his way to Kapilavatthu. Whatever the case, having been given the sad news, Kassapa and the monks with him hurried on to Kusinārā.

After a series of elaborate ceremonies, the Mallas carried the Buddha's body into their town through the north gate, along the streets, out by the east gate and from there to the Makuṭa Bandhana Shrine, where they cremated it. Once the funeral pyre had cooled, they took what remained of the bones to their assembly hall so everyone could pay respects to them. Meanwhile, news of the Buddha's demise had been spreading, and representatives from various kingdoms, chiefdoms and clans began arriving in Kusinārā to claim the mortal remains. The Sakyans wanted them because, as their representative said: "The Tathāgata was the greatest of our clan." The envoy of the king of Magadha said that his master was entitled to the ashes because he was of the warrior caste, as was the Buddha. The Mallas of Kusinārā, arguing from the standpoint of possession being nine-tenths of the law, said: "The Tathāgata attained final Nirvana in the precincts of our town, and we will not give up his bones." In all, eight claimants were involved in this unseemly dispute, the others being the Licchavis, the Buliyas of Allakappa, the Koliyas of Rāmagāma, the Mallas of Pāvā, and a mysterious brahmin from Veṭhadīpa known only from this single reference in the Tipitaka.[2] Given that the Buddha had

2. Veṭhadīpa may be the modern Bettiah in West Champaran District.

spent much of his last two decades in Kosala, it is curious that no representative from there was amongst the claimants.

A brahmin named Doṇa happened to be visiting Kusinārā, and he offered to arbitrate between the quarrelling parties.[3] He addressed the assembled worthies, saying: "The Buddha's teaching is about patience, and it is not right that strife should come from sharing out the remains of this best of men. Let us all come together in harmony and peace and in a spirit of friendship divide the remains into eight." This appeal was accepted, probably reluctantly by some, and it was agreed that Doṇa should divide the remains according to what he thought fair. This he did, and as a gesture of gratitude for his services, he was given the vessel (*kumbha*) in which the remains had been held and from which he had measured them out.[4] The division having been made to everyone's satisfaction, an envoy from the Moriya clan turned up and demanded a portion of the remains, and Doṇa came to the rescue again, suggesting that these latecomers be given the ashes from the funeral pyre. This was done, and each recipient undertook to build a stupa over their share.[5]

After the Buddha's funeral there was some discussion amongst the monks about what the future might hold for them personally, for the

---

3. D.II,166. Doṇa had met the Buddha years before, A.II,37; III,223. His name could be a shortened form of *doṇamāpaka*, a royal revenue officer tasked with measuring out the king's share of the harvest using a wooden vessel called a *doṇa*. According to Olivelle, 2004 p.458, a *doṇa* had a capacity of about 5 litres. See also Srinivasan pp. 49-51, 90-92 and 166.

4. It could be conjectured that Doṇa placed the Buddha's ashes in one of the monks' alms bowls rather than in a container used for some mundane purpose. This would have been more appropriate, considering the Malla's and the monks' wish to have a fitting funeral for the Tathāgata - solemn and dignified. The Tipitaka provides little information about what Buddhist alms bowls were like at that time, but there is one in the State Museum in Lucknow, India. It is of the pottery known as Northern Black Polished Ware, which was produced around the time and in the region the Buddha lived, and its shape and size are almost the same as today's standard Burmese monks' bowls. These Burmese bowls hold 4 ½ litres, very close to Olivelle's estimation of a *doṇa* measure, and would have easily held the Buddha's ashes. The remains of the average human male after cremation weigh about 2 ½ kgs.

5. On the possible identification of the stupa built by Doṇa see Dhammika 2008, pp. 174-175 and Patil pp.40-41,86,121.

monastic Saṅgha in general, and especially for the Buddha's Dhamma. Mahā Kassapa suggested that some attempt should be made to preserve the Dhamma for the benefit of future generations. Subhadda's casual but potentially dangerous comment had added urgency to Kassapa's plan. It is also possible that Kassapa and the others remembered what had happened when Mahāvīra had died some years before: his followers had broken up into quarrelling factions. So it was decided that a meeting, a council in fact, of all the monks who had attained awakening should take place, so that some effort could be made to preserve what the Buddha had taught them. The monks in Kusinārā agreed to go in different directions to spread the word that such a council would take place in Rājagaha during the coming rainy season. Given that such a large number of monks in a city – even one as large as Rājagaha – could make it difficult to get alms and accommodations, all other monks were to be asked not to come or, if they were already there, to vacate the city.

By the beginning of the rainy season, several hundred monks turned up – the Tipitaka gives the conventional five hundred as the number – and over the following months met regularly at the Sattapaṇṇa Cave, which is situated on the steep northern side of Vebhāra Hill, now called Vaibhara.[6]

The leading figures in the council were the gruff and abstemious Mahā Kassapa, the more easy-going and approachable Ānanda, and Upāli, an expert in monastic discipline. There had been tensions between Ānanda and Kassapa in the past, with the latter criticising Ānanda for being too accommodating towards nuns and not being strict enough with the novices under his tutelage.[7] When Kassapa gave his recommendations for who should attend the council, he pointedly did not mention Ānanda, until other monks pointed out that he should be present, given that he had been so close to the Buddha for so long

6. Vin.II,76. The cave is actually two fissures, one larger than the other, in the side of a high, jagged cliff near the top of the hill. When Buddhist pilgrims visit the site today, they often wonder how several hundred monks could have fitted into either or even both these fissures. The council was held at, not in, the cave, likely in a hall built on the wide platform extending outward from the foot of the cliff.

7. S.II,215-218.

and had heard so many things he had said. The presence of these two contrasting personalities may have been responsible for the decision to include a range of material in what would become the Tipitaka – not just teachings relevant to monks, which Kassapa would have favoured, but other teachings important to the laity, which Ānanda would have seen the importance of.[8]

The accounts of how the council proceeded are too cursory to get an idea of exactly what took place. It certainly would have been difficult for the participants to learn by heart all, or even the most important of the Buddha's discourses in the time the council lasted. However, there is evidence that some monks, nuns and lay people too had memorized and were able to chant them even while the Buddha was still alive. For example, the Buddha described a certain devout layman from Sāvatthī as being "learned and a preserver of the texts" (*bahussuto āgatāgamo*), meaning that he would have been able to recite a significant number of discourses from memory. The nun Thullanandā was similarly well-trained, being known as a reciter (*bhāṇika*).[9] When Soṇa was asked by the Buddha to recite some discourses, he did so faultlessly, earning the Buddha's praise, despite having been a monk for only a few months. Having been a devout layman, he may have learned some of the discourses even before his ordination.[10] It was mentioned previously the woman Khajjutarā remembered and passes on all the discourses the Buddha gave during one of his stays in Kosambi. It is also not known how the suttas selected and committed to memory were arranged, but it was probably according to their length.

Once, a group of monks had approached the Buddha and told him they had decided to travel to the western region and reside there for a while.[11] He advised them to consult with Sāriputta before leaving, which they did. After learning of their intentions, Sāriputta said to them:

---

8. Tilakaratne pp.229-257 has some interesting observations on this matter and its possible implications.

9. Vin.IV,158; IV,254.

10. Ud.59. See also pages 161-162.

11. *Pacchābhūmaṃ janapadaṃ.* This would have included what is now Pakistan's Punjab and parts of eastern Afghanistan, then known as Gandhāra, which became a predominantly Buddhist region by the early centuries CE. These monks must have been amongst the first missionaries there.

> "There are inquiring nobles and brahmins, householders and ascetics who are sure to question a monk when he goes to foreign parts, because such people are learned. They will ask, 'Who is your teacher?' and 'What does he teach?' So I hope you have learned the teachings well, studied, grasped, thought about and gone deep into them, so that when you answer you will say what the Lord has taught and not misrepresent him."

Sāriputta then suggested to them some salient aspects of the Dhamma that they could use to introduce the teachings to people they would meet.[12]

These monks were not the only ones to take the Buddha's teachings to distant parts. After the monk Puṇṇa had learned the Dhamma well, he told the Buddha that he intended to go and reside in Sunāparanta, a region known for its wild and violent inhabitants.[13] The Buddha warned him that he ran the risk of being manhandled or worse, but undeterred, the fearless and determined monk went anyway. The Tipitaka says he converted many of Sunāparanta's inhabitants to the Dhamma and eventually died there.[14]

These two stories are instructive because they show that monks, and probably nuns too, were taking the Buddha's instructions to spread the Dhamma seriously, even while he was still alive. After his passing and the First Council, this missionary endeavour became even more dynamic, and within a few centuries Buddhism had become a major religion in India and went on to have a presence beyond it in other parts of Asia. In the last hundred years, the Buddha and what he taught have begun to win admiration and acceptance in the West, despite almost unimaginable differences between today's world and the Buddha's. It would seem that his teachings were, as he claimed, timeless (*akāliko*).

---

12. S.III,6-9.

13. M.III,268-270. Several later Pāḷi and Sanskrit sources say that Puṇṇa was born in Suppāraka, the modern Sopara, which if correct, would mean that Sunāparanta must have been the coastal region north of Mumbai. The ruins of a very ancient stupa can be found near Wagholi Naka Road on the western side of Sopara.

14. M.III,268-270.

Appendix I
Towns and Cities Visited by the Buddha

Ālavī

The Buddha stayed in this town on a number of occasions, and tradition says he spent his sixteenth rainy season there as well. A shrine nearby called Aggāḷava provided basic accommodation for wandering *samaṇa*s and was where the Buddha usually lodged when visiting Ālavī. It may have been where a yakkha named Āḷavaka was worshipped by the locals.[1] The monk Vaṅgīsa, highly regarded for composing beautiful verses, sometimes stayed at this shrine too.[2] One of the Buddha's most devout and enthusiastic lay disciples, Hatthaka, was from Ālavī and was responsible for attracting large numbers of people to the Dhamma, something the Buddha praised him for.[3] Ālavī is mentioned in the Jain scriptures, where it is known as Ālabhiyā, and was visited by Mahāvīra several times.[4]

Ālavī has been identified with the modern town of Airwa, off the Agra-Lucknow Expressway about twenty-eight kilometers from Etawah in Uttar Pradesh. The extensive ruins of Buddhist and Jain temples that could be seen at the end of the nineteenth century have now mostly disappeared because of locals taking their stones and bricks for building purposes.

Bārāṇasī

Bārāṇasī is located on the left bank of the Ganges and is now known by the people who live there as Banares or Kāsi, and officially as Varanasi. It was the capital of the former kingdom of Kāsi. Today, and for at least the last millennium and a half, the city has been considered the most sacred place in Hinduism, although in early Buddhist and

1. D.III,205. See Chakrabarti 2007 p.75.
2. S.I,188; Tha.1227-1251.
3. A.IV,216-220.
4. *Viyāhapaṇṇatti* 11,12.

pre-Buddhist texts there is no evidence of it being held in such regard. The Buddha mentioned places people would visit in order to bathe in the Ganges, but Bārāṇasī is not amongst them.[5] Kāsi had been conquered by Kosala, perhaps during Gotama's youth or earlier, and faded into a provincial city, although it remained an important centre for trade, particularly for luxury goods.[6] The Buddha spent almost no time in Bārāṇasī itself, but he proclaimed his Dhamma for the first time at a deer reserve called Isipatana, about a yojana north of the city, and returned there several times afterwards, judging by the number of suttas he delivered there.[7] Senior monks such as Sāriputta and Mahākoṭṭhita visited Isipatana too, perhaps because of the Buddha's encouragement that all disciples should go at least once in their lives to the places where the pivotal events in his life took place, one of which was Isipatana.[8]

Isipatana, now called Sarnath, grew into a great monastic centre and flourished right up to Indian Buddhism's last days. No monastery was ever founded in Bārāṇasī itself during the Buddha's time, and although Buddhism had a presence there in later centuries, it was always overshadowed by Hinduism. Tradition says Pārśva, the founder of Jainism, was born in Bārāṇasī on Vesākhā, attained awakening and passed away on that day too, just as the Buddha was said to have done.

Parts of the ancient Bārāṇasī have been excavated at Rajghat.

Bhaddiya

At some point during Gotama's youth, the kingdom of Aṅga had been incorporated into Magadha, although whether it was by force, a treaty arrangement or a marriage alliance is not known. The Buddha's many tours through the land occasionally took him to places in Aṅga, such as Bhaddiya, Āpaṇa, Assapura and its principal city Campā. When in Bhaddiya, he would usually stay in a park or grove called Jātiyā. The town was the home of the layman Meṇḍaka, a generous supporter of the

5. M.I,39.
6. A.I,248; A.III,391.
7. E.g., A.I,279; III,320; S.III,66: V,406.
8. D.II,141.

monastic community and famous for his extraordinary psychic abilities.[9] On leaving Bhaddiya, the Buddha set out for a tour of Aṅguttarāpa, a district of Aṅga north of the Ganges.[10] During another of his visits, he was invited for a meal to the house of Meṇḍaka's grandson, and after it was finished, he was asked to offer some advice to several soon-to-be brides concerning how they should behave in their new home.[11] Bhadria, the modern Bhaddiya, is a small hamlet in the Godda District of Jharkhand.

Campā

Campā was the capital of the small state of Aṅga to the east of Magadha and was situated on the right bank of the Ganges. Despite having become a part of Magadha, Aṅga's king kept his life and at least some of his wealth because he was able to make generous religious donations. The texts mention that he was still alive after the Buddha had died.[12]

People in the Middle Land had heard of the ocean, although few had ever actually seen it, other than the more intrepid of the merchants of Campā. The city was the major port for riverine traffic, and ships from there sailed down the Ganges to the sea and beyond to south India and South-east Asia. One of the landmarks of the city was the large lake or reservoir which a former queen, Gaggarā by name, had excavated. A grove of campaka trees (*Magnolia champaca*) grew around the lake, and during the Buddha's several visits to the city, he chose to reside in this grove. Campā was the only city frequented by the Buddha in which no monastery was founded during his lifetime, although in later centuries it became an important centre of Buddhism. Campā is identified today with the large mound called Campanagar on the western edge of the modern town of Bhagalpur in Bihar, and Queen Gaggarā's lake still exists too, although much silted up, and is now known as Bherva Lake.[13]

---

9. Vin.I,240.
10. Pandey, p.97, thinks Aṅguttarāpa was somewhere in modern Purina District.
11. A.III,36-38.
12. M.II,163.
13. See Sinha,1979, pp.90-96.

Gayā

This town is situated on the left bank of the wide and shallow Palgu River, about eleven kilometers from Uruvelā, now known as Bodh Gayā. Even before the Buddha, pilgrims were coming to Gayā to bathe in the river during the Spring Festival (*gayāphaggu*), in the belief that it would wash away any evil they had done.[14] It was also a gathering place for brahmin ascetics, who immersed themselves in the river three times a day and performed fire sacrifices.[15]

The Buddha visited Gayā only rarely, probably because it was a centre of Brahminism. On his way from Bārāṇasī to Rājagaha in the months after his awakening, he revisited Uruvelā, where he met, converted and ordained the three Kassapa brothers and all their disciples. They then accompanied him to a hill called Gayāsīsa, where he delivered his famous Ādittapariyāya Sutta to them.[16] The Tipitaka says that from the top of the hill, the Buddha could see crowds of ascetics doing their ablutions and tending their sacred fires, which prompted him to comment: "One is not made pure by water, even though many come here to bathe. Having truth and Dhamma makes one pure and a true brahmin."[17] When the Chinese pilgrim Xuanzang visited Gayā in the seventh century, he noticed a stupa on the hill, probably marking the place where the sutta was taught.

When someone told the nun Puṇṇikā that ritual ablutions would cleanse them of evil, her reply added an element of logic and humour to the Buddha's comments on the subject.

> "Whoever told you this just added ignorance to ignorance...If this were true, then all the frogs would go to heaven, as would the nāgas, crocodiles, and other aquatic creatures. Those who butcher sheep and pigs, fishermen and hunters, thieves, executioners and other evil-doers, would be free from evil simply by washing in water. And if rivers

---

14. M.I,39. Held on the 1st of Phagguṇa (the full moon), later known as Vasantotsava and today as Holi.
15. Tha.345.
16. Vin.I,34-35.
17. Ud.6.

washed away your evil, they could also wash away good you had done, and you would have neither."[18]

Other than the Palgu, the most sacred place in Gayā at that time was a bathing tank called Brahmasara in Hindu sources and Maṇḍalavāpi in Buddhist literature. On its bank was a tower-like structure made of stone slabs riveted together, which later Hindu texts call Brahmayūpa and the Tipitaka knows as Ṭaṅkitamañca, and which was the abode of a menacing yakkha named Sūciloma, Needle Hair. When the Buddha was staying at this Ṭaṅkitamañca, Sūciloma and one of his yakkha friends attempted to frighten him, although without success. Somewhat surprised, Sūciloma asked the Buddha what caused fear, lust, hatred and other negative mental states, and the Buddha gave a short but insightful reply.[19] This story may have originated in an incident where the Buddha spent a few days, perhaps a night, at a yakkha shrine which locals were too terrified to approach, causing amazement among them.

Today, and for well over a thousand years, Hindus have come to Gayā to perform the *śrāddha* ceremony, which involves offering rice balls (*piṇḍadāna*) to their departed parents, in the belief that it will guarantee their comfort in the afterlife. This ceremony is referred to in the Tipitaka, although there is no mention of Gayā being the main place to do it until the beginning of the Common Era.[20]

It is difficult now to identify the Brahmasara tank amongst some seven others in and around the city, but it may have been Surya Kund or Ransagar Kund. Gayāsīsa, now known as Brahmayoni Hill, is located on the south-west edge of the city.

Kajaṅgalā

Kajaṅgalā was a town marking the eastern-most edge of the Middle Land and is now known as Kankjol. Today the Ganges is about ten kilometers east of the town although it may have been much closer in ancient times and considered the actual border rather than the town itself. The Buddha described it as being a *nigama*, a word of uncertain

18. Thi.240-243.
19. S.I,207-208.
20. E.g., A.I,166; D.I,97.

meaning sometimes translated as 'market town', 'township' or 'large town', and as being in the eastern district (*paccantima janapada*).[21] Given Kajaṇgalā's distance from the main centres of the Buddha's activities, it is likely that he only went there once. He might have done this after one of his occasional visits to Campā, which lies a hundred kilometers north-west of it, or alternatively from Bhaddiya, which would have involved a journey of nearly sixty kilometers.

The impression of a single visit by the Buddha is strengthened by the fact that the Tipitaka records only two discourses given by him there. In one of these, he had a discussion with a young student of a brahmin scholar named Pārāsariya.[22] The other discourse took place while he was staying in a bamboo grove near the town. A group of lay disciples approached a certain nun and asked her to elaborate on the meaning of one of the Buddha's discourses that he had given while at Sāvatthī.[23] She told them that although she had neither heard the Buddha deliver this discourse nor had learned it from a senior monk, she would do her best to explain it, which she proceeded to do. Later, these lay disciples went to see the Buddha and recounted to him what the nun had explained to them; he endorsed everything she had said, adding; "If you had asked me about it, I would have explained it exactly as she did."[24] High praise indeed!

This story raises a few questions. Did the Buddha repeat his discourse while he was in Kajaṇgalā, or did the lay disciples already know it by heart or hear it from someone else? As the Buddha was in town, why did they not approach him for an explanation of it rather than the nun? And particularly, given that the nun was so erudite and wise, why was her name not recorded?[25]

Kajaṇgalā's main claim to fame in the centuries after the Buddha was it being the hometown of the monk Nāgasena, the main protagonist of the *Milindapañha*.[26] Whether Nāgasena was an actual historical character or not is an open question, but either way, associating him

---

21. See Wagal,1995 pp.20-23, Vin.I,197.
22. M.III,298.
23. A.V,48-54.
24. A.V,54-58.
25. See Bodhi 2012, p.1839, note 2012.
26. Mil.10.p.231

with Kajaṅgalā suggests that the town had a Buddhist presence and also was significant for Buddhists. This is confirmed by Xuanzang, who visited the place during his pilgrimage and found half a dozen monasteries in the district, although the town itself was in ruins.

Kaṇṇakujja

Kaṇṇakujja was a large town on the right bank of the Ganges and is now known as Kannauj. The Buddha passed through this place at least once but must have only stayed briefly because there is no record of him giving any talks there.[27] During the Gupta dynasty, Kaṇṇakujja grew into the largest and most important city in northern India and remained so for centuries. Xuanzang visited it and described its many monasteries and temples, one of which enshrined what was believed to be a tooth of the Buddha. The modern town is partly built on the huge mounds which are now the only evidence of the ancient city. Only minor archaeological excavations have so far been done at Kannauj.

Kesaputta

Kesaputta was the main town of a clan of people known as the Kāḷāmas. The Tipitaka says that it was in Kosala, which seems odd, as the town was a short distance east of the Gandak River, which would have formed the natural border between the two states. It may be that, like the Sakyans, the Kāḷāmas maintained some independence while being under the suzerainty of Kosala. Judging by his name, Āḷāra Kāḷāma, Gotama's first teacher, may have come from the Kāḷāma lands. During one of the Buddha's visits to Kesaputta, the locals explained to him their confusion concerning the competing claims of the various wandering teachers who visited there. The Buddha's reply to this is recorded in the famous Kesaputtiya Sutta, popularly known as the Kāḷāma Sutta.[28] Kesaputta is now identified with the small town of Kesariya, some twenty-five kilometers north-north-west of Vesālī. A short distance south of the town is a huge ruined stupa.[29]

27. Vin.III,11.
28. A.I,188-189.
29. See Sinha 2019 pp.27-31.

Kosambī

On the southern edge of the Middle Land lay the kingdom of Vaṃsā, with its capital at Kosambī. This city was strategically situated on the left bank of the Yamuna River, about a five-day walk from Payāga, the confluence of the Ganges and Yamuna rivers, which allowed the kingdom to control the riverine traffic. It was also located at the northern end of the Dakkhiṇāpatha, the great highway for traders and travellers coming from or going to the Deccan, i.e., central India. Both of these factors made Vaṃsā rich, powerful and a major influence in the politics of the Middle Land.

A merchant named Ghosita donated land for the establishment of a monastery in the city, which was named after him. In 1950, archaeologists uncovered the ruins of this Ghositārāma and verified its identity by an inscription and several clay sealings mentioning its name.[30] Another monastery, on the outskirts of the city, was the Badarikārāma, about which there is almost no information.[31] Tradition mentions two other monasteries in the city, Kukkuṭārāma and Pāvārikarama, but neither they nor the circumstances surrounding their founding are mentioned in the Tipitaka.[32] It is possible that this silence and the fact that the Buddha preached few discourses in Kosambī had something to do with the major rift within the Saṅgha which took place in the city.

Several locations in the vicinity of the city were favourite haunts for the Buddha – for example, the Siṃsapā Wood, where he delivered one of his most memorable discourses and the Pārileyyaka Forest where it is said he was ministered to by an elephant.[33] This second place may have been where the village of Pali, sometimes Pali Uparhar, is now, about four kilometers west of Kosambī. We read that Ānanda and a group of monks went from Kosambī to inspect the Pilakkha Tree Cave and while there they met a large group of wandering ascetics. This must refer to one of the caves or rock overhangs on Prabhosa Hill some

---

30. Ghosh 1956, pp.20-21.

31. S.III,126; Vin.IV,16.

32. For recently discovered inscriptions pointing to the existence of the Kukkuṭārāma, see Salomon and Marino, pp.34-35.

33. Ud.41-42; S.III,94-95; V,437.

eight kilometers west of Kosambī. Pabhosa may be the Maṅkula Hill where the commentaries say the Buddha spent his sixth rainy season. Archaeological evidence shows that this hill was the abode of ascetics for centuries.[34]

Udena, the king of Vaṃsā during much of the Buddha's career, had little interest in religion, and no dialogues between him and the Buddha have been preserved. However, the king once visited the Ghositārāma and had a talk with the monk Piṇḍola Bhāradvāja, who later tradition says was the son of the king's court chaplain.[35] It would seem that after the Buddha's demise Ānanda made Kosambī his base and from there continued to promote the doctrines of his beloved teacher.[36]

Kusinārā

Kusinārā was one of the two principal towns of the Mallas, the other being Pāvā. The fact that these people identified themselves according to which of the two towns they came from indicates that there was some kind of division between them.[37] Ānanda famously described Kusinārā as *kuḍḍa nagaraka, ujjaṅgala nagaraka, sākhā nagaraka*[38] which Rhys Davids translated as "this little wattle-and-daub town, in this town in the midst of the jungle, this branch township." Subsequent translators have followed the gist of this, giving the impression that Kusinārā was a wretched and dismal place. Some of the variations include "this sorry little town" (Chalmers); "this mean place, this uncivilized township in the midst of the jungle, a mere outpost of the province" (Vajirā and Story); "this miserable little town...right in the jungle in the back of beyond" (Walsh); "this small town, this barren town, this branch town" (Anandajoti); and "a little hamlet, a jungle hamlet, a branch hamlet" (Sujāto). These last two translations follow the wording of the Pali more closely than the others.

Nonetheless, there are problems with what branch, *sākhā*, could mean in this context. In English it would mean off the main route,

34. M.I,513. See Fuhrer pp.240-244.
35. S.IV,110-113.
36. See Ireland 1976, pp.114-117.
37. D. II,165.
38. D.II,146.

usually in reference to a path, road or railway. But, far from being off the main road, it is fairly certain that Kusinārā was situated right on the main road running from Magadha and Vajji to Kosala's capital at Sāvatthī and beyond, the northern equivalent of and roughly parallel to the Uttarāpatha, what later came to be called the Grand Trunk Road. Also, no town or village in the Tipitaka, or in any other Indian literature, to the best of my knowledge, is ever described as being *sākhā*, which is always used in reference to bush or tree branches. *Kuḍḍa* is from the Sanskrit *kuḍyā*, meaning 'a wall', and could be related to the Sanskrit *ksuṇṇa* ('to grind') and the Pali *cuṇṇa* ('powder'). Both meanings might be relevant to Kusinārā and may refer to the defences of the town – a wall or rampart – or to the lime plaster coating that was put over mud bricks to protect them from rain.[39] *Ujjaṅgala* can refer to hard or compact soil or mud. Modern visitors to Kusinārā will note that the soil around the town is not noticeably hard or barren (or no more so than anywhere else in northern Uttar Pradesh); in fact, it is fertile and productive. Thus, in relation to Kusinārā, *ujjaṅgala* may refer to the rammed earth or mud used in ramparts. Likewise, *sākhā* could well refer to the branches of thorny bushes that were cut and used for defensive purposes[40] or, alternatively, to a palisade running along the top of a rammed earth rampart.

If this interpretation is correct, Ānanda's comparison of the town with the great cities of the time was that it was a small place with basic or antiquated defences, the main cities having more impressive and substantial ones of stone and bricks. Ānanda's concern, as he clearly stated, was that there were not enough wealthy people in Kusinārā who could arrange a fitting funeral for the Buddha, not that the town was a miserable backwater.

When the Buddha visited Kusinārā, he usually stayed at the Baliharaṇavanasaṇḍa, the Wood of Offering, probably a grove of trees some of which the Mallas considered sacred.[41] Another place he sometimes stayed was called Upavattana, where there was a grove of sal trees (*Shorea robusta*), two of which were conspicuous because of their

39. Vin.III,81 mentions a *kuḍḍa* of burnt brick for a monastery being built.
40. Vin.II,154; Ja. I,240.
41. A.I,274: V,79.

size and, apparently, because they were growing close to each other.[42] It was under these two trees that the Buddha passed away. Another location mentioned as being in the vicinity of Kusinārā was the Makuṭa Bandhana Shrine, where the Buddha's body was taken to be cremated.[43]

Since the late 19th century, several archaeological excavations have been done at the stupa built over the sites of the Buddha's death, the monasteries that grew up around it, and at the cremation stupa. So far, however, no attempt has been made to locate and excavate the actual town of Kusinārā, and as the modern town is growing, this will be increasingly difficult to do in the future.

Madhurā

This city, now spelled Mathura, was the capital of the kingdom of Surasena and represents the furthest west the Buddha ever went which can still be identified. He only ever visited it once, probably because it was some way beyond the western edge of the Middle Land and also because he formed a poor impression of the place. He complained that it was dusty, filled with fierce dogs and yakkhas, its streets were uneven and its inhabitants were tardy when it came to giving alms.[44] On his way back from Madhurā, while on the main road to Verañjā, he met a group of men and women and, while sitting at the foot of a wayside tree, gave them a talk on conjugal relations.[45] The only other monk who visited the city during the Buddha's time was Mahā Kaccāna, who had a discussion with the king on the subject of caste and another one with a brahmin who had reproached him for not respecting brahmins by standing up for them.[46] While in Mathurā, Kaccāna lodged in the Gundā Forest, which may have later become the site of one of the city's many monasteries and which made it one of the major centres of Buddhism in northern India.[47]

From 1853 to 1977, important antiquities of both Buddhism and Jainism were unearthed from the many ancient sites in and around Mathurā.

---

42. Ud.37; D.II,137.
43. D.II,163. See Vogel, pp.43-58.
44. A.III,256.
45. A.II,57.
46. M.II,83; A.I,67.
47. On the history of Buddhism in Madhurā see Jaini 2001, pp.349 ff.

Pāṭaligāma

This village was located on the south bank of the Ganges and was the main crossing place between Magadha and Vajji. As such, it would have also been an important trading mart and customs post. Its name means "the village (*gāma*) of the patali tree (*pāṭali*)," the *Sterospermum chelonoides*, a common, medium-sized tree with fragrant mauve-coloured flowers. In later centuries, when it grew into a city, it was known as Pāṭaliputta.[48] When the Buddha stayed in the village during his last journey, he made a curious prediction about it. "For as long as the Aryan realm endures, Pāṭaliputta will be a principal city, its merchants opening boxes brought from afar. But the city will face three threats – from fire; from floods; and from internal dissension."[49]

The first part of this prediction could be a play on the phrase *puṭa bhedana*, which can mean a box, crate or container being opened or the seed pod of a tree breaking open. The seed pods of the patali tree are between 30 and 60 cm long, cylindrical in shape, ribbed and, when dry, crack or split open to release their seeds. As for the last part of the Buddha's prediction, archaeological investigation of the site of the ancient city in 1905 revealed, amongst other things, a layer of silt nearly three meters thick, above which was a thick layer of ash, indicating that the city had suffered at least one catastrophic flood, probably several, and a major conflagration.[50]

When the Buddha left the village to continue his journey north, the citizens decided to name the gate through which he left Gotama Gate and the place from where he embarked to cross the river Gotama Ford. About a century and a half later, Pāṭaligāma not only grew into a large city but became the capital of the mighty Mauryan Empire. King Asoka convened the Third Buddhist Council there; a precedent for this was the Jain's council held in the city during the

48. Pali *putta* and Sanskrit *putra* both mean son. On the possible origin of this part of the name and why it might have been used see Schlingloff, p.44.

49. D.II,87-88.

50. D. B. Spooner, *Annual Report of the Archaeological Survey of India*, 1905-1906; 'Mr. Ratan Tata's Excavations at Pataliputra', *Archaeological Survey of India Annual Report, 1912–13*, 1916.) A. S. Altekar and V. Mishra, *Report on the Kumrahar Excavations, 1951-55*, 1959.

reign of Asoka's grandfather Chandragupta. The Greek ambassador Megasthenes, who lived in Pāṭaliputta for several years, left a detailed description of it. The modern city Patna is built over the ancient site.

A discourse in the Majjhima Nikāya mentions that a brahmin named Ghoṭamukha built an assembly hall for the Saṅgha in Pāṭaliputta and adds that this occurred sometime after the Buddha's passing. That the discourse uses the name Pāṭaliputta rather than the earlier name Pāṭaligāma, indicates that the compilers of the Tipitaka were careful to distinguish between discourses dating from the Buddha's time and those from a later period, in this case possibly decades later.[51]

Pāvā

Towards the northern edge of the Middle Land lived a group of people known as the Mallas, one branch of whom had their chief town in Kusinārā and the other branch their chief town in Pāvā, because of which they were known as the Pāveyyakā Mallas. Both towns were on the main road leading from Magadha, through the Vajjian lands and then turning west and continuing all the way to Sāvatthī and beyond. When the disciples of Bāvari left Sāvatthī on their way to Vesālī in the hope of meeting the Buddha, they passed through Setavya, Kusinārā and Pāvā, and the Buddha travelled on this same road on his way to Kusinārā, but from its southern end and in the opposite direction.[52] During one of the Buddha's visits to Pāvā, he was invited to inaugurate the town's new assembly hall by spending the night in it.[53] It seems that the Pāveyyakā Mallas took to the Buddha's Dhamma with considerable enthusiasm, as at least thirty of them became monks, and the town's inhabitants claimed and received a portion of his ashes after his passing.[54]

---

51. M.II,163.
52. Sn.1012-1013. Setavya is probably now Siswania in Basti District, Uttar Pradesh, about ninety kilometers south-west of Kusinārā. The modern town is situated on the Kuwano River, known as the Sundarikā in the Tipitaka. See Mani pp.43-50.
53. D.III,207.
54. Vin.I, 253; D.II,165.

Pāvā's significance for Buddhists is due to the Buddha having spent his penultimate night and eaten his last meal in the town. It is also important to Jains because Mahāvīra died there, a fact confirmed by the Tipitaka.[55]

So far Pāvā has defied identification. The main candidates for it are Padrauna and Sathiyaon.[56] But the first of these is about twenty kilometers and the second twenty-five kilometers from Kusinārā, quite a distance for the sick and ailing Buddha to walk in a day. Further, Padrauna is north-east of Kusinārā, meaning that it is right off the ancient road, and an inscription found at Sathiyaon showed that its ancient name was Sresthigama, not Pāvā. Of late, it is being claimed that the ruins at Fazilnagar represent Pāvā, probably to attract tourists and pilgrims. Excavations conducted in the early 1980s showed that the ruins there are of a Hindu temple first built in the fifth or sixth century CE and enlarged from the thirteenth century onwards.[57] The Jains identify Pāvā with the town of Pavapur, some twenty kilometers north-east of Rajgir.[58]

Rājagaha

Rājagaha, the King's Abode, was the largest city in the most powerful kingdom of the time, Magadha. It also went by the name Giribaja, the Hill Fort, and is now known as Rajgir. Tradition says the city was laid out by the semi-mythical architect and town planner Mahā Govinda.[59] It is surrounded on all sides by several steep, rugged hills, which today are covered with low trees and stands of thorny bamboo, although in the fifth century there may have been thicker and greener cover. Numerous locations in and around the city mentioned by the Buddha can still be identified – the Robbers Cliff, from which convicted thieves were hurled; Jīvaka's Mango Orchard; and the Sattapaṇṇa Cave, where the First Buddhist Council was held. His favourite places to sojourn when visiting Rājagaha were the Vultures Peak, a rocky outcrop on the

---

55. *Kalpa Sūtra* V,147; D.III,210.
56. On these two places see Chakrabarti, 2001, p.211 and Bajpai pp.39-44.
57. See Chakrabarti, 2001, pp.211-213.
58. This confusion was perhaps caused by the abandonment of many Jain sites in northern India during Muslim persecution of the $11^{th}/12^{th}$ centuries.
59. Mvu. III,208-209.

slopes of the much higher Mt. Vepulla, and the Bamboo Grove, a royal park a little beyond the city's north gate. The Tapodārāma hot springs, which Moggallāna praised for its beautiful surroundings and sweet water, is now a public bath within a Hindu temple.[60] The remains of the stupa built by Ajātasattu to enshrine his share of the Buddha's ashes can still be seen as can the serpentine Sappini River although now much silted up and smaller. The Laṭṭhivana and nearby it the Kapota Cave both to the west of the city, the Sukarakhata Cave on the Vultures Peak, and the Indasāla Cave to its east, have also been identified.[61] This last place was the scene for one of the Buddha's most profound dialogues, the Sakkapañha Sutta.

According to the Tipitaka, the five hills of Rājagaha were Vebhāra, Paṇḍava, Vepulla, Gijjhakuta and Isigili.[62] Unfortunately, other later texts give different names for these hills, making it difficult to identify Paṇḍava, where Gotama stayed during his first visit to the city.[63] Impressive walls, the remains of which are still visible, snake along the top of the hills, and the city gates were, we are told, closed every night.

The first place we hear of Gotama being after he renounced the world is on, or perhaps at the foot of, the east side of Paṇḍava.[64] He had probably gone to Rājagaha to make contact with the many ascetics who lived in the groves, caves and rock shelters in the city's environs. Such ascetics were not attracted to Rājagaha because it was a centre of power but because of its intellectual and religious life. The large population also meant that getting a regular supply of alms or patronage was guaranteed. Rājagaha had been a centre of Jain activity even before Gotama arrived there, and Mahāvīra is said to have spent fourteen rainy seasons around the city and at nearby Nāḷandā.[65] Magadha's king at the time, Bimbisāra, was on good terms with the Buddha, and early tradition claims that he became a Buddhist, although Jain texts claim that he became a Jain. It is more likely that Bimbisāra patronized all sects, and each claimed him as their own, the Buddhists included. It is

60. Vin.III,108. See Sen,1918 pp.113-135.
61. A.I,185;Ud.39; M.I,497; D.II,263;Vin.I,35.
62. M.III,68.
63. The whole issue is discussed by Pandey, pp.31-38.
64. Sn.417.
65. *Kalpa Sūtra* V,122, also Jaini 2001, p.349ff.

significant that while the Tipitaka records numerous dialogues between the Buddha and King Pasenadi of Kosala, they have none between him and Bimbisāra.

The Buddha visited Rājagaha numerous times, spending his third, fourth, seventeenth and twentieth rainy seasons there and beginning his final journey from there some twelve months before his death.

Sāketa

South of Sāvatthī, by a direct and reasonably straight road, was Sāketa. Although it is not quite certain, it seems likely that Ayojjhā was either an alternative name for Sāketa or that they were two cities adjoining each other, much as the modern cities of Ayodhya and Faizabad do.[66] Confusing the matter is the Vinaya's mention of a ferry operating between the two places, suggesting that they were on opposite banks of the Sarabhū River (the modern Sarayu, sometimes also called Ghaghra).[67] Some ancient sources say they are different names for the same place, while others are unclear.[68] Sāketa had been the capital of Kosala before Sāvatthī, and the distance between them, approximately eighty kilometers, could be covered in a day by horse or, for the king and his officials, by a relay of seven chariots.[69] The Buddha occasionally visited Sāketa, as did several of his senior disciples. During one such visit, the wealthy merchant Kāḷaka, a patron of the Jains, invited the Buddha to his home for a meal and, impressed by what the Buddha had to say, offered him a plot of land and built a monastery on it. It became the only Buddhist monastery in the city.[70]

In the Nageshwarnath Temple in modern Ayodhya is part of an Asokan pillar now being used as an altar, and directly behind the temple is a large mound, almost certainly the remains of a stupa. This may well be the site of the monastery built by Kāḷaka, although only excavations will verify this.

66. S.III,140.
67. Vin.IV,65; 228.
68. Pathak, p.55.
69. M.I,149.
70. A.II,24.

Saṅkassa

Now called Sankisa, this town is mentioned only once in the Tipitaka as a place the Buddha passed through while on his way from Verañjā to Payāga.[71] In later centuries it became famous as the scene of a spectacular miracle which legend says the Buddha performed. Originally, the town was surrounded by two roughly circular fortifications, the outer one being a rampart about five kilometers in circumference and the inner one, also circular, being of brick. The inner wall enclosed the town where there are now two mounds, the smaller one being the remains of a stupa. Nearby is an elephant capital that once crowned a pillar erected by King Asoka; the pillar itself is now missing.

Sāvatthī

The city where the Buddha spent more time than any other was Sāvatthī, the capital of Kosala, now identified with the extensive ruins at Sahet Mahet in Uttar Pradesh.[72] This city was roughly crescent-shaped, the Aciravatī River flowing along the inner curve of the crescent. Unlike Rājagaha, there were no hills to protect the approaches to the city, so in their place high ramparts served this purpose. At one time or another, these ramparts were fortified with a palisade or a brick wall running along their top. The Buddha's most important patrons were from Sāvatthī – King Pasenadi and his queen Mallikā and the wealthy merchant Sudattha, known by the moniker Anāthapiṇḍaka.

It is not surprising, therefore, that more monasteries were founded in and around Sāvatthī during the Buddha's lifetime than in any other city. There were three altogether – the Pubbārāma, the Rājakārāma and, most famous of all, the Jetavana, about a kilometre south-west of the main gate of the city. The hall that Queen Mallikā built in one of her parks and which was open to ascetics of all sects, became the venue of a meeting between Keśin and Gautama, each representing one of the two branches of Jainism. The venue for this meeting is mentioned in both the Tipitaka and the Jain texts.[73]

---

71. Vin.III,11.
72. Law,1939.
73. See Chapter 3, note 25.

Approximately eight hundred of the Buddha's discourses were delivered in Sāvatthī. It is interesting that the Buddha favoured Sāvatthī over Rājagaha or Vesālī as the main centre of his activities during the last two decades of his life. The reasons for this may have been because of the patronage afforded to him by Kosala's royal family and perhaps also because the language spoken there was the same as, or similar to, his own. The fact that the city was only a four or five-day walk from Kapilavatthu, his hometown, may have been a factor also. Little systematic archaeological investigation has been conducted in Sāvatthī yet, but a series of major excavations have been carried out at Jetavana since its identification in 1863.

Suṃsumāragira

Suṃsumāragira, Crocodile Hill, was a town situated on the right bank of the Ganges and had been the capital of the Bhaggā chiefdom until its absorption into the kingdom of Vaṃsā. The Buddha visited the city several times, usually staying in the nearby Bhesakalā Grove and, according to the tradition, spent his eighth rainy season there as well. This grove was within walking distance of the home of two of his most devoted disciples, the couple Nakulapitā and his wife Nakulamātā.[74] During one of his visits to the town, Prince Bodhi, the son of King Udena and probably governor of Bhaggā, invited him and the monks staying with him for a meal in his recently completed palace.[75] Mahāvīra visited Suṃsumāragira on several occasions too and spent his twelfth rainy season there.

Suṃsumāragira is identified with Chunar, which is about twenty kilometers up the Ganges from Varanasi, and is well known for the impressive fortress now occupying the top of the hill.

Ukkācelā

Those crossing the Ganges at Pāṭaligāma would arrive at Ukkācelā, the border and customs post of the Vajjian confederacy. The Buddha must have passed through the town many times during his tours of this part

---

74. E.g., A. II,61; S.III,1.
75. M.II, 91.

of the country, although only one talk he gave there has been recorded in the Tipitaka. In it, perhaps appropriately, he told of a cowherd who drove his cattle over the river in the last month of the rainy season, when the river was in full flood, at a location called Suvidehā, where there was no ford. The cattle huddled together in the middle of the river and drowned. He then made the point that listening to or having faith in teachers who knew nothing about this world or the next, about what is and is not the realm of death, etc. would result in problems.[76] The modern town of Hajjipur is identified as the site of the ancient town. Later tradition says that after Ānanda died, his ashes were shared between Magadha and the Licchavis. The remains of the stupa built by the Licchavīs at Ukkācalā can be found in the Rambhadra district of Hajjipur.

Uruvelā

Uruvelā was the small village on whose outskirts the Buddha attained awakening. After this momentous event, he sojourned there for several weeks, then made his way to Isipatana to meet his five former companions and proclaim his Dhamma to them. Then he returned to Uruvelā, encountered and converted the three Kassapa brothers and then left with them for Rājagaha, apparently never to visit the village again. Amongst the few details the Tipitaka provides about Uruvelā is that it was on the banks of the Nerañjarā River at a crossing place, that it was nestled in a pleasant rural countryside, and that it was connected by road to the nearby town of Gayā.[77] The Buddha described it as an army village (*senānigama*) probably meaning that the revenue from it was used by the state to help finance the army.[78] He also mentioned several trees in and around the village, particularly the pipal tree under which he was sitting when he had his awakening experience, and a banyan tree frequented by goatherds and their animals during the midday heat, and where he chose to stay for a week.[79]

76. M.I,225.
77. M.I.166-167.
78. See *Arthaśāstra* II,35,1.
79. Vin.I,1-2.

During his last hours, the Buddha said that a devout disciple should try to visit at least once in their lives the places where the four pivotal events in his life happened, and one of these places was Uruvelā.[80] As a result, within a century of his passing, the village grew into a major destination for pilgrims and became known variously as Sambodhi, Bodhimaṇḍa, Vajrāsana, and from about the 18th century onwards, as Bodh Gaya. The actual village of Uruvelā came to be called Taradih, a Hindi contraction of Tārā Devi, after a temple to this Mahāyāna deity was built nearby in about the 11th century. Situated a little to the south-west of the Mahābodhi Temple, Taradih was demolished in the late 1970s and rebuilt some distance away so that archaeological excavations could be done at the site. These excavations, carried out between 1980 and 1990, revealed that Uruvelā was first occupied during the Neolithic period, that it had originally been closer to the river, and that it showed evidence of a Buddhist presence there right up to the 12th century. Unfortunately, a full report of the excavations is yet to be published.[81]

Today Bodh Gaya is a bustling town visited by pilgrims and tourists from all over the world.

Verañjā

Verañjā was a large town where tradition says the Buddha spent the three months of his twelfth rainy season, although he may have visited it on several other occasions as well.[82] The town marked the furthermost extent of most of the Buddha's teaching journeys, and the only time he went beyond it was his single visit to Madhurā. During one of his stays in Verañjā, there was a famine in the district, and food tickets were being issued, probably by the town council, guilds or local philanthropists. The Buddha and the monks staying with him were reduced to eating grain given to them by horse merchants, who usually fed it to their animals. Before it could be eaten, it had to be steamed and then pounded in a mortar. The Buddha praised the monks for eating such fare, saying that they were setting a good example for future

80. D.II,140.
81. See Joshi 1990, pp.7-9.
82. A.IV; 197-198.

generations of monks who might disdain such coarse food.[83] Verañjā can be identified with the huge mound at Atranji Khera, about thirteen kilometers north of Etah in Uttar Pradesh.[84]

Vesālī

East of Kosala and divided from it by the Gandak River was a confederacy comprising eight small chiefdoms, or nine according to Jain sources, which had united to protect themselves from Kosala to their west and their bigger neighbour, Magadha, to the south. The dominant clans in this arrangement were the Vajjis, the Licchavis and the Videhās. The Licchavis' main city Vesālī acted as the political and administrative capital of the confederacy.

There were numerous shrines in and around the city, such as the Sārananda and the Cāpāla shrines. Others – the Bahuputta; Gotamaka; Udena and the Sattambaka shrines – were located at the four cardinal points around the city, probably a little beyond its walls.[85] The Tipitaka mentions the Buddha often spending a day's sojourn at one or another of these shrines. However, his favourite place to stay while visiting Vesālī was the Kūṭāgārasālā, the Peaked Roofed Hall, beyond the city's northern suburbs on the edge of the Mahāvana, the great forest that stretched almost unbroken up to the Himalayan foothills.[86] This hall must have been within easy walking distance of the city, as the Buddha would sometimes take a stroll from there to some of the locations in the city.[87] There was an infirmary nearby, and he would occasionally visit the patients there.[88] It was while staying at the Kūṭāgārasālā that the Buddha announced his impending death three months hence.[89] He favoured the Kūṭāgārasālā because it offered some respite from the continual stream of people who would come to see him, which even for an awakened person could become tiresome after a while.

83. Vin.III,6.
84. Sarao 1990, p.103.
85. D.II,117 ff; III,9.
86. E.g., A. II,191; V,86; D.I,150; M.II,252; S.I,230.
87. A.III,167; IV,308; D.II,119; S.V,258.
88. A.III,142; S.IV,210.
89. D.II,120.

That the Buddha had a particular affection for Vesālī and its people, and they for him, is apparent from the Tipitaka. Once, while he was spending a quiet day with Ānanda at one of the city's shrines, he expressed his appreciation for its many landmarks, and when he left it on his final journey, he looked back at Vesālī and mentioned wistfully that it would be the last time he would see it.[90] On another occasion, he was spending the day in the Mahāvana when a group of Licchavi youths out hunting saw him. They unstrung their bows, called their dogs to heel and, after bowing to the Buddha, stood quietly gazing at him. A townsman happened to witness this and expressed his surprise to the Buddha that these youth, usually so bad-mannered and boisterous, could become so reverential and quiet.[91] The Buddha praised the Licchavis for their simple and healthy, almost Spartan, habits – using blocks of wood as pillows; sleeping on hard beds; rising before sunrise; and being physically active. As long as they maintained such practices, he said, they would never fall victim to an invader.[92] This was one of two occasions when the Buddha expressed his hope that the Vajjians would be able to maintain their independence.

According to most Jain sources, Mahāvīra was born in Vesālī and visited it many times. He also spent eight rainy seasons in there.

Little of the remains of Vesālī can be seen today, as the area has been inundated by the nearby Gandak River many times over the centuries. However, the foundation of the stupa built to enshrine the Licchavis' share of the Buddha's ashes was discovered in the 1950s. The stupa was made of earth, with a diameter of 1.15 meters, about 3 ½ meters high, and was estimated to date from 550-450 BCE. It had also been enlarged three times over the proceeding centuries. A small stone casket was found in the original stupa containing ash, a punch-marked coin, some beads and a small sheet of gold foil. A breach in the original stupa seemed to confirm the Buddhist tradition that King Asoka opened the first stupas and removed some of the relics from them.[93] A much larger stupa surrounded by numerous smaller ones, and with one of King Asoka's

90. D.II, 102; II,122.
91. A.III,75-76.
92. S.II,268.
93. Sinha and Roy,1969, pp.16-23.

mighty pillars nearby, can also still be seen. Exactly what this stupa commemorates is not known. It may have been part of the monastic complex built in later centuries at Ambapāli's mango orchard.

Appendix II
The Buddha and the Upaniṣads

Kamma and its related concept of rebirth are two of the central doctrines of Buddhism, but they are also amongst the most misunderstood – by both Buddhists themselves and consequently by non-Buddhists too. The most widespread of these misunderstandings is that kamma and rebirth were universally believed in ancient India, and the Buddha simply took them for granted and incorporated them into his Dhamma. The usual claim is that he copied these doctrines from the *Upaniṣads*. Both of these assumptions are problematic, not only because the evidence for this claim is far from clear but also because they raise doubts about the assertion that the Buddha's Dhamma was an outcome of his personal realization. In what follows, each of these assumptions will be examined.

The Tipitaka itself offers ample evidence that kamma and rebirth were by no means widely accepted in India in the fifth century BCE. Brahmins continued to conduct the orthodox Vedic funeral rites and "lift [the deceased] up, call upon his name, and conduct him to heaven." Two young brahmins the Buddha met told him they had been taught that one went into the presence of Brahmā (*sahavyatā*) after death.[1] The Samaññaphala Sutta gives an overview of the doctrines of six of the most prominent non-Vedic teachers of the Buddha's time, and only one of them taught a form of kamma.[2] Likewise, there are frequent criticisms in both Buddhist and Jain scriptures of those who denied kamma and rebirth. For example, the popular teacher Makkhali Gosāla taught: "There is no kamma, no deed, no [point in making an] effort."[3] The Buddha mentioned several current beliefs he considered to be false, one of them being that everything that happens is due to the will of a supreme deity and another that things have no discernible cause.[4] Some teachers rejected kamma and rebirth as relatively new and

1. S.IV,312; D.I,235.
2. D.I,52-59.
3. A.I,286.
4. A.I,173.

non-traditional ideas, while others, such as Prince Pāyāsi, dismissed them on rational grounds. Seeing no empirical evidence for them, this educated sceptic came to the conclusion that: "There is no other world, there are no spontaneously born beings, nor is there any fruit or result of good or evil deeds."[5] Even centuries after the Buddha, Aśvaghoṣa was able to write that "some maintain there is rebirth while others say with confidence that there is not" (Bc.IX,45).

The Vedas, the oldest and foundational scriptures of Brahminism and later of Hinduism too, show no knowledge of either kamma or rebirth. The word *kamma* (Sanskrit *karma*) occurs in the Vedas often, although not in the sense of moral causation but in its original meaning of working, doing or, particularly, of performing Vedic rituals. According to the Vedas, the individual's destiny after death was determined by performing certain rituals and by the gods. At death the individual was not reborn; he or she went to the world of the fathers (*pitṛloka*), an indistinct type of heaven where they were sustained by offerings (*śrāddha*) made by the deceased's son. This was why it was crucial for a man to sire at least one son. This concept is mentioned, for example, in *Ṛgveda* 10.14,2; *Taittirīya Brahmaṇa* 1.5,5,6 and *Āpastamba Dharmasūtra* 2.24,1-7. One's position in the world of the fathers depends on the merit created by performing sacrifices.

What of the *Upaniṣads*? For the Buddha to have copied, borrowed or even been influenced by any Upanisadic ideas, these texts would have had to predate him, and it is by no means easy to demonstrate that this is the case. The reality is that the dates of the *Upaniṣads*, and of the Buddha too, are at best guess work. This makes it very uncertain about which came first. Complicating the issue further is the fact that few *Upaniṣads* are homogeneous; most had material added to them after their initial composition, sometimes as late as several centuries afterward. However, the general consensus amongst scholars is that the earliest *Upaniṣads* are probably the *Bṛhadāraṇyaka*, the *Chāndogya*, the *Kauṣītaki* and perhaps the *Aitareya*, and that they predate the Buddha, or at least their core material predates the Buddha. For the sake of argument, let us accept this. To assert that these texts influenced the Buddha, two things would be needed, apart from predating him.

5. D.II,316.

(a) The Buddha would have had to have access to them and (b) they would have to teach concepts of kamma and rebirth the same or recognisably similar to the Buddha's presentation of these ideas.

The internal evidence from the early *Upaniṣads* indicates that they were composed mainly in Madra, Matsya, Uśinara, Pañcālā, Kuru, Videha, Kosala and Kāsi, some of them more so in some places than others. There is no record of the Buddha ever having visited the first four of these regions; he only ever went to Kuru and to Videha once,[6] although he did spend much time in Kosala and at least some time around Bārānasī, the capital of Kāsi. But interestingly, of the four *Upaniṣads* thought to predate the Buddha, none of them mention Kosala and only the *Bṛhadāraṇyaka* and the *Kauṣītaki* mention Kāsi, and only once each. This strongly suggests that the Buddha spent little or no time in the regions where the supposedly earliest *Upaniṣads* were being taught.

Another thing that needs to be taken into account is Upanisadic esotericism. Upanisadic doctrines, like the Vedas before them, were from the very beginning considered secret and meant only for a small inner circle of initiates. The *Kaṭha* says that if a brahmin keeps the teaching secret, he will have eternal life (3,7), which of course also cancels out the idea of kamma. The *Śvetāśvatara* calls its doctrines "the supreme secret" (*paramaṃ guhyaṃ*) which should never be revealed to anyone who is not tranquil, a son or a pupil (6,22). The *Chāndogya* says: "A father should reveal this formulation of truth only to his eldest son or to a worthy student, and never to anyone else..." (3,11,5-6) because its teachings are secret (*guhya ādeśa*, 3,5,2). Indeed, the very word *upaniṣad* means 'to sit near' and implies secrecy, i.e., sitting near the teacher as he explained his teaching so that the uninitiated could not hear it. Even centuries after the Buddha, the *Manusmṛti* referred to the sacred texts, probably meaning the *Upaniṣads*, as confidential or hidden (*rahasya*. 2,140; 165).[7] Given this, it is unlikely that the Buddha, the worst type of heretic in the estimation of most brahmins, would have known any Upanisadic doctrines, although it could be argued that he had heard a second-hand version of them.

---

6. M.II,74; 54.
7. See Black, p. 101 ff.

The Buddha's frequent claim that his Dhamma was for all and that he did not have a "teacher's fist" (*ācariya muṭṭhi*) which keeps something back could be taken as evidence that he at least knew about Upanisadic secrecy.[8] It is, however, more likely that he was contrasting his Dhamma with the Vedas, which by his time were mainly available only to brahmins and perhaps to some of the warrior caste. He described the Vedic hymns as being "veiled" (*paṭicchanna*).[9]

The next thing that needs to be examined is whether the *Upaniṣads*, particularly the supposedly pre-Buddhist ones, teach kamma and rebirth or something like the Buddhist versions of them. The *Upaniṣads* teach a range of post-mortem destinies and what determines them, but only some of these resemble the Buddhist understanding of them and only in the vaguest terms. For example, the *Kauṣītaki* says that when people die they all go to the moon, which is the gateway to heaven. In order to pass, they have to answer a question. Those who cannot answer this question become rain, which falls to earth, and then they become worms, insects, fish, birds, lions or humans, according to their kamma. Those who can answer the question enter heaven and go into the presence of Brahmā (1.2). Whether kamma here means moral causation or the proper performance of Vedic rituals is unclear, but it very likely means the latter. The *Chāndogya* teaches something similar, but when the dead fall to the earth as rain, they become plants which, when a man eats them, pass with his semen into his wife's womb and become a new being. Interestingly, the *Chāndogya* also says that "this [teaching] has not been known to brahmins before"; in other words, it was something new to the Vedic tradition.

The *Bṛhadāraṇyaka* posits several possible destinies after death and how they can be obtained. According to Pravāhaṇa, those who love truth pass through the moon and the sun to the region of lightning and from there into the world of Brahman. Those who have performed the sacrifice and given gifts to brahmins go the world of the fathers and from there to the sun, where the gods feed on them. After that, they pass into the sky, the wind and the rain, which falls to the earth, where they become food again, which someone offers into the sacrificial fire,

---

8. D.II,100.
9. A.I,282.

from where they go up to heaven. Those who are unaware of these two destinies become worms, insects or snakes (6.2,15-16). In another passage, when asked what happens to a person after death, Yājñavalkya denied rebirth, saying, "Once he is born, he cannot be born again" (*jāta eva na jāyate*) and then adds that the departed are sustained by, amongst other things, offerings made to them by their sons and relatives, the traditional Vedic view (3.9,28).

As for kamma, there are a few sections of the *Bṛhadāraṇyaka* where Yājñavalkya does expound something resembling the Buddha's teaching of kamma, in the sense of moral causation, although only briefly and without any details. But then he makes it clear that this is a secret teaching (3.2.13). But why should this be so? Perhaps because all Upanisadic doctrines were secret but also perhaps because, not being part of traditional Vedic thought, Yājñavalkya wanted to avoid accusations of unorthodoxy. Complicating the issue is that another passage in the *Bṛhadāraṇyaka* clearly denies kamma as a form of moral causation, asserts the traditional Vedic belief that one's post-mortem destiny is determined by having a son, and asserts that the highest post-mortem state is to go to heaven. "There are three worlds – that of men, that of the fathers and that of the gods. The world of men is obtained through having a son, not by any other means. The world of the fathers is obtained by rituals and the world of the gods by knowledge. The best of these clearly is the world of the gods, and that is why it is highly praised" (1. 5, 16). Elsewhere, the *Bṛhadāraṇyaka* asserts yet another theory – that when the individual dies, he goes to the wind, from there to the sun, then to the moon, which he ascends out of, and arrives in a world without heat or cold, to abide there forever (5.10,1).

The *Kauṣītaki*'s and the *Bṛhadāraṇyaka*'s notion of 'rebirth' is never called that, but is more accurately referred to as transference or transmission (*saṃpratti* or *saṃpradāna*). According to these *Upaniṣads*, when a man is dying, his son should lie on top of him, their various organs touching each other, and then the father should say, "I place my breath in you," to which the son should reply, "I place your breath in me," and this then continues in the same way for sight, hearing, tasting, action, mind, intelligence and so on (2,15;1.5.17). By this means, the father was thought to live on in some way in his son, again underlining the crucial role of a son in a person's post-mortem state. From a genetic perspective, a child is a continuation of its parents – although both of them, rather than just one – and of their physical features not their psychological makeup. Thus, this Upanisadic concept bears no similarity to either the Buddhist or Jain doctrines of rebirth.

The *Śvetāśvatara* rejects a variety of explanations, including kamma, and maintains that actually everything is controlled by God (1.2-3). *Upaniṣads* such as the *Taittirīya* and the *Kauṣītaki* do mention forms of kamma and rebirth, often seemingly tentatively and sometimes only in the vaguest terms.

With all these competing claims and explanations, it is hardly surprising that the *Kaṭha* actually says that no one knows what happens to a person after he or she dies (1.20-24). The upshot of all this is that the few *Upaniṣads* that do teach something like kamma and rebirth are undecided about these ideas and present them as just some of many possible explanations which have not yet been fully worked out or accepted. Clearly, these ideas were new ones to the Vedic theology drawn from somewhere else. One is tempted to think that it was not that the Buddha adopted kamma and rebirth from the *Upaniṣads* but rather that the authors of the *Upaniṣads* were being influenced by Buddhism, and probably Jainism too.[10]

The earliest unambiguous and detailed mention of kamma and rebirth is asserted in the Jain scriptures. Jainism pre-dates Buddhism by perhaps a decade, and its founder, Mahāvīra, and his teachings are frequently mentioned in the Tipitaka. However, while being a recognizable kamma concept, the Jain doctrine of kamma differs in important ways from the Buddhist one. For example, Jainism teaches that every action, intentional or not, creates kamma, and that kamma is a kind of material substance (*paudgalika*) that adheres to the soul and drags it down. Jainism also posits a soul passing from one life to the next, something that the Buddha rejected. It is certainly possible that the Buddha was influenced by the Jain doctrines of kamma and rebirth, but it is equally clear that if he was, he did not simply take them for granted and unthinkingly and uncritically adopt them. It is much more likely that Mahāvīra's spiritual insights gave him a partial vision of kamma and rebirth, while the Buddha's awakening gave him a complete understanding of them.

10. Jaini 2001, pp.50-51.

By about the turn of the first millennium, diverse ideas about kamma and rebirth were on their way to being integrated into what would become Hinduism. But at that time, and even later, these ideas were by no means universally accepted. Hinduism generally developed or absorbed new concepts without abandoning earlier ones, meaning that it presents a wide range of sometimes contrasting, even contradictory, doctrines on most matters. Even when some theories of kamma and rebirth became widely accepted in Hinduism, they fitted into it somewhat awkwardly, often jarring with other doctrines. The belief that the gods can and do intervene in human affairs, that devotion (*bhakti*) to a particular god leads to salvation, that evil can be washed away by bathing in sacred rivers, that performing certain rituals, visiting holy shrines or passing away in Varanasi guarantees salvation clearly cancel out the idea of kamma.

Some spiritual movements in Hinduism rejected kamma in favour of fate (*daiva*), while others maintained that the individual's destiny was determined by time (*kāla*), inherent nature (*svabhāva*), chance (*yadṛccha*) or that it is predetermined (*bhāvivaśāt*). Many passages in the *Dharmasūtras* and the *Purāṇas* mention kamma while in the next breath recommending various ways it can be circumvented or negated. And on the functioning of rebirth, the *Purāṇas* and other early Hindu texts present a truly bewildering range of theories, each contradicting the other. The prologue of the *Manusmṛti*, for example, says: "As they come into existence one after another, beings follow their individual behaviour as assigned to them by the Lord. Aggression or peacefulness, gentleness or cruelty, goodness or evil, honesty or dishonesty, whatever is assigned to each as they are created sticks straight away to that being" (1.28-29). And yet, in several other places in the same text, it maintains that a person's post-mortem destiny will be determined by how they acted, either good or bad, i.e., by their kamma (e.g.12.8-9; 2,249;11,48; 12,16-23).

The *Caraka Saṁhitā*, one of the two seminal texts on Ayurveda (circa first century BCE/second century CE), correctly pointed out that not everyone believed in rebirth and that even the Hindu scriptures presented different post-mortem theories. It says: "There are some people who trust only what they can see, and because rebirth is something beyond the senses, they do not believe in it. There are others, only because of their strong religious faith, who believe they will be reborn. But the scriptures are themselves divided in this matter" (I,11). Thus, it is not far wrong to say that Hinduism does not teach a doctrine of kamma and rebirth – it teaches dozens of them, and they are but some amongst a multiplicity of explanations for why things occur and what happens to the individual after death. The Buddha's doctrines of kamma and rebirth, by contrast, are fully developed, fit harmoniously together with his other teachings and are explained in a clear and consistent way.

Addendum

Page 102. Offcuts of cloth, rags or shrouds picked up in cemeteries would be sewn together to make such robes (Vin.I,282). The Buddha described how a monk might notice a rag by the roadside, hold it down with one foot, use the other foot to spread it out, then tear off the usable part and keep it for later (A.III,187). Concerning such robes, the Buddha said that when a monk begins to experience the joys of meditation, his rags robes will seem to him like beautifully-colored apparel (A.IV,230).

Page 116. Recent research has shown that regular visits to hospital patients by their loved ones and friends is a significant factor in the speed of their recovery, although of course this depends on the seriousness of the patient's sickness. It is not surprising therefore to find that the Buddha often visited the sick to show his concern for their well-being, and that his monks followed his example. He also encouraged his lay disciples to console their sick fellow disciples so as to lessen any fear or anxiety they might have (e.g. S.V,408-409; A.III,295-298).

Page 118, note 78. It seems the Buddha not only knew something about medicine but on occasions would even prescribe certain treatments for particular medical problems. For example, the monk Belaṭṭhasīsa developed scabs from which a discharge would ooze causing his robe to stick to his body so that those nursing him had to repeatedly moisten the robe with water to get it off. Seeing this problem, the Buddha recommended putting chunam, clay and dried cow dung on the scabs to absorb and dry up the discharge so that it could no longer stick to the robe (Vin.I,202).

Page 145. It might be possible to get some idea about how tall the Buddha was. Once, when responding to an observation about the nature of the world, the Buddha opined that the world could be found "within this *vyāma*-long body" (*imasmiññeva vāymamatte kaḷevare*, S.I,62). The *Arthaśāstra*, the *Samarāṇga Sūtradhāra*, the *Aśvalāyanagrhya Sūtra* and several other ancient sources agree that 84 *aṅgulis* made a *vyāma* and that a vyāma was the distance between the middle fingers of a man standing with outstretched arms, i.e. an arm span. This would be equivalent to a fathom, or 6 feet or 1.8288 m. Whether the Buddha meant that humans in general were about a *vyāma* tall or that he himself was is unclear, but the "this" body suggests the latter and perhaps that he was pointing to himself as he made this observation. If this conjecture is correct, it would mean that the Buddha was about 6 feet tall.

Page 168–169. The arched harp (*vīṇā*) consisted of the resonator box with a parchment stretched over it (*cammapokkhara*), the belly (*doṇi*), the arm (*daṇḍa*), strings (*tanti*) and the head (*upavīṇā*). There were two types; the seven-stringed was plucked with the fingernails while the nine-stringed was played with a plectrum (*koṇa*), usually made of ivory (Ja.II,252; IV,470; S.IV,197; Mil.53). One of the strings was known as the bee string (*bhamara-tanti*) because its deep resonant hum resembled that of the bumble bee. A harp could be tuned to the high pitch (*uttama-mucchanāya mucchetvā vādesi*), the middle pitch (*majjhima-mucchanāya*) or with slack strings (*sithila*, Ja. II,249). Refined music was played by an orchestra of five instruments (Th.398), these being the arched harp, flute, drum, cymbals and clappers.

The Buddha commented that an arched harp in the hands of skilled musicians could produce music he described as "captivating, melodious and enchanting" (S.IV,197). On hearing Pañcasikha sing to the accompaniment of his harp, the Buddha commented that "the sound of your strings blends well with your voice and the sound of your voice blends well with the sound of your strings" (D.II,267).

Page 212, note 16. The Jātaka describes the symptoms of someone suffering from diarrhoea thus... "his body burned, his stomach churned, there was bloody diarrhoea and as food went in it came straight out" (Ja. IV, 171).

Abbreviations

Pali and Sanskrit Texts

A	Aṅguttara Nikāya, ed. R. Morris, E. Hardy, PTS London 1885-1900.
Bc	Buddhacarita, ed. and trans. E. H. Johnston, Calcutta 1935.
Bv-a	Madhuratthavilāsinī, ed. I. B. Horner, 1946.
D	Dīgha Nikāya, ed. T. W. Rhys Davids, J. E. Carpenter, PTS London 1890-1911.
Dhp	Dhammapada, ed. O. Von Hinüber, K. R. Norman, PTS Oxford 1994.
Dhp-a	Dhammapada-aṭṭhakathā, ed. H. C. Norman, PTS London 1906-14.
It	Itivuttaka, ed. E. Windisch, PTS London 1889.
Ja	Jātaka with commentary, ed. V. Fausbøll, PTS London 1877-96.
Jn	Jātaka Nidānakathā, ed. V. Fausbøll, PTS London 1877-96.
Kv	Kathāvatthu, ed. A. C. Taylor, PTS London, vol. I 1894, vol. II 1897.
M	Majjhima Nikāya, ed. V. Trenckner, R. Chalmers, PTS London 1887-1902.
Mhv	Mahāvaṃsa, ed. W. Geiger, PTS London 1908.
Mil	Milindapañho, ed. V. Trenckner, PTS London 1880.
Mvu	Mahāvastu, ed. E. Senart, Paris 1882-1897.
S	Saṃyutta Nikāya, ed. L. Feer, PTS London 1884-98.
Sn	Sutta Nipāta, ed. D. Andersen, H. Smith, PTS London 1913.
Tha, Thi	Theragātha and Therīgāthā, ed. H. Oldenberg, R. Pischel, 2nd edition, PTS London 1966.
Ud	Udāna, ed. P. Steinthal, PTS London 1885.
Ud-a	Paramatthadīpanī, ed. F. L, Woodward, PTS London 1926.
Vin	Vinaya Piṭaka, ed. H. Oldenberg, PTS London 1879-83.

Bibliography

Agrawala, V. S. *India as Known to Pāṇini*, second edition, 1963.

Ali, Daud. *Courtly Culture and Political Life in Early Medieval India*, 2004.

Allen, Charles. *The Buddha and Dr Führer*, 2008.

Anālayo. *A Comparative Study of the Majjhima Nikāya*, Vol.I and II, 2011.

- 'The Historical Value of the Pāli Discourses', *Indo-Iranian Journal*, 55 (3), 2012.

- 'A Note on the Term Theravāda', *Buddhist Studies Review*, 2013.

- 'The Four Assemblies in Pāli Buddhism', B.L.W. Khin, V. Samarawickrama, and T.H. Soon (eds.), *K Sri Dhammananda, Essays in Honor of his Centenary*, *Vol.2*, 2018.

Apte, V. M. *Social and Religious Life in the Grihyasutras*, 1939.

Armstrong, Karen. *Buddha*, 2004.

Bailey, Greg and Mabbett, Ian. *The Sociology of Early Buddhism*, 2003.

Bajpai, K. D. 'Location of Pava', *Purātattva*, No.16, 1985-86.

Balbir, Nalini. 'Jain-Buddhist Dialogue – Material from the Pāli Scriptures', *Journal of the Pali Text Society*, Vol. XXVI, 2000.

Balcerowicz, Piotr. *Early Asceticism in India*, 2016.

Banerjee, N. R. 'Nagda 1955-57', *Memoirs of the Archaeological Survey of India*, 1986.

Barua, P. R. 'The Brahmin Doctrine of Sacrifice and Ritual in the Pali Canon', *Journal of the Asiatic Society of Pakistan*, Vol.I, 1956.

Basham, A. L. *History and Doctrine of the Ājīvakas, A Vanished Indian Religion*, 1951.

- 'The Background to the Rise of Buddhism', A. K. Naraian (ed.), *Studies in History of Buddhism*, 1980.

Bechert, H. (ed.). *Dating the Historical Buddha*, Part 1, 1991.

Black, Brian. 'The Rhetoric of Secrecy in the Upaniṣads', Steven E. Lindquist (ed.) *Religion and Identity in South Asia and Beyond*, 2013.

Bodhi, Bhikkhu. *In the Buddha's Words*, 2005.

- *The Numerical Discourses of the Buddha*, 2012.

- *The Buddha's Teachings on Social and Communal Harmony: An Anthology of Discourses from the Pāli Canon, 2016.*

Bronkhorst, Johannes. 'The Riddle of the Jains and Ājīvakas in Early Buddhist Literature', *Journal of Indian Philosophy*, 28, 2000.

- 'Literacy and Rationality in Ancient India', *Asiatische Studien/Etudes Asiatiques*, 56 (4) 2002.
- *Greater Magadha, Studies in the Culture of Early India*, 2007.
- *Buddhism in the Shadow of Brahmanism*, 2011.

Chakrabarti, Dilip K. 'Rajagaha: An Early Historic Site in India', *World Archaeology*, Vol.7 No.3, 1975.
- *Archaeological Geography of the Ganga Plain. The Lower and the Middle Ganga*, 2001.
- *Archaeological Geography of the Ganga Plain. The Upper Ganga*, 2007.

Chakravarti, U. *The Social Dimensions of Early Buddhism*, 1987.

Chandra, Pratap. 'Was Early Buddhism Influenced by the Upanisads?' *Philosophy East and West* 21/3, 1971.

Cousins. L.S. 'Pali Oral Literature', Philip Denwood and Alexander Piatigorsky (eds.), *Buddhist Studies Ancient and Modern*, 1983.

de Silva, Lily. 'Ministering to the Sick and Counselling the Terminally Ill', N. K. Wagle and F. Watanabe (eds.) *Studies on Buddhism in Honor of A. K. Warder*, 1993.

Deva, Krishna. 'The Antiquity of Sites Related to the Buddha', Satish Chandra (ed.) *Studies in Archaeology and History*, 2003.

Dhammajoti, Bhikkhu. 'The Sixteen-mode Mindfulness of Breathing', *Journal of the Centre for Buddhist Studies, Sri Lanka*, 2008.

Dhammika, S. *Middle Land Middle Way*, revised edition, 2008.
- *To Eat or not to Eat Meat*, revised edition, 2016.
- *Jesus and the Buddha, A Study of their Commonalities and Contrasts*, 2018a.
- *Nature and the Environment in Early Buddhism* (revised edition), 2018b.
- *The View from the West*, 2018c.

Dyson, Tim. *A Population History of India*, 2018.

Eltschinger, Vincent. *Caste and Buddhist Philosophy*, 2012.

Erdosy, Georg. 'City States of North India and Pakistan at the Time of the Buddha', F. Raymond Allchin (ed.), *The Archaeology of Early Historic South Asia*, 1995.

Falk, Harry. *Aśokan Sites and Artefacts*, 2006.
- 'The Ashes of the Buddha', *Bulletin of the Asia Institute*, 2013.

Fick, Richard. *The Social Organisation in North-east India in Buddha's Time*, reprint 1972.

Fleet, J. F. 'The Inscription on the Piprawa Vase', *Journal of the Royal Asiatic Society* Vol. 38 issue 1, 1906.

Fuhrer, A. 'Pabhosa Inscriptions', *Epigraphia Indica* Vol.II, 1894

Ghosh, A. (ed). *Indian Archaeology 1955-56*, 1956.

- 'Buddhist Inscription from Kausambi', D, C. Sircar (ed.), *Epigraphia Indica, 1961-1962*, 1963.

Gillon, Brendan S. 'An Early Buddhist Text on Logic: *Fang Bian Xin Lun*', *Argumentation* 22, No.1, 2008.

Gokhale, B. G. *The Brahmins in Early Buddhist Literature*, 1970.

- 'The Merchant in Ancient India', *Journal of the American Oriental Society*, 97.2, 1977.

- 'Early Buddhism and the Urban Revolution', *Journal of the International Association of Buddhist Studies*, 5/2. 1982.

Gombrich, Richard. 'Bodies like Old Carts', *Journal of the Pali Text Society*, XI, 1987.

- *Theravada Buddhism*, 1988.

- *How Buddhism Began*, 1996.

- *What the Buddha Thought*, 2009.

- *Buddhism and Pali*, 2018.

Heirman, Ann and Torck, Mathieu. *A Pure Mind in a Clean Body: Bodily Care in the Buddhist Monasteries of Ancient India and China*, 2012.

Hinüber, Oskar von. 'The Buddha as an Historical Person', *Journal of the International Association of Buddhist Studies* Vol. 42, 2019.

- 'Hoary Past and Hazy Memory. On the History of Early Buddhist Texts', *Journal of the International Association of Buddhist Studies*, Vol.29, 2. 2006.

Hoey, W. 'The Five Rivers of the Buddhists', *Journal of the Royal Asiatic Society*, 1907.

Ireland, John D. 'The Kosambī Suttas', *Pali Buddhist Review*, Vol.1, No. 2, 1976.

- 'Sūkaramaddava, the Buddha's Last Meal', *Buddhist Studies Review*, Vol,10, No.1 1993.

Jacobi, Hermann. *Jain Sūtras*, Part 1, 1884.

Jain, Jagdishchandra. *Life in Ancient India as Depicted in the Jain Canon and Commentaries*, 1984.

Jaini, Padmanabh, S. *The Jaina Path of Purification*, 1998.

- 'Śamaṇas: Their Conflict with Brahmanical Society', *Collected Papers on Buddhist Studies*, 2001.

Jamison, Stephanie and Brereton, Joel, P. *The Rigveda, The Earliest Religious Poetry of India*, Vols. I, II, and III, 2014.

Jayaswal, K. P. *An Imperial History of India*, 1934.

Jayatilleke, K. N. *Early Buddhist Theory of Knowledge*, 1963.

Jha, D. N. 'Brahmanical Intolerance in Early India', *Social Scientist*, Vol. 44, No. 5/6, 2016.

Joshi, Jagat, Pati (ed.) *Indian Archaeology – A Review 1985-86*, 1990.

Joshi, Lal. *Discerning the Buddha, A Study of Buddhism and of the Brahmanical Hindu Attitude to It*,1983.

Karpin, Stefan. 'The Buddha Taught in Pali: A Working Hypothesis', *Journal of the Oxford Centre of Buddhist Studies*, 2019.

Kaul, Shonaleeka. *Imagining the Urban, Sanskrit and the City in Early India*, 2010.

Kennet, D, Rao, J. V. and Bai, M. Kasturi. *Excavations at Paithan, Maharashtra*, 2020.

Kosambi, D. D. 'Ancient Kosala and Magadha', *Journal of the Bombay Branch of the Royal Asiatic Society*, 1952.

Kumar, D. *Archaeology of Vaisali*, 1986.

Lal, M. *Settlement History and the Rise of Civilization in the Ganga-Yamuna Doab*, 1984a.

- 'Summary of Four Seasons of Exploration in Kanpur District, Uttar Pradesh', *Man and Environment 8*, 1984b.

- 'Population Distribution and its Movement During the Second-First Millennium B.C. in the Indo-Gangetic Divide and Upper Ganga Plain', *Purātattva*, 1987–8.

Law, B. C. *Geography of Early Buddhism*, 1932.

- *Sravasti in Indian Literature*, 1939.

Levman, Bryan Geoffrey. '*Sakāya niruttiyā* revisited', *Bulletin D'Etudes Indiennes*, 2008-2009.

- 'The *muṇḍa/muṇḍaka* crux: What does the word mean?' *Canadian Journal of Buddhist Studies*, No.7, 2011.

- 'Cultural Remnants of the Indigenous Peoples in the Buddhist Scriptures', *Buddhist Studies Review*, 30, 2. 2013.

- 'The Historical Buddha: Response to Drewes', *Canadian Journal of Buddhist Studies*, No.14, 2019.

- *Pāli, the Language*, 2020.

- *Pāli and Buddhism: Language and Linage*, 2021.

Ling, Trevor. *The Buddha, Buddhist Civilization in India and Ceylon*, 1973.

Liyanaratane, Jinadasa. 'Pāli Canonical Passages of Importance for the History of Indian Medicine', *Journal of the Pali Text Society*, XXII, 1996.

Majumdar, R. C. *Corporate Life in Ancient India*, 1922.

Malalasekera, G. P. and Jayatilleke, K. N. *Buddhism and the Race Question*, 1958.

Mani, B. R. 'Identification of Setavyā, the Ancient City of Kosala, with Siswania', *Purātattva*, No.21, 1990-1991.

Manne, J. 'The Dīgha Nikāya Debates: Debating Practices at the time of the Buddha', *Buddhist Studies Review*, 9.2, 1992.

Marshall, J. *The Monuments of Sāñchī*, Vol. I, (reprint) 1983.

Masefield, Peter and Revire, Nicolas. 'On the Buddha's 'Kammic Fluff': The Last Meal Revisited', *Journal of the Oxford Centre for Buddhist Studies*, Vol.20, 2021.

Mettananda and Hinüber, Oskar von. 'The Cause of the Buddha's Death: The last Meal of the Buddha', Appendix, A Note on *sūkaramaddava*', *Journal of the Pali Text Society*, XXVI. 2000.

Mitra, Debala. *Excavations at Tilaura-Kot and Kodan and Explorations in the Nepalese Tarai*, 1972.

Mohanty, Gopinath, *et al.* 'Tapussa and Bhallika of Orissa, their Historicity and Nativity', *Orissa Review*, Nov. 2007.

Nakamura, Hajime. *Gotama Buddha, A Biography Based on the Most Reliable Texts*, Vol. I, 2000 and II, 2005.

Neelis, Jason. *Early Buddhist Transmission and Trade Networks*, 2011.

Norman K. R. 'The Origin of Pāli and its Position among the Indo-European Languages', *Journal of Pali and Buddhist Studies*, Vol. I. March, 1988.

- 'Aspects of Early Buddhism', David Seyfort Ruegg and Lambert Schmithausen (eds.), *The Earliest Buddhism and Madhyamaka*, 1990.

- 'A Philological Approach to Buddhism', *The Buddhist Forum*, Vol. V. 1997.

- 'Theravada Buddhism and Brahmanical Hinduism: Brahmanical Terms in Buddhist Guise', *The Buddhist Forum* Vol.VII, 2012.

Oldenberg, Hermann. *The Grihya-Sūtras. Rules of Vedic Domestic Ceremonies*. Part I, 1886 and II, 1892.

- *Buddha, His Life, His Doctrine, His Order*, 1882.

Olivelle, Patrick. *Saṃnyasa Upaniṣads*, 1992.

- *The Āśrāma System*, 1993.

- *The Early Upaniṣads*, 1998.
- *Dharmasūtras, The Law Codes of Ancient India*, 1999.
- *The Law Code of Manu*, 2004.
- *Kings, Governance, and Law in Ancient India*, 2013.

Pande, G, C. *Śramaṇa Tradition, Its History and Contribution to Indian Society*, 1978.

Pandey, M. S. *The Historical Geography and Topography of Bihar*, 1963

Pathak, Vishuddhanand. *History of Kosala up to the Rise of the Mauryas*, 1963.

Patil, D. R. *Antiquarian Remains of Bihar*, 1963.

Pollock, Sheldon. 'Axialism and Empire', Jóhann Páll Árnason, S. N. Eisenstadt and Björn Wittrock (eds.), *Axial Civilizations and World History*, 2005.

Postel, M. *Ear Ornaments of Ancient India*, 1989.

Prakash, Om. *Food and Drink in Ancient India*, 1961.

Prasad, R. C. *Archaeology of Champa and Vikramasila*, 1987.

Prets, Ernst. 'Theories of Debate, Proof and Counter-proof in the Early Indian Dialectical Tradition', Piotr Balcerowitz and Marek Mejor (eds.), *Studia Indologiczne 7*, 2000.

Puri, B. N. *India in the Time of Patañjali*, 1957.

Rhys Davids, C. A. F. *The Psalms of the Early Buddhists*, Vol. II, 1913.

Rhys Davids, T. W. *Dialogues of the Buddha*, Part 1, 1899.
- *Buddhist India*, 1903.
- *Dialogues of the Buddha*, Part III, 1921.

Roy, Kumkum. *The Emergence of Monarchy in North India, Eighth to Fourth Centuries BC*, 1994.

Roy, T. N. 'Sanitary Arrangements in Northern Black Polished Ware Period, Archaeology and History', B.M. Pande *et al* (eds.), *Essay in Memory of Shri A. Ghosh*. Vol.I, 1987.

Salomon, Richard and Marino, Joseph. 'Observations on the Deorkothar Inscriptions and Their Significance for the Evaluation of Buddhist Historical Traditions', *Annual Report of The International Research Institute for Advanced Buddhology at Soka University* 17: 27-39, 2014.

Sarao, K. T. S. *The Origin and Nature of Ancient Indian Buddhism*,1989.
- *Urban Centres and Urbanisation as Reflected in the Pāli Vinaya and Sutta Piṭakas*, 1990.

Schlieter, Jens. 'Did the Buddha Emerge from a Brahmanic Environment? The Early Evaluation of "Noble Brahmans" and the "Ideological System" of Brahmanism', Volkhard Krech and Marion Steinicke (eds.) *Dynamics in the History between Asia and Europe*, Vol. I, 2012.

Schlingloff, Dieter. *Fortified Cities of Ancient India, A Comparative Study*, 2014.

Schubring, Walther (ed.). *Isibhāsiyāiṃ: A Jaina Text of Early Period*, 1974.

Sen, Chitrabhanu. *A Dictionary of the Vedic Rituals Based on the Śrauta and Grihya Sūtras*, 1978.

Sen. D. N. 'Sites in Rajgir Associated with the Buddha and His Disciples', *Journal of the Bihar and Orissa Research Society*, Vol.IV Part II, 1918.

Shama, G. R. 'Excavations at Kauśāmbī (1949-50)', *Memoirs of the Archaeological Survey of India*, 1969.

Sharma, R. S. 'Material Background of the Rise of Buddhism', Mohit Sen and M. B. Rao (eds.), *Das Kapital Centenary Volume*, 1968.

Singh, Upinder. *Political Violence in Ancient India*. 2017.

Sinha, B. P. 'Excavations at Champa', *Archaeology and Art of India*, 1979.

Sinha, B. P. and Roy, Sita Ram. *Vaiśālī Excavations* 1958-1962, 1969.

Sinha, B. P. and Narain, L. A. *Pātaliputra Excavations 1955-56*, 1970.

Sinha, Ishani. 'Kesariya Stupa: Recently Excavated Architectural Marvel', *Proceeding of the International Conference on Archaeology, History and Heritage*, Vol.1, 2019.

Sinha, K. K. *Excavations at Sravasti:1959*, 1967.

Sinha, Prakash. 'Buddhist Sites of the Age of Buddha: Archaeological Evidence on Dating and Urbanization', G. C. Pande (ed.) *Life, Thought and Culture in India (from c. 600 BC to c. AD 300)*, Vol. I Part 2, 2001.

Sircar, D. C. 'Mahāmāyūrī List of Yaksas', *Journal of Ancient Indian History*, Vol. V, Parts 1-2, 1971-72.

Srinivasan, Saradha. *Mensuration in Ancient India*, 1979.

Srivastava, K. M. *The Discovery of Kapilavastu*, 1986.

Strickland, K.M, Coningham, R.A.E. (et el.). 'Ancient *Lumminigame*: A Preliminary Report on Recent Archaeological Investigations at Lumbini's Village Mound.' *Ancient Nepal*, 2016.

Sujato, Bhikkhu and Brahmali, Bhikkhu. *The Authenticity of the Early Buddhist Texts*, 2014.

Tatia, N. 'The Interaction of Jainism and Buddhism', A. K. Narain, (ed.), *Studies in History*, 1980.

Tatz, Mark. *Buddhism and Healing, Demiéville's Article "Byo" from Hobogirin*, 1985.

Thanissaro, Bhikkhu. *The Buddha Smiles, Humor in the Pali Canon*, 2015.

Thaplyal, K. K. *Village and Village Life in Ancient India*, 2004.

Tilakaratne, Asanga. 'Personality Differences of Arahants and the Origins of Theravada', Asanga Tilakaratne, Toshiichi Endo, *et al*, (eds.), *Dhamma-Vinaya: Essays in Honour of Venerable Professor Dhammavihari*, 2005.

Upasak, C. S. *Dictionary of Early Buddhist Monastic Terms*, 1975.

Verardi, Giovanni. *Hardships and Downfall of Buddhism in India*, 2011.

Vishnu, Asha. *Material Life in Northern India, Based on an Archaeological Study*, 1993.

Vogel, J. 'Notes on Excavations at Kasia', *Archeological Survey of India Annual Report,1904-5*, 1908.

Wagle, N, K. 'Minor Rites and Rituals Attributed to the Brahmins in the Nikāya Texts of the Pali Canon', *Journal of the Oriental Institute of Baroda* Vol. XVII, 1968.

- *Society at the Time of the Buddha*, 1995.

Warder, A. K. 'On the relationships between Buddhism and other Contemporary Systems', *Bulletin of the School of Oriental and African Studies*,18. 1956.

Wasson, R. G. and O'Flaherty Wendy Doniger. 'The Buddha's Last Meal', *Botanical Museum Leaflets, Harvard University*, Vol. 29, No.3, 1983.

Wezler, Albrecht. 'On the Problem of the Contribution of Ascetics and Buddhist Monks to the Development of Indian Medicine', *Journal of the European Āyurvedic Society*, 1995.

Wijayaratna, Mohan. *Buddhist Monastic Life according to the Texts of the Theravāda Tradition*, 1990.

Wijesekera, O. H. de A. 'Buddhist Evidence for the Early Existence of Drama'. *Indian Historical Quarterly*, Vol.17 No.2, 1941.

Witzel, Michael. 'The Case of the Shattered Head', *Studien zurIndologie und Iranistik* 13/14:363–415, 1987.

Wujastyk, Dominik. 'The Spikes in the Ears of the Ascetics: An Illustrated Tale in Buddhism and Jainism', *Oriental Art*, New Series Vol. XXX, No.2, 1984.

- 'The Evidence for Hospitals in Early India', in *History of Science in South Asia*, 10, 2022.

Wynne, Alexander. 'The Oral Transmission of Early Buddhist Literature', *Journal of the International Association of Buddhist Studies*, 27 (1) 2004.

- *The Origin of Buddhist Meditation*, 2007.

- 'Did the Buddha Exist?', *Journal of the Oxford Centre of Buddhist Studies*, Vol.16, 2019.

Zysk, Kenneth. *Asceticism and Healing in Ancient India*, 1998.

Index

M

N

O

P

R

S

T

U

V

W

Y

ABOUT PARIYATTI

Pariyatti is dedicated to providing affordable access to authentic teachings of the Buddha about the Dhamma theory (*pariyatti*) and practice (*paṭipatti*) of Vipassana meditation. A 501(c)(3) non-profit charitable organization since 2002, Pariyatti is sustained by contributions from individuals who appreciate and want to share the incalculable value of the Dhamma teachings. We invite you to visit www.pariyatti.org to learn about our programs, services, and ways to support publishing and other undertakings.

Pariyatti Publishing Imprints

Vipassana Research Publications (focus on Vipassana as taught by S.N. Goenka in the tradition of Sayagyi U Ba Khin)

BPS Pariyatti Editions (selected titles from the Buddhist Publication Society, copublished by Pariyatti)

MPA Pariyatti Editions (selected titles from the Myanmar Pitaka Association, copublished by Pariyatti)

Pariyatti Digital Editions (audio and video titles, including discourses)

Pariyatti Press (classic titles returned to print and inspirational writing by contemporary authors)

Pariyatti enriches the world by

- disseminating the words of the Buddha,
- providing sustenance for the seeker's journey,
- illuminating the meditator's path.

www.ingramcontent.com/pod-product-compliance
Lightning Source LLC
Chambersburg PA
CBHW021046090426
42738CB00006B/209
9781681725963